DATE DUE			
May 22'67			
Jan 18'68			
May 22'68			
Oct 15'68			
Apr 8 '69			
May 14'69			
Nov 17'69			
Dec 9 '69			
Apr 6 70			
Nov 17 70			
Dec 8 70			
Nov 27'72			
Oct 29 '73			
Sep 25 '75			
Dec 8 '75			
Apr 12'76			
May 11 78			
Apr 26 79			
GAYLORD			PRINTED IN U.S.A.

BETTY JANE TROTTER, Ed.D., Teachers College, Columbia University, is Associate Professor of Physical Education for Women, San Jose State College. She previously taught at North Texas State University. During her time there she became Editor of *The Bulletin* of the Texas Association for Health, Physical Education, and Recreation and was named by Governor Price Daniel to the Texas Youth Fitness Council. Dr. Trotter is a member of both the American and California Associations for Health, Physical Education, and Recreation and is National Official—Volleyball, Women's National Officials Rating Committee.

VOLLEYBALL
For Girls and Women

Betty Jane Trotter
San Jose State College

THE RONALD PRESS COMPANY • NEW YORK

Library of Congress Catalog Card Number: 65–17093

PRINTED IN THE UNITED STATES OF AMERICA

To my Father and my Mother
Mr. and Mrs. Emert Arthur Trotter

Foreword

Since its invention about the turn of the present century, volleyball has developed into one of the most frequently played and best loved games in the world. There is scarcely a school, college, club, or recreational organization in this or any other country where the game is not played as a part of a comprehensive program of physical education or recreation.

One of the characteristics of a truly great game lies in the extent to which it can be adapted to meet desired educational, recreational, competitive, or health goals. Where adaptability is concerned, few, if any, athletic activities surpass the game of volleyball. It can be played with pleasure and profit under sex-limited conditions or in mixed groups over a long span of life, thereby providing unlimited opportunities for healthful physical exercise and release from the pressures of workaday living.

Although adaptability is one of the outstanding characteristics of volleyball, it may also be a factor in retarding the development of other important aspects of the game. One frequently voiced criticism of volleyball is that game rules often are so severely breached in the interests of social, recreational, and/or health outcomes that the development of game skills and strategy are relegated to a position of secondary importance.

Athletic games develop their greatest potential when there is vigorous, meaningful competition under the guidance of expert teachers, working with participants who vie with others for team membership, with strict adherence to the rules in an atmosphere of purposeful work necessitated by a demanding schedule of games. While volleyball is played under the above conditions in many foreign lands and in YMCA's, clubs, and recreational organizations in this country, interinstitutional competition has been relatively slow to develop in the schools and colleges in the United States. When compared with competitive basketball, for example, which is about the same chronological age, volleyball lags considerably behind. Similar comparisons may be made with other traditional school and college athletic sports.

For games to develop their greatest potential, expert, dedicated teachers are an imperative necessity. Unfortunately, the quality of instruction in volleyball is not up to the standards set by the teachers of other school and college games and sports. Some of the responsibility for this situation lies with the teacher education institutions. Where only a modicum of game knowledge and skill is required of future volleyball teachers, the product in the field is likely to be inferior.

In upgrading the quality of instruction in volleyball, as well as in other athletic activities, expertly written textbooks are indispensable. *Volleyball —For Girls and Women* is such a text. The author of this book speaks with the authority of many years of experience as a player and as teacher of volleyball and one who is a highly successful professional person in the field of teacher education.

HARRY A. SCOTT
Carmel, California

Acknowledgment

Regardless of the fact that only one name usually appears on the title page, no author is solely responsible for a finished book. Certainly, *Volleyball—For Girls and Women* is no exception. Outstanding among its many contributors have been:

Dr. Harry A. Scott, whose inspiration and leadership in physical education and whose professional writings in the area of competitive sports for schools and colleges made him a natural and logical choice to author the Foreword;

Miss Gayle L. Frary, a former student and extramural volleyball competitor and now a respected colleague, who combined knowledge and love of the game with creative flair and artistic skill to produce the invaluable illustrations of this book;

Mrs. Ray E. Holbert, whose experience in manuscript typing and interest in this project promoted feelings of security conducive to the final accomplishment;

The members of the 1963–1964 San Jose State College extramural volleyball team, whose dedication to and skill in the game have been an infectious incentive to all who have seen them in demonstration and competition, and who have patiently served as subjects for the photographic illustrations; and

All volleyball students and team members, former and present, who have insisted that this book be written.

To all I owe my heartfelt gratitude.

Betty Jane Trotter

April, 1965
San Jose, California

Contents

INTRODUCTION

1

Volleyball:
History and Benefits

At the end of the War Between the States virtually no organized sports existed in the United States of America. Yet it was in this turbulent period of reconstruction, when the entire country struggled to gain its composure after the siege of internal strife, that two new sports were originated by Americans. These two sports not only captured the imagination of their countrymen, but also spread abroad to gain the interest and enthusiasm of the entire civilized world.

THE HISTORY OF VOLLEYBALL

Basketball was a mere infant, although a rapidly growing and gusty one, when William G. Morgan, in the year, 1895, introduced his new game of volleyball, which he called Mintonette. Mr. Morgan, the physical director of the Young Men's Christian Association center of Holyoke, Massachusetts, also had a specific purpose in mind when he originated his new game. Just as Dr. Naismith had hoped to produce a game which would help to fill the long winter months of the Northeast with an indoor-type, vigorous activity, Mr. Morgan was searching for an indoor game that was challenging to the young and old alike but not quite so vigorous as the game of basketball.

While some denied that volleyball was an original creation of Mr. Morgan, and pointed out the similarities between the game and battledore and shuttlecock, and even tennis, others accepted his work in developing and promoting the game as they did the work of Dr. Naismith with basketball.

THE NEW GAME

In its original version, the game of volleyball was played with the inflated rubber bladder of a soccer ball. By using the hands in much the same way

3

as a racquet is used, the object was to hit the ball over a tennis net elevated to its regulation height. It was soon discovered that the bladder was too light and the net was too low. The next change in the game involved the lifting of the net to a higher level and use of the newly developed basketball. However, it was soon discovered that this ball was too heavy to be batted over the net and eventually a special ball was developed for the new game. In the original rules players were allowed to let the ball bounce, but there was no privilege in catching. The bounce rule was soon eliminated, and the basic rules of the game have since remained fairly intact.

EARLY GROWTH

Within the year after its introduction, Mr. Morgan staged an exhibition game at the YMCA Physical Directors' Conference held in Springfield, Massachusetts, and at that time turned over a hand-written copy of the rules to the men in attendance there. Gaining the enthusiasm and support of the YMCA physical directors gave great initiative to the promotion and growth of the game, and it was not long before it was being presented in activity programs sponsored by this organization throughout the country. The first official volleyball rules were included in the *Handbook of the Athletic League of YMCA's of North America* in 1897, and the first rules committee was a group of YMCA physical directors who made recommendations for rule changes at each annual conference.[2]

Additional impetus was given to the spread of the game when Dr. Elwood Brown, the director of the American Expeditionary Forces in the Orient and International Secretary of the YMCA, inserted instructions for it in the booklet, "Far Eastern Games," in Manila of the Philippine Islands, in 1913. Meantime, back in the United States, interest in the game by schools, colleges, universities, and other institutions and organizations led to an invitation to the National Collegiate Athletic Association, in 1916, to join the YMCA in establishing a joint set of rules. The efforts of the two organizations were published that year in the *Spalding Blue Cover Volleyball Rule Book*.[3]

THE DECADE OF THE 1920'S

The decade of the 1920's resulted in additional progress in the growth and development of the new game. By 1922, enough teams scattered throughout the country were playing volleyball to hold a national tournament, sponsored by the YMCA, in Brooklyn. With twenty-seven teams

---

[1] Katherine W. Montgomery, *Volley Ball for Women* (New York: The Ronald Press Co., 1934), p. 1.

[2] Harold T. Friermood and Marshall L. Walters, "Selected Highlights from the History of Volleyball," *The 1963 Annual Official Volleyball Rules* (Berne, Indiana: The United States Volleyball Association, 1962), p. 109.

[3] *Ibid.*

from eleven states competing, the Pittsburgh, Pennsylvania, branch emerged victorious.[4] In the same year the Playground Association and the Boy Scouts of America were invited to participate in the formulation of the annual rules and by 1925, the rules group was enlarged to include representatives of the Army, the Navy, and a committee committed to the interests of industrial organizations and high schools. During the same year the American Playground and Recreation Association reported the existence of 703 volleyball leagues and 3,834 teams in operation throughout the country.

One of the most significant developments of the 1920's was the adoption of volleyball as an official activity by the National Amateur Athletic Federation in 1923, and the subsequent appointment of a member of the Women's Division as a representative to the Official Volley Ball Rules Committee. By 1926 special rules appeared for girls and women in the Red Cover Series of the Spalding Athletic Library.[5] In the meantime, the National Section on Women's Athletics (NSWA), a division of the American Physical Education Association, set about to establish a completely different set of rules for girls and women, which they felt would be more in keeping with the principles and standards of their organization. Until 1937, the NSWA included their volleyball rules in a grouping of athletic games. In that year volleyball was moved to major sport status, and the rules for the game were published in a dual-purpose book along with softball. When the NSWA changed its name to become the National Section for Girls and Women's Sports (NSGWS), volleyball rules became the primary emphasis in a separate book, which also included instruction in some minor recreational activities. More recently the NSGWS has become the Division of Girls and Women's Sports (DGWS), still a part of the parent organization, now known as the American Association for Health, Physical Education, and Recreation, and the official *Volleyball Guide* is an entity, including not only rules, but also standards, instructions in officiating, and professional teaching and coaching articles for the game. The current rules, devised by this organization and to be referred to in this text as the DGWS rules, are most often used by schools, colleges, and universities.

THE FOUNDING OF THE UNITED STATES VOLLEYBALL ASSOCIATION

A second significant happening of the 1920's was the formation of the United States Volleyball Association (USVBA) in 1928. The first president of the newly found organization was Dr. George J. Fisher, who gave continued direction as chief executive for 24 years. The USVBA is composed of the following member organizations: general representation of the American Association for Health, Physical Education, and Recreation, special

---

[4] Robert E. Laveaga, *Volleyball.* 2d ed. (New York: The Ronald Press Co., 1960), p. 5.
[5] Montgomery, *op. cit.,* p. 4.

representation from the Division for Girls and Women's Sports, the American Turners, the Armed Forces (the Army, Navy, and Air Force), the Boys' Clubs of America, the Boy Scouts of America, the National Amateur Athletic Federation, the National Collegiate Athletic Association, the National Council of the YMCA, the National Federation of State High School Associations, the National Jewish Welfare Board, the National Recreation Association, and the Physical Education Society of the YMCA.[6]

PURPOSES OF THE USVBA

The avowed purposes of the USVBA are: to encourage cooperative efforts among national groups interested in the promotion of volleyball; to represent the United States' volleyball interests in national and international sports organizations; to promote interest in the game; to increase the number of participants in organized play and competition at all ability levels; to formulate, publish, and distribute official playing rules; to certify qualified game officials; and to stress good sportsmanship among players, officials, and spectators.[7]

In addition to the United States, the USVBA serves Puerto Rico and the Canal Zone. The rules composed by this organization are intended for use by boys and men and girls and women alike. In most non-educational organizations and institutions they are accepted as the official rules for girls and women, and for purposes of this text will be referred to as the USVBA rules. In actuality, during recent years the DGWS and USVBA rules have moved closer and closer toward each other, and currently are different only in respect to positioning when the ball is put into play on the service; the restraining line behind which USVBA players must spike when they occupy playing positions of backs; and the interchange of positions after the service as allowable under the USVBA rules.

One of the first official acts of the newly formed USVBA was to conduct in the same year as its founding, 1928, the first Open championship in conjunction with the seventh annual National YMCA championships. The winning team was the Houston, Texas, YMCA. Currently, the USVBA conducts the following tournaments each year: the United States Open, the Senior YMCA, the YMCA Masters (for men 35 years and older), Collegiate, Women's Open, and competition for the divisions of the Armed Forces.

GROWTH IN THE 1930's

The 1930's not only showed marked increase in the number of teams and participants in organized play throughout the country, but also indicated development in other aspects concerning the game. The first book on the game, *Volleyball—A Man's Game,* was written by Robert E. Laveaga,

---

[6] Harold T. Friermood, "Volleyball Goes Modern," *Journal of the American Association for Health, Physical Education, and Recreation,* XXIV (May, 1953), 11.
[7] *Ibid.*

and was published in 1933. In the next year came the beginning of recognition and approval of nationally ranked officials. Five years later, in 1939, representatives of volleyball players were appointed, for the first time, to serve on the USVBA Board of Directors.[8]

THE ARMED FORCES AND POSTWAR VOLLEYBALL

When the American doughboys of the World War I went overseas, they took with them to their military camps the game of volleyball and to them goes the credit for establishing it as a recreational activity in many of the countries in which they were stationed. However, the armed forces serving in the Second World War saw service in a much larger theater of war, and volleyball was first taught in friendly territories and then among the peoples of the conquered areas as millions of servicemen engaged in the game as part of their physical training, as well as a popular recreational activity. At the close of World War II, an All-Army championship tournament was held and has since become an annual event. In 1953, the Air Force followed suit by establishing an All-Air Force championship tournament to be held annually.

Other developments in the postwar years included the introduction of the publication, the *International Volleyball Review*, with Dr. David Gordon and Harry E. Wilson as editors, in 1946, and the resuming of the national championships in that same year. The USVBA meeting held in connection with the championships was of particular significance because Avery Brundage, president of the United States Olympic Committee, was invited to attend to advise the organization on the procedure to be followed in getting volleyball recognized as an Olympic sport.[9] In the following year, the USVBA, represented by two members, attended the organization meeting of the International Volleyball Federation in Paris, France, and there established charter membership for the United States, along with twelve other countries, in the new international group. In the next year, 1948, Harry E. Wilson, editor of the *International Volleyball Review*, took a team of United States players on a goodwill tour of France, Switzerland, Italy, Czechoslovakia, Western Germany, Belgium, and Holland. For the twelve men within the touring group it was a learning, as well as a goodwill, mission, and they returned home impressed with the quality of the European style of play and with the vigorous and skilled competitive ability of the game for women abroad.[10]

It was in the following year, 1949, as if striving to meet the challenge offered by their European counterparts, that the women's division was added to the national USVBA championships held in Los Angeles. During the same year a collegiate unit of competition was held, and the first World

[8] Friermood and Walters, *op. cit.,* p. 109.
[9] *Ibid.,* pp. 109–10.
[10] Friermood, *op. cit.,* 37.

Championship matches were held in Prague, Czechoslovakia, with the Union of Soviet Socialist Republics (Russia) emerging the victor. The United States was not represented by a team, and there was no competition for women. However, in 1952, when the second World Championships for men were held in Moscow, there was a division of competition for women, and the Soviet Union won in both men's and women's play. In the finals conducted in Dynamo Stadium, 40,000 spectators came to observe the matches. At this time some 31 countries were members of the International Volleyball Federation, and the organization undertook to have an exhibition volleyball game staged in the Olympics held in Helsinki. They were not successful in this attempt.[11]

During the same year of 1952, the volleyball committee of the American Amateur Union recommended to the USVBA special consultation on coed and girls and women's volleyball. Together the two organizations met in Columbus, Ohio, on the day before the annual Board of Directors meeting of the USVBA. Further unification of the efforts of both groups in promoting and controlling play for women resulted from the conference, and a decision was made to devote space in the *Annual Reference Guide and Official Rules* to the game for girls and women.[12]

INTERNATIONAL COMPETITION

The status of volleyball as a truly international sport is borne out by outstanding events of succeeding years. When the Pan American Games were held in Mexico City in 1955, volleyball was added to the program of activities and tickets to the matches, the only sport in which such interest was exhibited, were sold out weeks in advance. Eventually, Mexico City riot squads had to be called out to prevent would-be spectators, unable to secure tickets, from knocking down doors and breaking windows to see the games. The World Championship matches were held again in 1956 in Paris, France; in 1960, Sao Paulo, Brazil; in 1962, Moscow; and in 1963, a return to Sao Paulo. The most important single event in the growth and development of the game of volleyball in the 1950's came in 1957, when it was designated as an official Olympic team sport by the International Olympic Committee meeting in Sophia, Bulgaria. This decision was followed in 1962 by one which established competition for women, as well as men, for the Olympic games program to be held in Tokyo, Japan, in October of 1964.[13]

CURRENT STATUS IN THE UNITED STATES

It is almost a paradox that the United States, the country in which volleyball originated, gives the game nothing like the spectator support that it

[11] *Ibid.*
[12] *Ibid.*, 28.
[13] Friermood and Walters, *op. cit.*, p. 110.

receives abroad. In this country volleyball does not even begin to compete with football, baseball, or basketball in drawing a paying public. Crowds of 5,000, such as the one that attended the finals of the National Collegiate tournament held in Springfield, Massachusetts, in 1951, are the exception rather than the rule.[14]

On the other hand, the picture of volleyball as a participant sport in the United States could not be brighter. Boys and girls across the land receive their initial exposure to the skills of volleyball at an early age in many lead-up games included in elementary school programs of physical education. At the upper elementary school level and in the junior high school, they receive instruction in the game per se. On the high school level volleyball is, almost without exception, a part of the instructional and intramural program for girls and boys alike. In some states and areas it is an extramural and interscholastic event for both sexes, and some state athletic associations go so far as to sponsor state tournaments in the sport. In other states volleyball is included at the district, or first unit of competition, and regional, or second, level, but is not an event for statewide competition.

At the collegiate level the adoption of volleyball as a major sport by the National Collegiate Athletic Association and its inclusion as an Olympic event has done much to boost its stock among athletic departments in the colleges and universities. Collegiate varsity leaders for men include Springfield College, the University of Southern California, Florida State University, Earlham College, the University of California, the University of Washington, George Williams College, Whittier College, Ball State, Ohio State University, Iowa State University, and Dartmouth University.[15] In addition, volleyball is keeping pace as an event in today's current trend toward an increase in extramural and limited intercollegiate competitive experiences for women.

√ In addition, volleyball flourishes as an activity in competitive leagues formed by recreation departments, churches, and industrial and civic organizations throughout the country. Arranged for men and women alike, and often in coeducational groups, these programs occupy a major portion of the physical-recreational leisure-time pursuits of these adults. But it is not only in organized programs that volleyball is gaining and maintaining numbers of participants. Backyard volleyball, with a net elevated on regulation standards or between two trees, volleyball on asphalt playground surfaces and in grassy plots, and volleyball on wooded pavilions and sandy beaches dot the American scene from the eastern seaboard states to sunny Hawaii and from the courts of Alaska to the southernmost tip of Florida.

Thus, it should come to no one but the most casual of observers as a surprise that volleyball is not only the number one participant sport in the United States but is also the fastest growing. These facts were substantiated

---

[14] William T. Odeneal, "Volleyball—Major Sport," *Journal of the American Association for Health, Physical Education, and Recreation,* XXV (January, 1954), 8.

[15] *Ibid.*

by a sports participation survey conducted in 1963 by the Athletic Institute and made known in a national press release in 1964. The survey showed that 60 million Americans were involved in participation in the game of volleyball. This number represented triple the total revealed in a similar study made in 1961.

BENEFITS

As volleyball has grown to the leadership role in the participant sports of the United States, it is of utmost importance that professions concerned with the direction of instructional, intramural, and interscholastic or intercollegiate programs in schools, colleges, and universities, and in the recreational and competitive programs of non-educational institutions and organizations, as well as the lay participant, know, understand, and appreciate the physical, recreational, and educational benefits to be derived through practice and play.

PHYSICAL ABILITIES

Although physical fitness was one of the first values to be recognized in participation in sports by boys and men, it was some time before the same objective was held for girls and women. Indeed, at one time any participation in athletic events was frowned upon by educators, physical educators, and even medical authorities as being responsible for the development of undesirable physical attributes. Today, however, evidence supports the view that the potential physical-biological values in sports, including volleyball, are the same for girls and boys. Therefore, as the girl or woman practices to perfect her technique, and as she improves her skills in the actual playing of the game, she also adds to her physical strength, her muscular coordinations, and her capacity for physical endurance.

Strength. Scientific research has shown that the modern American woman lacks desired strength in three major sets of muscles: the arms and shoulders, the abdominals, and the feet. Certainly, in the development of the former, the arm and shoulder musculature, volleyball has an opportunity to make one of its most significant contributions. The entire game is based on skills—volleying, serving, "digging," spiking, and blocking—which call these muscles into play. Too, the feet are exercised continuously in the walking, running, sliding, and jumping necessary to practice and play, and if proper instruction is given in correct use, strength is sure to accrue. Although the abdominals are not as clearly involved as are the arm and shoulder muscles and feet, they are definitely related to the game skills which call upon close control of the body, such as the basic movement of jumping, which is essential to good spiking and blocking. Beside the three major areas of muscular weakness, participation in volleyball leads to the development of back, leg, and hand muscles to a significant degree.

Endurance. Although volleyball was originated for the purpose of a game not quite so strenuous and vigorous as basketball, the game of today has developed to the extent that players must undergo rigorous programs of conditioning and training in order to gain and maintain the standard of endurance required for competitive play. In skilled play the drain upon the cardiovascular reserves of the competitors matches that of many other athletic contests. Therefore, students going beyond any more than the merest of basic instruction must engage in supplementary physical activities which will help to prepare them for the occasion of full participation and competition. Information concerning supplementary programs of conditioning and training is presented in Chapter 10.

Other Physical Considerations. In addition to strength and endurance, the two primary factors in physical fitness, volleyball has potential benefits in the development of agility, through walking, running, sliding, leaping, and jumping; flexibility, through the twisting, turning, bending, squatting, crouching, and stretching involved in the performance of game skills; balance, through the gaining and maintaining of proper positions for the execution of all skills and landing after a spike or the block; and coordination, beginning with the most simple and progressing through the most complex game skills. Gracefulness and poise, traditionally valued as feminine characteristics and closely related to ability, flexibility, balance, and coordination, are other desirable physical attributes to be sought in the game.

RECREATIONAL SKILLS

It is a recognized psychological principle that human beings continue pursuit of those things that they can do well. Therefore, it is easy to associate this principle with the fact that volleyball is the nation's number one participant sport and is also the fastest growing. Volleyball is, essentially, a game low in the number of fundamental skills which must be learned before enjoyment can take place. Therefore, the average student can be expected, with reasonable instruction, to gain enough skill so that she can meet some success in play. Thus, volleyball becomes a popular activity for the voluntary phases of school and college programs of physical education as students wish to continue extraclass participation in activities in which they are, to some degree at least, successful. For many of them volleyball will also represent the major physical-recreational activity of their adult lives.

Volleyball as a Leisure-Time Activity. In order to understand the role of volleyball as a major leisure-time pursuit of the American people, it is important to evaluate it by several universally recognized criteria. First of all, does volleyball appeal to the creative and adventuresome spirit, a long established characteristic of the citizenry? Surely this requirement is fully met. What is more exciting than the polished finesse of a well-skilled team at play; the spectacular qualities of a well-aimed spike, which research has shown to travel up to 100 miles per hour in competitive play; the oft-brilliant work of defending players in overcoming such scoring threats; and the perfected beauty of the pass, set, and serving techniques?

Age of Participants.   Second, is age a prohibitive factor in the playing of the game? Certainly, it is not in volleyball. Children in the elementary school years begin playing modified versions of the game, and by the time they have reached the upper elementary school or junior high school levels they are able to engage fully in the team game. Neither is old age a handicap. Men, especially, continue active participation for many years, even as senior citizens. Women, too, are able to engage in this game for a much longer period of time than they are other physical-recreational activities.

Sex of Participants.   Is the playing of the game restricted to the two sexes separately? Volleyball is the only team sport in which men and women and boys and girls can participate together with any real sense of satisfaction. In fact, increased interest in the combined game, especially at the school and college levels, has resulted in the production of a set of rules, by the Division of Girls and Women's Sports, to guide such competition. The rules are such that the number of men and women on a team is equalized and emphasis is given to the women's role in the game by making it mandatory that at least one of the three contacts on each side of the net be made by one of the women players. Also gaining in popularity is mixed Volleyball Doubles (see page 155). An increasingly recognized social value is for girls and women to attain skills and to be competent to engage in friendly competition in mixed groups in order to be good companions to the opposite sex. Furthermore, social relationships are considerably improved if a woman is an intelligent spectator at a variety of sports events. Too, as the need for the American family to find mutual interests increases, volleyball presents itself as an activity in which the whole family, young and old, male and female, can engage. Also related to the same principle is the fact that equipment for the game can be easily established in the backyard or on the beach.

Number of Participants.   Does the number of participants involved limit volleyball as a recreational game? The number, twelve, who must be involved to make a game official does reduce the ranking of volleyball when it is to be compared with individual and dual sports. On the other hand, it is not as difficult to find the twelve players for volleyball as it is to find the eighteen necessary for softball or the twenty-two for soccer or field hockey. In addition, modified versions of the game, such as Trio Volleyball and Volleyball Doubles (see pages 82 and 155), call for much smaller numbers of participants while retaining a great deal of the exciting and exacting aspects of regulation game play.

Seasons of the Sport. Is participation in the game of volleyball relegated to one season? Absolutely not; in fact, in most areas of the country the game is played year-round, often as an indoor activity, often as an outdoor activity, and often under both conditions. Thus, volleyball ranks high in regard to this criterion, and this is in sharp contrast to other sports which are definitely products of the summer, fall, winter, or spring months.

Indoor or Outdoor Sport. Must volleyball be played as either an indoor or outdoor sport? Again, volleyball is an activity which can be played both indoors and outdoors, depending largely upon the area of the country and the weather conditions there. That the game can be played under both conditions raises its value as a recreational activity, for many sports are confined to an either-or location. For example, indoor baseball and field hockey are all but impossible, while outdoor badminton and basketball leave a lot to be desired.

Cost of Participation. Is the cost of participation prohibitive? In this day of extended leisure time, the ability of the working classes to afford certain recreational pursuits has not kept pace with the amount of time they have free for such pursuits. Some of today's most popular activities —namely, golf, bowling, boating, water-skiing, and skiing—are quite expensive. Volleyball, in contrast, demands very little in the way of personal equipment and memberships in league-sponsored play are available at a very nominal fee. Inexpensive nets and balls can be obtained for backyard and beach-type recreational play, and a rope stretched between two trees will suffice for a net if that appears too costly.

KNOWLEDGE AND UNDERSTANDINGS

In addition to the physical abilities and recreational skills to be developed through participation in the game of volleyball, volleyball represents both a direct and indirect body of knowledge which has meaningful potential in the gaining of understandings which enable the individual to live a more well-rounded and productive life.

The Game Itself. Directly, knowledge concerning the game itself is sufficient to offer mental challenge to the participant. Involved is knowledge of the rules of the game; of the standards and regulations governing recommended participation and competition; of the individual skills necessary for basic and advanced play; of the team strategies possible in both offensive and defensive play; and of scoring and officiating. Understandings in these areas enrich the participation experience and lend educational import to the game.

The Cultural Role.   Knowledge and understanding of the historical role that volleyball has played in the socialization and culturalization process of the American people, and especially its contributions in helping the girl and woman to find her rights as an equal citizen, should lead each participant to a better attitude toward, and appreciation of, the game. As an uniquely American sport, volleyball is, indeed, a part of the cultural heritage.

Fitness and Skills.   As instruction in volleyball in institutional programs will have as primary objectives the building of physical fitness and recreational skills, it is of the essence that students not only attain these objectives, but that they gain concurrently knowledge and understandings concerning them as both immediate and long-range values. Thus, a foundation will be laid during instruction in the game to serve as continuing motivation for physical-recreational activity and the importance of fitness in all aspects of day-by-day living.

Self and Others.   As the participant in volleyball acts and interacts in the social laboratory that the game provides, she will be gaining knowledge which will lead her to not only a better understanding of herself, her drives, and her motivations, but also a better understanding of others. She will learn standards of safety which are necessary for game play to be pleasant and free from undue risk. She will engage in the game according to the levels of etiquette and courtesy required by the leadership, and as she does so, she will be invited to compare these standards with those of socially accepted general behavior.

ATTITUDES AND APPRECIATIONS

As participants engage in challenging experiences in volleyball, they are more likely to be developing the know-how of effective self-management. Volleyball represents an opportunity for players to acquire, through practice, play, and competition, attitudes and appreciations, as well as abilities, skills, and knowledge and understandings, which are essential to democratic living. An excellent laboratory for sportsmanship-citizenship learning can be established when there is effective planning and administration by the volleyball leadership.

Ethical Behavior.   The opportunity to learn ethical behavior is offered the individual who participates in a volleyball group, instructional or voluntary, as she learns her social role and gains appropriate attitudes toward social groups and institutions. However, if the volleyball player learns ethical behavior, she must consistently practice it and must want to learn it. The importance of good adult supervision cannot be overemphasized in developing the proper attitudes toward, and appreciations of, team play, cooperation, consideration of others, working together, planning together, realization of individual relationship to group effort, mental alertness, willingness to make personal sacrifices for the good of the group, initiative, resourcefulness, and loyalty.

Acceptance and Belonging. Participation in volleyball provides an opportunity for satisfying the human desire of belonging to a group. When the volleyball experience is educationally sound, the individual gains recognition and status within the group and thereby important values in adequate personality development.

New Adventure. In a society characterized by mechanization, industrialization, and urbanization, chances to feel the excitement to be found in new adventures and experiences are rapidly diminishing. Vandalism and other forms of juvenile delinquency are increasingly used to fill this void. Volleyball, along with other sports experiences, can provide that excitement, to a limited degree within the instructional program, increasingly so in intramural and extramural offerings, and to a climactic degree in interscholastic, intercollegiate, and postschool competition.

Competition and Cooperation. In volleyball the individual has a chance to participate in an activity that requires cooperation essential to individual and group progress and, at the same time, offers the conflict and competition necessary in the development of the personality and the determination of status. The participant, then, has a chance to experience both aspects in their proper proportions and relationships and has an opportunity to develop a healthy attitude in respect to them.

RELATIVE MERITS OF PROGRAMS

Instructional. The volleyball instructional program should be organized to provide for all levels of ability and experience among students. As familiarity with an activity tends to increase participation, every effort should be made to teach the game in such a way that there is emphasis on immediate and future use of skills, strategies, rules, knowledges, understandings, and favorable attitudes.

Voluntary. The volleyball to be found in the instructional program, beginning, intermediate, or advanced, is not enough. A willing interest which motivates the student to participate in a voluntary program ensures her the opportunity to engage in the sport on a more realistic basis. Upper elementary age children will profit from limited voluntary programs in volleyball. In secondary schools, colleges, and universities the voluntary program will assume increasing importance, and the intramural, extramural, and interscholastic or intercollegiate phases should be used to augment the instructional program.

Intramural. Intramural volleyball should provide opportunity for reinforcing the skills and interests begun in the earlier instructional program. Competition within the intramural program should be fun; should enhance the educational experience through the satisfactions involved in being chosen to represent a group; and should motivate the participant to increased effort to perfect skills, become well conditioned, and otherwise prepare to give a good account of herself in the game. Guidelines which can be followed in the development of sound instructional and intramural programs of volleyball are to be found in Chapters 7, 8, and 9.

Extramural. As early as the junior high school level, students with increasing social interests and more highly developed skills can profit from extramural volleyball experiences with students from other schools. Extramural experiences in volleyball should be open to all girls on the high school level and all women on the college level who desire them. Indeed, this type of volleyball competition is particularly suitable for the girl or woman who has the drive but not the superior skill for interscholastic or intercollegiate competition.

Interscholastic-Intercollegiate Programs. Programs of interscholastic and modified programs of intercollegiate volleyball should be maintained for the accelerated player to satisfy her needs and interests in representing a school, college, or university on an athletic team. While opportunity to try out on an equal basis should be open to all, it is expected that only the gifted volleyball player will have opportunity to gain the educational values inherent in this type of competition, and that this participation will come only when she is ready physically, socially, mentally, emotionally, and healthwise.

To those who would deny this type of competition to the girl or woman let it be said that education for *all* must include the few who are superior in skill as well as the many who have average, or less than average, ability, and it is only through this type of competition that provision can be made for the special needs of the gifted. Just as some boys and men want to excel, so do some girls and women need evidence of superiority to sustain their self-respect.

Postschool Competition. In the competitive volleyball leagues sponsored by recreation departments, church, and industrial and civic organizations are to be found the women who need continuing experiences in the game at this level. They participate and compete out of their own desire, and from within this group come some of the most loyal and staunch supporters of the game. The physical, recreational, and educational values experienced in educational types of programs should continue, and be enhanced, at this level. Guidelines in the sound conduct of competitive programs for schools, colleges, and universities and non-educational institutions and organizations are outlined in Chapter 10.

INDIVIDUAL SKILLS:
Presentation and Practice

There is little doubt that one of the major reasons why volleyball is the most popular participant sport in America, and also the fastest growing, is that the number of skills which must be perfected to enjoy the game in recreational play is relatively small. Basically, with some technique in putting the ball into play, the service, and in volleying it over the net, the would-be player is ready to perform in a game of sorts. However, this same truism is also the reason why many students, more often girls and women, finish high school and go to college with a rather thorough dislike for the game. These students had their first exposure to the game of volleyball during the late elementary school, or early junior high school years, and continued participation in instructional units in the team sport during high school, and discouragingly found little change in the skills and strategy introduced along the way.

Unfortunately, many physical education teachers at the junior high school, high school, and even college and university levels have used volleyball as a "filler"-type activity within the program—that is, one to accommodate large numbers of students without any real attention to the development of the exciting, interesting, and skillful game that it can, and should, be. Thus, instruction, when any, has been geared to that of a "messy-mass" game where seven, eight, nine, and more players are crowded onto a regulation court, with little chance to really handle the ball, and haphazardly poke or push the ball over the net.

Often the cause of such low quality instruction is the fact that the volleyball teacher herself does not know the game: the fundamental skills and interesting practices in which to help students develop them; its strategies of sparkling offensive and keen defensive play; or how to teach it in such a way that it becomes a thrilling sports experience in which the student wishes to continue as an active participant rather than being willing to remove herself entirely from the game or to the sidelines as a passive spectator.

To be a successful participant in any sport, the individual player must have mastered to some reasonable degree the fundamental skills. Volleyball is no exception. Although the girl or woman may choose volleyball as a favorite activity because it is a team game, and she does not have to perform as an individual, she must be responsible for her share of the team's efforts, and if she is to be an asset rather than a liability, she must accept this responsibility with all its implications. Therefore, she must know, understand the uses, and be ready to perform all of the basic individual skills.

2

Ball-Handling Skills

Each and every player on a volleyball team, regardless of its nature—instructional, recreational, or competitive—is a ball-handler. Therefore, she must be able not only to handle the ball, but to handle it with purpose according to the dictates of the play situation.

THE VOLLEY

The basic ball-handling skill in the game of volleyball is the volley. The type of volley to be used at a particular time in the game depends upon the demands of the situation. In passing and setting the ball, the skilled player will concentrate almost exclusively on the overhead volley or one of its modifications, and the beginning player should be encouraged to do the same. However, in passing the ball in beginning units of instruction and in recreational play, an underhand volley should be acceptable.

THE OVERHEAD VOLLEY AS A PASS

Every girl or woman on the team must have volleying skill that enables her to be a good passer. The Pass is the beginning of the attack, regardless of the offensive pattern of play developed by the team. No good offensive play can possibly result without a sound beginning in a good pass. There is a natural tendency to play down the importance of the volley-pass, when it is compared to the more spectacular skills of the spike and the block. However, any experienced player, teacher, coach, official, or spectator knows that the Pass—emphasizing the proper distance to the Key-Set; the necessary height to permit that player to get under the ball and be waiting for it, and the reduction of spin and force—is an absolute essential. It is also known that the player who has been able to master this skill has worked long and hard, for despite its apparent ease, it requires dedicated and diligent practice to perfect.

The most difficult overhead volley-pass to make is the one that must

21

accompany the responsibility in receiving the service. To take the power and spin out of a strategically served ball, to bring it under complete control, and to start the ball moving toward the Key-Set in such a way that she can set the ball to a spiker is the objective in this initial contact. As the ball leaves the hand of the server, or is last contacted by a member of the opposing team during a rally of net-crossing plays, the receiving team must make a judgment as to which player will be responsible for the initial contact, and the appropriate player must move to be in position, ready, and waiting for the ball.

Body Position (see Fig. 2–1). As the player moves to be ready to use the overhead volley in passing the ball, she should assume a position in which the balls of both feet equally support the weight of the body. The heels are kept in contact with the court surface, but the player must not allow any of her body weight to settle back onto the heels. Both feet should be pointed in the direction of the intended play. The legs will be separated with the knees slightly flexed. One foot is forward, usually the left foot in the right-handed player, so that the basic position of feet and legs resembles the familiar forward-stride position used in many sports. The trunk of the body should tilt slightly forward.

There are two basic positions for the arms and elbows in executing the overhead volley-pass. In the first, the elbows are bent and the arms are held in front of the body with the forearms and upper arms forming a flexible oval. The second position recommends that the elbows be held slightly to the front of the body and in alignment with the shoulders. The first position is popular among girls' and women's teams as they wait in team formation to receive the service. However, there is usually a noticeable change to the second position immediately prior to contacting the ball. The hands are placed approximately chest high with the thumbs pointed in toward each other, almost touching, and downward. The wrists are flexed and are extended backward so that the palms of the hands are upward from the floor. The fingers are spread wide and, with the palms and the heels of the hands, are capable of forming a secure resting place for the ball.

The position of the head and neck is regulated by the flight pattern of the ball. A descriptive guide to follow is to let the ball fall toward the upturned face, with the eyes never leaving their concentration on the flight pattern, until contact can be made just before the ball would strike the nose.

The Action. As the ball approaches, the extended arms are withdrawn, following the ball into the body until it reaches the face level. At that point there is a complete extension of the arms and throughout the body. All eight fingers and the two thumbs should contact the ball simultaneously, making a definite and clear rebound from the fleshy pads near the ends of the fingers and thumbs. The wrists extend to a maximum in line with the forearms and arms, accompanied by a rotation of the wrists and hands inward. From the forward tilting position, the body extends so that a slight arch forms in the back. The knees straighten and there is a forward and upward shift of body weight behind the ball.

THE UNDERHAND VOLLEY AS A PASS

If the volleyball player cannot move to be ready and waiting to execute an overhead volley in passing the ball and is unable to handle the ball in the same manner from a squatting or kneeling position, an obvious alternate way to attempt the play is through use of an underhand volley. However, although both the USVBA and the DGWS rules still legalize the underhand volley, it is extremely difficult to perform without committing a ball-handling violation. Therefore, officials in competitive play for girls and women, as well as for boys and men, tend to call all open-palm, underhand contacts as holding or catching the ball.

In purely recreational play and in beginning units of instruction, where ball-handling violations need not be quite so strictly enforced, it is recommended that the two-hand underhand volley be permitted and offered as an alternate volley for passing purposes. As students progress from beginning to intermediate and advanced levels of play, they should be encouraged to use the overhead volley whenever possible, dropping down into a squatting or even a kneeling position to play the low ball, and to substitute a

Fig. 2–1. Waiting to volley overhead.   **Fig. 2–2.** Waiting to volley underhand.

"dig" for those plays in which it is impossible to move to meet the ball above the head.

The Body Position (see Fig. 2–2). The feet are in a forward-stride position which comfortably accommodates the weight of the body as the knees and hips are bent into a crouching or squatting position. The weight of the body is forward on the balls of both feet. The arms are held out in front of the body and are flexed at the elbow. The hands are turned so that the palms are upward. The little fingers of each hand are held parallel with each other and the thumbs are turned outward. The fingers are slightly spread and are held in a state of tension. The head, accommodating the eyes, moves to follow the flight pattern of the ball.

The Action. The ball should be contacted as it drops below the waistline. The movement pattern of the body follows a complete extension, beginning in the feet and continuing until the snap of the finger pads against the surface of the ball. The weight of the body shifts from the back foot to the front foot. In fact, the heel of the back foot will become elevated from the court surface. The knees straighten with a forceful action; the hips are lifted to a regular standing position; the arms are raised upward and rotated outward; the wrists are snapped; and the fleshy parts of the fingers briefly contact the surface of the ball. The ball must rebound from the finger pads immediately and any contact of the ball with the palms or the heel of the hands must be carefully avoided.

THE OVERHEAD VOLLEY AS A SET

If a good overhead volley is important in the Pass, or the beginning of the attacking play, it is absolutely essential in the Set. The Set is the second contact of the ball and the objective of this volley is to get the ball from the Key-Set to the spiker in such a way that she can spike it in the most effective manner. As the second of the three contacts that a team has with the ball on its side of the court, the Set holds the attack together. Probably the most desirable characteristic in a player who is to Set the ball to the spiker is that she be consistent in her overhead volleying ability. To be consistent does not mean that she will be playing the ball each time in the same way. On the contrary, being consistent as a Key-Set means being able to vary the height, the distance, the direction, and the position of the ball in relationship to the net without losing anything in the way of control.

Again, the overhead volley-set may not be as spectacular as the spike, the block, or even the pick-up, but everyone who knows the game and has experience as a player or spectator appreciates the skillful play of a talented Set. As the supporting play of the Key-Set is observed in the game, it is with full recognition that this girl or woman has worked long and hard with the spiker or spikers who compose her attacking unit. First, she learned to set the ball with consistency to a height of 10 to 12 feet so that it reaches its highest point at the middle of the distance between her and the spiker. Then, she learned to adjust the Set to the net, keeping it parallel and some 12 to 18 inches away for the taller spikers and parallel and 24 to 30 inches away for the shorter spikers. Ultimately, she learned to vary heights, distances, and directions to prevent blockers on the opposing team from fully anticipating the pattern to be used in the setting-spiking attack.

Body Position and Action.   Just as members on the team will be coached to allow the Key-Set to make the second contact on the ball whenever possible, the Key-Set must be coached to move wherever she must to be ready and waiting to play the ball with a good overhead volley. She must also be ready to signal her intentions to her teammates in order to keep any overanxious member from moving in to play the ball in a way which, at best, would probably be defensive in nature.

The basic body position and the action of the overhead volley-set is the same as that for the Pass. However, there should be additional stress on playing the ball above the face, and one way to give this emphasis is to teach and coach the player to look through the triangle formed by the fingers and thumbs on her two hands as she plays the ball (see Fig. 2–3). A second emphasis should be on getting more arch in the back as the ball is

Fig. 2–3.   Setting for the spiker.

contacted so that there is more power involved and a better chance for the desirable high volley.

THE REVERSE VOLLEY AS A SET

The reverse volley, or "back set," as it is frequently called, is receiving quite a bit of attention in competitive play for girls and women. In the Pair-Partner (Three-Three), Two-for-One (Four-Two) and Five-to-One systems of play, it is used to take advantage of a spiker in the right forward position. The reverse volley is a modification of the overhead volley in which the Key-Set, usually playing the center forward position, volleys the ball directly over her own head to a spiker. Part of its value as a surprise weapon lies in the fact that the Key-Set is in the same position she normally uses to play the ball to the spiker on her left, usually her Key-Spiker. Therefore, it is difficult for the blockers to anticipate and to move to the best position to act against the spiker.

Body Position and Action. The basic body position for the overhead volley is used in the reverse volley. However, there are some modifications. First, the player allows the head and neck to move up and back to follow the flight pattern of the ball, but instead of lining up the contact with the moment just before the ball would fall on to the nose, the forehead is used as the guide. The arms extend to a position over the top of the head drawing the back into a more arched position. The wrists are flexed back more fully so that the fingers get into the contact and control of the ball more than do the thumbs. As the ball is touched, the fingers spread out into a straightened and extended position (see Fig. 2–4). The rest of the body follows the same movement pattern as for a regular overhead volley.

Fig. 2–4.   Reverse setting for the spiker.

CROSS SET AND OVER SET

The cross set and the over set are two additional modifications of the overhead volley gaining prominence in the girls' and women's competitive game. The cross set refers to the set made by the Key-Set in the left forward position or in the center forward position when she is making the volley to a spiker in the center forward or in the right forward position and wants the ball to cross in front of the spiker's body so that she can play it with her right hand (see Fig. 2–5). This particular set requires an overhead volley that is very accurate in its relationship to the net and is high or low according to the height of the spiker and the wishes of the offense in varying the attack. The over set refers to a set made by the Key-Set when she is playing the position of left forward and wants to volley the ball to the right forward to be spiked or by the Key-Set when she is playing the position of right forward and wants to volley the ball to the left forward position to be spiked (see Fig. 2–6). In either case the overhead volley must be modified with additional height and distance so that it passes over the top of the head of the center forward. The effectiveness of this particular play in the game depends upon the faking motion of the center forward, as well as the quality of the set and spike, so that the opposing blockers will not be able to decide which of the two players will be spiking the ball until it is too late to set up an effective blocking station. The cross set will be of use in the Pair-Partner, Two-for-One, and Five-to-One systems of play (see Chapter 5). The over set is of special value in the Two-for-One and Five-to-One systems, where the number of spikers is greater than that of the set players.

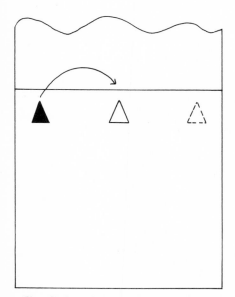
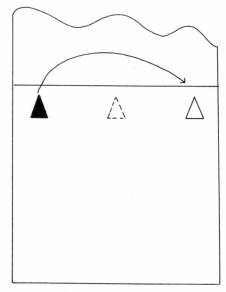

Fig. 2–5.   Cross setting to the spiker.   **Fig. 2–6.**   Over setting to the spiker.

METHODS OF PRESENTATION AND PRACTICE

One of the first concerns of the volleyball teacher in a beginning unit of instruction is to help any student who has a fear of the ball. Therefore, activity in the beginning unit should start with some elementary ball-handling procedures in which the student has an opportunity to experiment with the size, shape, and feel of a regulation and properly inflated ball. In these experimental procedures of lightly tossing, catching, rolling, and bouncing, the instructor should emphasize that the ball within itself is an inanimate object, without power to perform in any capacity. Following the same line of reasoning, she should indicate that the ball needs a "master" who can "tell" the ball what to do and be assured that it will react in the way that it has been directed.

DEMONSTRATION OF THE VOLLEYS

Because beginners will have little control over where the ball is received, the teacher will more than likely introduce the overhead and underhand volleys at the same time, very carefully pointing out the advantages of the overhead technique. Consequently, she will demonstrate both skills, beginning with the most desirable overhead, using a self-volley. A follow-up of the self-volley idea is to volley the ball against a solid wall surface whenever one is available. Then, she will use a student to throw, toss, or volley the ball toward her, and she will complete the demonstration as she returns the ball to the student assistant. During the introduction and the demonstration the teacher will carefully analyze or explain the starting position and the action involved in the volleys and will ask for questions before the students begin their practice.

PRACTICE FORMATIONS

The following is a suggested outline of practice formations, beginning with quite simple ones and progressing to the more complex, which can be used by the teacher in beginning, intermediate, and advanced units of instruction and by the coach working with a competitive group to practice and perfect volleying techniques:

1. Using the proper body position, including the triangle formed by the fingers and thumbs of the hands, have the players catch a ball that has been tossed by the teacher. As each girl has her turn, allow her to inspect briefly her hand position on the ball and repeat the major points of emphasis as outlined during the demonstration and analysis. Check to see that each girl holds the ball with the fleshy finger pads without allowing palms or the heels of the hands to make contact.

2. *"Give and Go."* Remembering all of the essential points in the body

position and the action of the volley, have the students to practice the action, at its regular speed, mimetically. As the signal "Give" is called, the students should flex their bodies into the body position, and on "Go," they complete the action necessary to execute a successful volley.

3. *Circle with a Purpose* (see Fig. 2–7). Divide the class temporarily into groups of no more than eight and no less than six. Each group stands in a circle formation approximately the size of the restraining circle on a basketball court. It is essential that the circle is not too large as the group begins to handle the ball or their volleys may fall short and lead to early frustration. The object is to pass the ball to any member within the circle except those who are at either side of the ball-handler. Allow either an overhead or underhand volley, emphasizing control of the ball, height (look at the net!), and the basic body principles. From the very beginning encourage students to volley with a purpose: to have someone in mind as they attempt to pass the ball; to face the direction they want the ball to go; and to assume responsibility for playing the ball when it comes in their direction by verbally sounding out with "Ball" or "Mine."

COMPETITION. Adding a competitive element to arouse and maintain interest, to raise group or team spirit, and to begin a will to win is important even in the most elementary of practice formations. First, beginning all groups at the same time with a verbal or whistle signal, see which one can keep the ball going the longest without a "miss." A miss will be letting the ball drop to the floor or hit any obstruction within the teaching station; players standing beside each other making successive contacts; a player hitting the ball twice in succession or committing a ball-handling violation. Encourage the students to recognize and enforce their own ball-handling violations. Whenever a miss occurs, the team is out of the competition and should kneel, squat, or sit so that they can watch the continuing teams and so that the teacher is better able to establish the winner. Offer several trials in the competition so that more than one team has a chance to win. Encourage teams which have lost out in the trial to watch the other teams finish to see if there is anything in the style of play which might be helpful

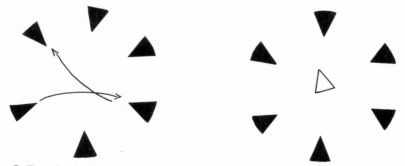

Fig. 2–7.   Circle with a purpose.   **Fig. 2–8.**   Captain-circle formation.

to their own group. If different teams win in the several trials, the teacher may find it profitable to conduct a championship trial with only the winners competing and the other groups watching for suggestions they can use in their own play.

Second, instead of calling out "Ball" or "Mine" as the ball is played, have the students number their consecutive successful contacts. The first player calls out "one"; the second player, "two"; the third player, "three," and so forth until the ball is missed. After a miss, the count must begin again at "one." Set a particular number for an objective and see which group can get to that number first. Begin all groups at the same time with a verbal or whistle signal. As the group reaches the set goal, it should sit, kneel, or squat so that the teacher is able to acknowledge the winner. Insist that counting be aloud. The misses are the same as those listed above. Increase the number-goal as the players' skills develop.

Third, set a particular and reasonable time limit and see how many consecutive successful contacts can be accumulated within the time allotted. Numbering aloud and starting over at one after a miss will be expected. At the end of the time limit, the teacher will check each group for its best number and will announce the winner, as well as recognize other groups with worthy scores. Misses are the same.

4. *Captain-Circle Formation* (see Fig. 2–8). After participation in circle with a purpose, each group will probably be able to name some player within its number who shows better than average skill. That player is invited to become the captain or leader and takes her place in the center of the circle. The captain begins by passing the ball to any player on the outside of the circle, but that player must reciprocate by returning the ball to the captain. Besides continuing emphasis on height, control, and body principles in handling the ball, placement and direction of the volley become objectives. The player in the circle must return the ball to her captain and, therefore, she must direct the placement of the pass. The teacher should emphasize the fact that good volleys will keep the captain in a fairly stationary position in which she will merely pivot on a base foot as she passes the ball to the outside of the circle.

COMPETITION. In competing within the circle-captain formation, add one additional miss: the failure to volley the ball alternately between the captain and a member of the outside circle. The other misses are the same as those described under "Circle with a Purpose." The competitive variations are also the same. However, one addition, the round-trip, may be used. In the round-trip a player in the outside of the circle starts the ball rather than the captain, and following the same procedure, the ball is volleyed in and out of the circle until it returns to the player who originally started it. The object is to see which group can complete a successful round-trip first. Whenever a miss occurs, the ball must be tossed back to the starting player to begin again. As players gain in their ball-handling skill, the number of round-trips can be increased. If the number designated is four, when the ball returns to the original player the first time, she calls out "one"; the second time, "two"; and so on, until "four" has been reached. A variation of the round-trip is to set a time limit and to see how many successful round-trips a team or group can accumulate. This round-trip variation has the additional advantage of keeping all groups active, rather than have them drop out after a miss or after successfully completing an objective.

5. *Captain-Semicircle Formation.* The captain-semicircle formation is a simple variation of the captain-circle formation outlined in number 4. The semicircle should be arranged around the captain so that each player is approximately the same distance away. The ball is alternately played by the leader and any member in the semicircle. The same purposes in height, control, distance, and placement of the volley are appropriate. The competitive possibilities outlined in connection with the captain-circle formation may be repeated in the captain-semicircle formation.

6. *Zigzag Formation* (see Fig. 2–9). In addition to height, control, and placement, one of the most desired objectives of the volley is to cover distance. Players must be able to grade the distance they pass the ball from the back line positions to the forwards, and the forwards must be able to grade the distance covered in the set so that the ball comes down between the Key-Set and the spiker. An excellent way to introduce regulating the

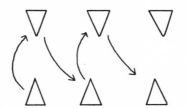

Fig. 2–9. Zigzag formation.

distance of the volley is through use of the zigzag formation. In this formation the team or group is evenly divided so that there are two lines with each player facing a partner. The objective is to begin the ball at the end of one line with a straight, or "zigging," volley across to the partner, who in turn will "zag" the ball on the diagonal back to the next player in the opposite line. Thus, the ball is volleyed up and down the lines. Begin players at a short distance from each other, approximately 6 to 8 feet, and back them up as they begin to develop control at the shorter distance. If there are appropriate line markings down on the gymnasium floor in an indoor teaching station, these can be used to good advantage by the teacher

in stressing control for a particular distance. Chalk lines drawn on outdoor playing surfaces will serve the same purpose. The teacher frequently
will need to call attention to the fact that height should not be sacrificed
in reaching distance. She will encourage the students to get the feel of
playing the ball up and over at a height approximating that of the net.

COMPETITION. In addition to those previously outlined under "Circle
with a Purpose" a miss will be failing to have each player hit the ball in turn
as it advances up and down the line. Although students will be encouraged
to stand behind the line to play the ball, stepping in front of the line is not
only permissible but expected when the volley falls short. All of the competition variations previously presented are possible within the framework
of the zigzag formation.

1. *Volley by Two's* (see Fig. 2–10). In volley by two's volleying enforces
the height of the net for the first time. Each girl works with a partner,

Fig. 2–10. Volley by two's.

with one standing on one side of the net and the other on the opposite side.
The object is to volley the ball back and forth across the net to each other.
During this type of practice the teacher is stressing the required height to
clear the net, the distance away from the net that a player should stand to
volley the ball over effectively, and the establishment of a good rhythm in
the volley. To accomplish the latter purpose, have the players count aloud
"and" as they contact the ball and "one," or the correct number as it increases, with the ball as it crosses over the net. Only in occasional teaching
situations will there be enough balls for each two players to have one.
Therefore, the teacher will need to devise a system for taking turns. One
suggestion is for an even number of partners to be assigned to each court,
and as one pair of partners miss, they give the ball to another twosome
awaiting their turn.

COMPETITION. Additional misses for volley by two's include: failing to
clear the net on the volley, stepping over the center line, and coming in
contact with the net. Competition variations will include keeping the ball
going the longest without a miss, numbering the volleys to see which pair
of players can get to a set number first, and setting a time limit and determining which twosome can build up the highest number of consecutive

successful volleys within the time allotment. Because of the limitations that may be placed on the class by the number of balls available, the last variation probably will have the most merit. Each set of partners would have an equal amount of time in which to participate and would be active continuously during the time allotment. The teacher may want to continue the competition by declaring a winning partnership on each court and by bringing those winners together to compete for a grand championship.

8. *Volley by Four's* (see Fig. 2–11). Two players line up on one side of the net to face two players assuming the same positions on the opposite side. To demonstrate volley by four's, the teacher may call upon two sets of winning competitors from volley by two's. One player on each side assumes the position of forward and the other assumes the position of back. The object is for the back player to begin play by volleying, or passing, the ball to the forward, who, in turn, attempts to volley the ball over the head of the forward on the opposite side of the net to the back. The back returns the ball to her own forward and the sequence of play is continued. The volleyball teacher may use volley by four's to introduce team play through emphasis that the forward-back combination is identical with full-team structure, which will be accomplished by adding two other sets of partners to each twosome. Thus, the back will be encouraged to play facing the net squarely and to study the opponents in action. The forward will be taught to assume a basic position with one shoulder into the net so that she, too, can watch her opponents, but, at the same time, can be ready and waiting for the volley-pass coming from her teammate behind her. The concept of "point" and "side-out" may also be introduced by having the team that puts the ball into play score a point when the other team is unable to legally return the ball and by giving the ball to the other twosome to put into play whenever the "serving" pair has failed in making a good return. Introducing the three-contact ruling will also be easily effected at this time.

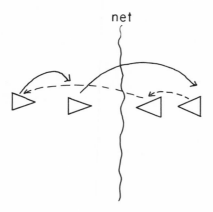

net

Fig. 2–11. Volley by four's.

COMPETITION. As the groups of four begin practice in this formation, competition should not be stressed. The forward should deliberately attempt to place the ball close to the back on the opposite side so that a good volleying rally can be established. However, as soon as the teacher feels that her class is ready, she should encourage the forwards to mix up the distance, height, and placement of their contacts so that the opposing players have difficulty in making a good return. Then, competition can be started with the awarding of point and side-out in the appropriate situations. When competition is in effect, it is advisable, for reasons of safety, not to have more than two groups participating on a court at any time. The teacher will provide for a system of rotation so that each player will have a chance to function as the back and as the forward.

9. *Volley Game.* When teaching in a beginning unit of instruction where one of the immediate objectives has been to help students overcome fear of the ball, the use of a Volley Game, before introducing the service, may prove quite effective. In Volley Game play is conducted as in regulation play, with the exception that the ball is put into play with a volley from the student occupying the right back position. Using the three contacts provided them, the "serving" team plays the ball to the opponents who in turn must legally return the ball to them. Volley Game can also be used by the teacher to emphasize team play, especially in regard to positioning the six players to cover the playing court and in the use of the three contacts to make the last play over the net more effective. At this time it is also possible to introduce such basic rules of the game as:

1. Right back puts the ball into play.
2. Rotation.
3. Court boundaries and balls landing on lines.
4. Three contacts.
5. Scoring.
6. Game (points and time) and match.
7. Fouls: ball-handling violations, more than three hits, two hits in succession by one player, net fouls, center-line violations, and body fouls.

COMPETITION. Competition in Volley Game will be handled as in a regular game with a predetermined indication as to whether the game will be played on a time basis, by points, or by a combination of the two. As a culminating experience of an early lesson in a beginner's unit, the teacher may elect to have the students participate in a full match of Volley Game.

10. *Shuttle Formation ("Hi! Ho!")* (see Fig. 2–12). In moving on to practice formations requiring more than beginning skill level in order to meet success, the volleyball teacher and coach will find merit in the use of the shuttle formation. In the shuttle the player has an opportunity to practice moving into position to make a good volley and then moving out so that another player has an opportunity at the ball. Volleyball is not a

Fig. 2–12. Shuttle formation.

stationary game, and each player should understand and have experience in moving before and after contacting the ball. A team or group, representing no more than eight players, is divided so that each half is lined up behind a leader. The leader puts the ball into play by passing it across the desired distance to the leader in the opposite line. She then moves, to her right-hand side to avoid being in the line of the next play, down to the end of the opposite line. In the meantime, the leader on the other side has moved in and returns the ball to the new leader in the original line. In addition to the value gained by moving into position and out, this formation should be used to develop rhythm and timing in the pass and for the set. It is suggested that as the first player contacts the ball she calls out some verbal signal such as "Hi!" and the leader in the opposite line responds with "Ho!" as she makes her contact. After the players are able to control the ball to the extent that there is uniformity in height, distance, and control, the "Hi-Ho" verbal sounds will fall into an even rhythmical pattern. The teacher or coach can arrange practice for setting within this formation by emphasizing a volley in which the player sends the ball almost straight into the air and a real move must be made from the opposing line to cover the ball. This type of volley is used in the game when the ball is set close and parallel with the net for the spiker to contact with a running approach.

COMPETITION. Competitions among the groups or teams in the shuttle formation can be conducted on the basis of seeing which team can keep the ball going the longest; setting a particular number of volleys as a goal and seeing which team can reach the number first; setting a time limit and determining which team can build up the highest number of consecutive successful volleys within that time; or establishing the round-trip variations.

11. *Shuttle Formation Across the Net.* Volleying within a shuttle formation with half of the group lined up on one side of the net and the other half on the opposite side can be used to emphasize a good rhythmical volley with the net enforcing the height quality. Instead of moving to the end of the opposite line after playing the ball, the leader merely moves to the end of her own line. Again, verbal signals will help to develop the desirable timing in contacting the ball.

COMPETITION. Competition among the various groups may be conducted in the same way as for the previous shuttle formation. In addition, competition may be arranged between the two halves of the group with the side which is able to have the appropriate player volley the ball over the net without a legal return from the other side to be given a point. The winner would be determined by the number of points a side could build up within a given time limit. For purposes of safety, no more than two groups should be competing on a court at a given time.

12. *Zigzag Across the Net.* The zigzag formation, described earlier, can be used to emphasize the distance of the volley, or pass, across the net and to enforce the minimum height. The group, or team, is divided so that each player faces a partner on the opposite side of the net. The ball begins with the end player on one side passing the ball straight across to her opposite player, who in turn "zags" the ball back to the second person in the original line. The play sequence follows in the same pattern up and down the lines.

COMPETITION. All of the variations previously mentioned for competing in the zigzag formation are appropriate for zigzag across the net. Because of the spread of players along the net, only one group should participate on a court at one time. It is not recommended that one side compete against the other in this formation since emphasis should be on playing the ball to each specific player in turn and not merely on getting the ball across the net.

13. *Wall Volley.* The volleyball teacher and coach should be prepared to take advantage of any solid wall surface which is available to her. Using the wall for volleying purposes has special merit in that it offers an individual practice procedure to the player. By placing target lines of net height, 10 feet high, and 12 feet high on the wall and restraining lines on the floor 3, 5, and 7 feet away, the teacher can encourage practice of the volley for control, height, and distance. The wall returns the ball in much the same way that it was contacted. Thus, the player can learn much about the spin and force she puts on her passes and sets to teammates. Many teachers have balls available at the teaching station so that students reporting early for class can begin individual practice against the wall. Many volleyball coaches use wall practice as a means of quickly warming up the fingers in each practice session.

COMPETITION. Although it is possible to use the same group competitive procedures for individual competition in the wall volley, it is recommended that the teacher, instead, select one or more of the available skill tests involving the wall volley for administration to her students. Such tests provide incentive to players wanting to improve ability and scores. Several of these tests are included in the section on skill testing at the end of Chapter 9.

14. *Self-volley.* When the teacher or coach is working in a teaching station where no wall space is available, she will find that a self-volley practice will serve many of the same purposes as that of wall volley practice. A special merit is that it allows good individual practice. In a self-volley practice the player volleys the ball over her own head, and as it returns

from its highest point, she continues to play it into the air. The player should be encouraged to keep to a fairly constant area of playing space; to work for varying heights, with a minimum height being the top of the net; to learn something about the quality of her contact in regard to force and spin; and to associate this type of volley with the one she will be using in the game as a set for the spiker.

COMPETITION. The self-volley can also be used for individual competitive purposes in much the same way as many of the group competitions. However, it should be administered as a skill test early in the instructional unit so that it motivates students to improve their own scores in self-practice. One skill test using the self-volley as the testing procedure, the Trotter Self-Volley Test, is presented on pages 184–85.

15. *Captain-Circle Moving.* One of the most spectacular volley practice formations, and one which can be used effectively as pregame warm-up in competition, is the captain-circle moving. The practice formation begins as a stationary pattern as described under captain-circle; however, as soon as the group is completely controlling the ball, on a verbal or whistle signal, it moves either clockwise or counterclockwise. Then, at every subsequent signal, each player reverses her direction by making a reverse turn on the balls of both feet or by making a half-pivot. If the coach or teacher is calling the direction changes, she should use a whistle for the signal. If the signal is to come from the group, it should be a verbal, "Change," and should be called by someone outside the circle rather than the captain. The captain, who is contacting the ball alternately, must concentrate on her play. The outside circle should move at a steady pace, a medium speed walk, and should attempt to keep the circumference of the circle fairly stable, with each player in the same approximate distance from the captain. When timing has been perfected, it is possible to change directions frequently, showing proficiency in moving to play the ball, to time passes, and to judge responsibility for play.

COMPETITION. Although the main purpose of this practice formation is to develop finesse in control of the volley, it can be adapted to provide the competitive variations: keeping it going the longest; setting a number of volleys as a goal and seeing which group is first able to reach that number; setting a time limit and determining which group can build up the highest number of successful consecutive contacts within the time limit; and variations of the round-trip procedure.

16. *Two-Ball Formations.* Practice formations in which two balls are controlled and volleyed by the group at the same time provide challenging advanced methods in perfecting the quality and timing of the pass or set. They can be used by intermediate, advanced, and competitive groups for demonstration purposes and pregame warm-up. Both the captain-circle formation and the captain-semicircle formation lend themselves to the use

of two balls. In either case, a definite pattern for passing to the circle or
semicircle must be followed. Within circle formation the captain and a
player in the outside of the circle contact the ball at the same time. As the
second contact is made, the captain will direct her ball to a player adjacent
to the original outside player, and in each consecutive contact, she will
move the ball around the circle to each player in turn. In the semicircle
formation, a player on the end will pass the ball at the same time that the
captain does, and the captain will direct her volleys to each player in turn
within the semicircle. Following this type of pattern, the captain is able
to keep her eyes on both balls at the same time. There is little value to be
gained in using these practice formations for competitive purposes.

17. *Reverse Volley by Three's* (see Fig. 2–13). Although the reverse
volley is often used by beginners as a defensive type of play when it becomes
necessary for a forward, on the third contact, to volley the ball over her
own head into the opponents' court, the use of a reverse volley in the game
as a setting skill is definitely of intermediate or advanced skill level. In
reverse volley by three's, the player who is trying to develop her reverse
volley skill is placed in the middle of two other players, usually the spikers
with whom she will be working in the game. As the practice formation
begins, she is directly facing one of the two players. The player she faces
begins by volleying the ball to the middle player. She then sets the ball
over her own head to the third player. Immediately after making the contact, the middle player turns to face the third player, receives her pass, and
back sets it to the player who started the formation. The practice continues
according to this sequence of contacts. Because this practice formation is
wearing upon the middle player, who will begin to feel symptoms of dizzi-
ness if it is prolonged, the teacher or coach should encourage frequent rotation of different players into the center position.

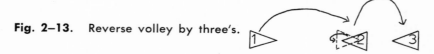

Fig. 2–13.   Reverse volley by three's.

COMPETITION. Competition among the groups—in keeping the ball
going the longest, working for the highest number of successful consecutive
volleys within a given time limit, and attempting to reach a designated
number of successful volleys first—is possible and desirable.

18. *Reverse Volley Shuttle* (see Fig. 2–14). The reverse volley shuttle
formation also emphasizes the development of the reverse volley as a setting
skill. A group of six to eight players are lined up in the following manner:
Two players stand in the middle of a regular shuttle formation, back to
back so that each one faces her half of the shuttle. The leader of one half
of the shuttle puts the ball into play by volleying it out to the player facing

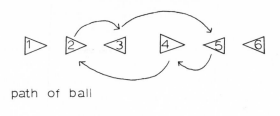

path of ball

rotation of players

Fig. 2–14.   Reverse volley shuttle.

her in the middle of the shuttle. That player, in turn, reverse volleys the ball over her own head and that of the player standing just behind her to the leader of the second half of the shuttle. The leader of the second half of the shuttle volleys the ball to the player in the middle facing her, and the sequence of contacts continues. However, new players continuously assume the middle positions in the shuttle in this manner: As soon as the original middle player reverse volleys the ball, she moves to her right to the end of her own half of the line, and the player who started as the leader in her half of the line moves forward to the middle position. There is ample time while the other half of the shuttle is making its appropriate ball contacts for this rotation to occur.

This formation requires a great deal of skill, as well as good reaction to responsibilities in changing of positions. To perform in this formation with finesse and control will be a challenge to even the most advanced of players.

COMPETITION.   All of the competitive formations previously outlined for volley practice are appropriate, but the teacher and coach will find that the round-trip variations are of special value.

19. *Pass-Set-Spike.*   Additional practices for the volley in the pass-set-spike sequence are presented with the spiking formations.

DIGS

While it is recommended that beginning classes and recreational volleyball groups be allowed to use the underhand volley in passing the ball, intermediate and advanced classes and competitive groups must have alternate skills in playing the ball which drops below the waistline. To be ready and waiting for the ball so that the overhead volley can be executed is the ideal contact in the volleyball pass. However, as the ideal contact is not always possible in skillful play, variations of the dig become the appropriate alternate for play under both DGWS and USVBA rules.

Digs are fast becoming essential ball-handling skills in good volleyball for girls and women. As the competitive groups are able to do more in the development of forceful spikes and services, the need for a variety of ways to keep the ball in play will increase. A sidearm service with its force and spin often has to be met with a dig rather than an overhead volley. The overhead and roundhouse services, with their force, spin, and difficult angles of penetration leave little opportunity to get set underneath the ball and be waiting to execute an overhead volley. A powerfully driven spike, untouched by blockers and still carrying a tremendous amount of momentum, usually requires a dig to pick up or "save" the play.

In addition to using the dig as a defensive play against the service and the spike, a dig is the surest way of playing a ball that must be recovered from the net. Good net recoveries necessitate playing the ball at a level lower than the waistline.

THE TWO-HANDED DIG

The two-handed dig is preferred over the one-handed dig because there is greater opportunity to control the ball. Certainly, the skilled player should perfect and use this skill against powerful services, spikes, and in the net recoveries which permit two players to contact the ball after it has gone into the net.

Body Position (see Fig. 2–15). As the dig is used as an emergency measure in playing the ball which cannot be met with an overhead volley, it is expected to serve the purpose of playing the ball that is falling toward the court surface. Therefore, the player will kneel or crouch so that the knees are in a flexed position. She will hold both arms out in front of the body so that the forearms are close and parallel with each other. The feet will be separated, with one foot slightly in front in a modification of the forward-stride position. The weight of the body will be distributed on the balls of both feet. The arms are flexed at the elbow. To secure the proper hand position, she will quickly make a fist out of one hand and will clasp the fisted hand with her other hand. The thumbs are on top side by side. An alternate hand position for the two-handed dig is to make the two hands come together with the fingers held against the palms of the hands, but in touch with each other. The thumbs are on top side by side. Some experts claim that this hand-heart position, so entitled because the hands assume

Fig. 2–15. The two-handed dig.

a heartlike shape (see Fig. 2–16), is easier to assume and relinquish because there is no actual clasping of the hands.

The Action. Meeting the ball in the dig must become an almost reflex action. As the player determines that she will not be able to execute an

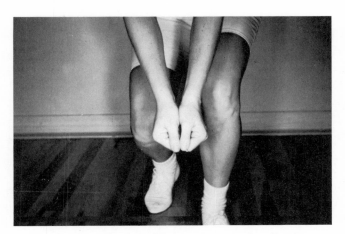

Fig. 2–16. The hand-heart position for the dig.

overhead volley, she drops into a kneeling position, keeping her eyes on the ball, and getting her arms and hands close to the floor. Her intentions should be to meet the ball soundly and squarely, intercepting it on its flight to the floor. The ball should be contacted as close to its center as possible. There is little action from the wrists and forearms. The original force of the ball rebounding from the solid surface formed by the arms gives the contacted ball enough momentum to carry it into the air and forward so that it is playable by a teammate. The knees and body straighten as the ball is met. With sufficient practice, skilled players will be able to manipulate the ball in such a way that it becomes a playable pass to the Key-Set, who, in turn, can set the ball to be spiked.

THE ONE-HANDED DIG

The one-handed dig is regarded as a skill to be used in even greater emergencies than those in which there is need for the two-handed dig. Some of these situations in the game are in meeting a service, such as the overhead or round-house, in which there is such tremendous force and sharp penetration that it is impossible to call a two-handed dig into play; in picking up a powerhouse spike, in which there is not time to react with a two-handed dig; and in the one-man defensive type of net recovery, in which the player attempting to recover the ball is the last legal player. The main purpose of the one-handed dig is to get the ball up into the air and playable by a teammate, or over the net as in the case of the one-man net recovery.

Body Position.   Because it is used as an emergency measure, there is little time or opportunity to concentrate on getting ready for the one-handed dig. Rather, a reflex action is required as the player drops to a kneeling or crouching position, with the feet separated and one foot forward. In this forward-stride position, the knees are flexed so that the player can get as close to the floor as possible without losing her balance. The weight of the body is distributed on the balls of both feet. The hand and arm to be used in performing the one-hand dig should be brought forward, close to the floor, so that the ball can be met squarely and as close to its center as possible. Two hand positions are possible. In the first, the fingers are brought up to the palm in a relaxed sort of position, and the attempt is made to hit the ball with the heel of the hand. In the second, the fingers are brought into tighter contact with the palm, and the ball is allowed to rebound from the heel and fingers simultaneously.

The Action.   The amount of action in the one-handed dig is limited in much the same way as for the two-handed dig. In other words, the force involved in the spiked or served ball is enough, as it rebounds from the hand in the dig, to carry the ball into the air and make it playable. A slight snap of the wrist as the ball is contacted serves to ensure the upward and forward flight pattern usually desired.

METHODS OF PRESENTATION AND PRACTICE

The teacher in intermediate and advanced instructional units in volleyball will use a demonstration to present the two-handed and one-handed digs. Although the two-handed and one-handed digs are similar in nature and in purpose, they should be presented first as separate skills. However, as many of the practice methods are the same, these are to be outlined together. As the teacher demonstrates the two skills, she will present both of the acceptable hand positions for each. The teacher should begin the demonstration by tossing the ball lightly into the air and then using the dig technique to play it again. She should also demonstrate the skill by having one of the members of the class toss the ball to her. Finally, she may follow with a demonstration of the digs against a wall surface. After striking the ball against the wall surface, the teacher waits for the ball to rebound from the floor and then returns it to the wall with the digging motion. During the presentation of the skills, the teacher will carefully outline their uses in the game and the major elements to be emphasized in the performance of each. After asking for questions, and answering them, she is ready to organize and conduct practices.

PRACTICE FORMATIONS

The following formations are suggested for practice of the digs, beginning with their introduction in an intermediate or advanced level class and continuing with formations suitable for competitive groups.

1. The students are allowed to experiment with the two hand positions recommended for each of the two types of digs. The teacher will make spot checks and necessary corrections, verbalizing the basic points to be remembered as she moves from student to student.

2. By using the dig which is being presented at the particular time, a mimetic practice of the basic position and the action may be conducted. So that the student can gain insight as to the feel of the skill as a whole, regular speed should be used. It may prove worthwhile later to break down the skill into parts for practice. The teacher may find the use of verbal clues, such as "give" to describe the basic position and "go" to describe the desirable action, effective with this type of practice.

3. Working in small informal groups, allow the student to experiment with tossing the ball into the air, dropping into the basic position, and making the dig contact.

4. *Toss and Dig by Two's.* Divide the participating group into partners and give each twosome a ball as far as the supply lasts. Have the partners stand 8 to 10 feet away from each other and have one player toss the

ball to her partner, who executes a dig, attempting to return the ball with distance and height control. Have the players repeat the process three to five times before they exchange duties. If the one-handed dig is being emphasized, have the players attempt the dig with the nondominant hand as often as the dominant hand. If the ball supply is limited, make sure that all students have an equal time to work with a ball, or move on to the zigzag formation, which provides practice in much the same way within the framework of a group.

5. *Zigzag Formation.* Place six to eight players in two lines, with each player facing a partner. The first player on one side of the line tosses the ball to her partner. The partner uses the appropriate dig to attempt to send the ball forward and upward, back to the original player. The second player in the original line follows the same procedure, tossing the ball to her partner, who returns with the dig. Play sequence follows this pattern until the end of the line has been reached. Then the players who had been tossing the ball become the players who execute the dig.

6. *Bounce and Dig by Two's.* Partners face each other at a distance of some 10 feet. One player drops the ball to the floor and, as it rebounds, gets underneath to dig-pass it to her partner. The partner, in turn, allows the ball to bounce and returns it with the dig, and the rally continues. In covering distance between the partners, height and control of the ball should not be sacrificed. Direct the ball into the air at least 8 feet so that the practice assimilates use of the skill during the game. If the ball supply is limited so that bounce and dig by two's is not feasible, use the zigzag formation to allow the same type of practice within a group.

7. *Wall Digging.* A solid wall surface, when one is available at the teaching or practice station, provides an excellent opportunity for working individually on the technique for the two digs. Encourage students who arrive early for class or practice or who stay after the scheduled session is over to use the wall for perfecting the digging skills. The player faces the wall squarely, drops the ball in front of her body, assumes the basic position, and digs the ball up and against the wall surface. As it rebounds, she moves to dig again after allowing the ball to bounce on the playing surface. Again, height, distance, and control should be emphasized. In this type of practice the player will have excellent opportunity to experiment with hand positioning for each of the two digs and with the momentum she must use in getting the ball into the air and playable.

8. *Circle Formation.* Using a regular circle formation, one player puts the ball into play by bouncing it against the floor and then digging it to one of the circle teammates. This player must also pass the ball with a one-handed or two-handed dig. The ball is repeatedly played in this manner. Each player must allow the ball to drop below the level of her own waistline before she makes contact with it.

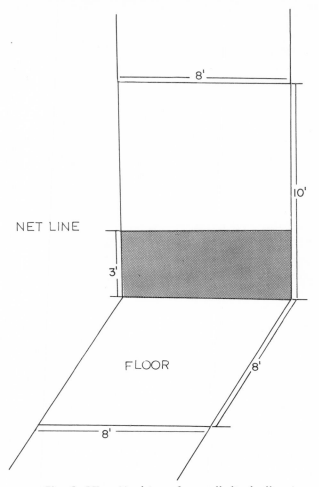

Fig. 2–17. Markings for wall-dig ball.

9. *Wall Dig-Ball.*[1]   Wall Dig-Ball is a volleyball skill game in which the two digging skills can be isolated and developed one at a time or can be combined and practiced simultaneously. A solid wall surface is necessary, and the wall and court surface have markings unique to this game (see Fig. 2–17). The rules for the game are:

1. Two players are opponents (later the game may be adapted to doubles play).
2. The ball is put into play behind the baseline with bounce and dig; it must hit above the net line on the wall; and it must rebound into the designated playing area.

[1] Ralph L. Wickstrom, "How to Teach the Underhand Pass in Volleyball," *Journal of the American Association for Health, Physical Education and Recreation,* XXX, 1 (January, 1959), 19–20.

3. The original player's opponent must return the ball to the appropriate area above the net line, using the designated digging skill.
4. The ball may be allowed to bounce only one time.
5. The opponents must continue to strike the ball alternately until one player or the other fails to make a legal play.
6. Scoring, as regards to point and side-out, is the same as the official game, and
7. A game consists of ten points.

The game of Wall Dig-Ball provides a novel way of practicing on a basic skill—by structuring the conditions under which the dig can be counted successful and by allowing competition in a stimulating way.

10. *Dig-Tennis.*[2] Dig-Tennis is another volleyball skill game which emphasizes the use of either, or both, of the digging techniques. Because it is played as a game and has a fun-type competitive element, it will motivate advanced players to work even more diligently on the perfection of skills. Two games may be conducted at one time on each volleyball court. The playing surface is evenly divided down the middle, and one pair of opponents face another on each half-court. The volleyball net is lowered to the regulation height for the game of tennis. The player putting the ball into play must stand behind the baseline on her side of the court and "serves" the ball by means of bounce and dig. Her opponent must allow the "service" to bounce and then she must return, using one of the underhand digging skills. After the service, the ball may or may not be allowed to bounce on one side of the net, but it must not be allowed to bounce more than once. All plays must be underhand. The ball is played back and forth across the net until one player is unable to return legally. Scoring is the same for the game of tennis with either the server or receiver capable of winning points, and one player serves for the entire game.

COMPETITION. In addition to the type of competition available through use of Wall Dig-Ball and Dig-Tennis, several of the previously mentioned practice formations lend themselves quite well to competition among the groups. These are: bounce and dig by two's, bounce and dig within the zigzag formation, wall digging, and circle formation. The principal variations of competition, presented in connection with the volley formations, are appropriate for these particular digging practice formations.

Other uses and methods of developing and practicing the dig will be presented with net recoveries and with the second-line defense against the spike, picking up or "saving."

KICKING THE BALL

Kicking the ball, which is permissible under the rules of the USVBA but not under DGWS rules, should be used only in the most extreme

[2] *Ibid.*

of emergencies. When it is absolutely impossible for the player to use one of the other ball-handling techniques, kicking the ball up into the air can be used to keep it in play. In performing this skill the player lifts her foot slightly off the floor and extends the toes so that there is no bend in the ankle. The ball is then allowed to rebound from this almost flat surface. Little impetus is given with the foot itself, and the object is to carry the ball into the air so that it becomes playable by a teammate.

3

Serving and Net Recovery

THE SERVE

The service, or putting the ball into play at the beginning of the game and after each point and side-out, is potentially the number one offensive weapon of the game of volleyball since a team must have the service in order to score points. Therefore, each player on a volleyball team should develop serving techniques which will enable her to put the opposing team immediately on the defensive.

The teacher of beginning volleyball units will work toward the development of the underhand service so that it becomes an effective game technique and will probably introduce the sidearm service to her students. The teacher on the intermediate level will review the underhand, adding appropriate variations; will continue instruction and development in the sidearm service; and will probably introduce the overhead service. The teacher on the advanced skill level and coaches of competitive groups will review the underhand and sidearm serving techniques, emphasizing variations in placement, power, and angle of penetration; will seek to perfect the overhead service and its appropriate variations; and among the more skilled players will encourage the development of a roundhouse, or hook, service.

UNDERHAND SERVICE

The underhand service skill is presented to students in beginning volleyball units because it is the easiest technique to learn and the easiest to control. The basic reason for the ease in the learning of the underhand serving skill is the similarity between it and many other movement patterns with which the student may already be familiar. An analysis of an underhand throw in softball, the delivery of a bowling ball, the out-of-hand serving skill in badminton, the pitching of horseshoes, and the one-hand underhand pass in basketball reveal many of the same essentials present in the underhand service.

48

Although the underhand service has definite advantages in being the easiest to learn and to control, it has two decided disadvantages. First, the force or power that can be directed behind the underhand service is minimal when compared to that possible in the other service skills. Secondly, the natural flight pattern of the ball carries it into the air and drops it into the opponents' court, so that the angle of penetration is easily predetermined and the receiving player can readily move into a position to return with a good overhead volley. Nevertheless, even the advanced player and competitor will make use of the underhand service as an interchangeable skill to be used to vary power, placement, and angle of ball penetration.

Basic Position. The player may stand anywhere she desires behind the baseline, provided that she is within the confines of an extension of each side line, and is no further away from the baseline than 6 feet. If she is right-handed, she will be standing with her shoulders facing the net squarely and will have the left foot forward. The right foot may be turned toward the net or may be turned slightly toward the right, so that the server feels well established in a firm forward-stride position. In the beginning stance the weight of the body is evenly distributed between the two feet and is forward on the balls of both feet. As the player brings the hand holding the ball into its proper position, the left knee becomes flexed, and the right knee should relax. The ball is allowed to rest on the palm of the left hand, and the player brings this hand down to a level close to the knee on the forward leg and slightly to the right. The fingers on the holding hand are extended toward the right and the thumb points straight forward. The serving hand may be lined up immediately behind the ball before the back-swing is taken, and this procedure is especially recommended for beginners as they are attempting to learn the service technique. The serving hand is held in one of three hand positions:

1. *Open Palm* (see Fig. 3–1). In this position the fingers are extended forward and held firmly together in a slightly curved surface, which permits the ball to be contacted first by the palm close to the heel of the hand and uses the fingers to give the final touch of direction and control to the ball.

Players may experiment with this hand position by making a strong open palm position out of the serving hand and then by using it to clap against the other hand. The rather hollow sound which results may lead to some interesting rhythmical patterns while the players are conducting this experimentation.

Most beginning players will feel that the open palm position is not as forceful as is one of the other hand positions. However, what it lacks in the way of power is more than compensated for in the amount of control that can be gained. It is highly recommended for beginning players, and skilled players usually return to it in preference over the other two.

2. *Closed Palm* (see Fig. 3–2). In this position the fingers on the serv-

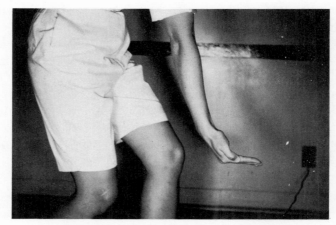

Fig. 3–1.   Open palm hand position.

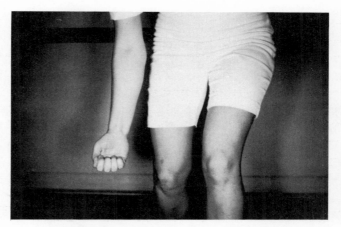

Fig. 3–2.   Closed palm hand position.

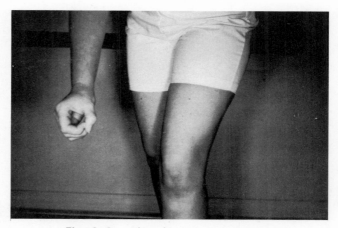

Fig. 3–3.   Thumb-circle hand position.

ing hand are curled forward so that they are in contact with the palm of the hand. As the ball is hit, there is an effort to make contact with the heel of the hand and the fingers at the same time. By reducing the amount of striking surface, some control over the direction of the ball is lost. Some power may be gained.

3. *Thumb-Circle Position* (see Fig. 3–3). This hand position is gained by having the thumb and fingers circle to come in contact with each other. The circle surface should be kept as large as possible. Therefore, the thumb will probably grip the first three fingers only. The thumb should be fully extended so that the thumb joint is reduced to a common level with the rest of the thumb and the index finger to avoid possible injury and at the same time to ensure more control of the ball. In the thumb-circle position, the striking surface becomes even more restricted and control becomes more difficult. However, most players will feel a power advantage.

The Action (see Fig. 3–4). The backswing is started by drawing the serving arm back, keeping the elbow straight until the arm is fully extended to shoulder height and parallel with the floor. As the arm moves into the backswing, the weight of the body will follow until it rests on the back, or right, foot. Both knees temporarily straighten. The eyes are kept on the ball and the player must make a conscious effort to keep the hand holding the ball in place. From the backswing the arm is brought forward as a pendulum, and the weight of the body is shifted on to the left foot at the point of contact. The ball is contacted slightly under its center point so that the player senses hitting forward and upward at the same time. The eyes remain on the ball, the holding arm and the serving arm keep elbow bending to a minimum, and the ball is clearly hit off the holding hand without any preliminary toss into the air. After the point of contact, the serving arm continues forward until it has reached approximate shoulder height and the right foot naturally steps from behind to forward in the follow-through.

As skill is gained in the underhand service, allow the players to experiment with changing the pace of the ball flight, the direction of the service, and the amount of power. Hitting the ball briefly and withdrawing the hand with little follow-through permits the ball to float through the air and is a deceptive change of pace. Swinging the serving arm forward with slight inward or outward rotations produces some change-up patterns in the flight of the ball. Adjusting the hand position to the closed palm and the thumb-circle results in added power and difficult to control spins.

SIDEARM SERVICE

While some experts look upon the sidearm service as a mere modification of the familiar underhand, many girls' and women's teams have par-

a   b

c   d

Fig. 3–4.   The underhand service. (a) Ready position. (b) The backswing.
(c) The point of contact. (d) The follow-through.

layed this technique into a separate skill with definite offensive possibilities. In comparing the sidearm with the underhand service, the obvious advantages are its increased power, the tremendous amount of spin on the ball, and the fact that the angle of penetration is one in which the ball travels parallel and close to the top of the net toward the baseline on the opponents' court. Because of its pattern of flight, it is difficult to judge whether the ball is going to land legally in bounds or whether it is an out-of-bounds ball. On the disadvantage side, the sidearm service is more difficult to control and direct with accuracy. The technique involved in the sidearm service skill is not quite as common in the basic movement pattern of sports skills. Therefore, the teacher or coach will not have as many word pictures or already coordinated neuromuscular skills to call upon when introducing the sidearm service. However, there are similar movement patterns in the drives in badminton and tennis and batting in softball and baseball.

Basic Position. The player may stand in any legal position behind the baseline. If she is right-handed, she will be standing with her left shoulder directed in toward the net. The two feet will be pointed toward the right side line, and the left foot will be placed slightly in front of the right. In the beginning position the weight of the body is evenly distributed between the two feet. Both knees are slightly flexed. The ball is held on the palm of the left hand, and the left arm is fully extended so that the ball is being held parallel with the left foot. The fingers on the holding hand are extended toward the right sideline and the thumb is toward the net. The serving hand may be properly aligned behind the ball before the backswing is taken. This procedure is highly recommended for the beginner. The same hand positions previously outlined for use in the underhand service are appropriate for the sidearm. The open palm position will furnish more control over the ball. The closed palm and thumb-circle positions will give added force.

The Action (see Fig. 3–5). The backswing is started by drawing the serving arm back at shoulder level height and parallel with the playing surface. The elbow is kept straight. The hand is in one of the three suggested hand positions. As the arm moves into the backswing, the weight of the body shifts onto the right foot. The hips rotate and the left knee bends toward the right. The eyes must be kept on the ball and attention must be given to the problem of keeping the holding hand in its original position. From the backswing the serving arm is brought forward, keeping the elbow straight and the swing horizontal and parallel with the floor at shoulder height. The ball is contacted at its center point, without any preliminary toss or release by the holding hand, so that the player senses the feeling of cleaning her hand in one instantaneous motion. At the point of contact

a

b

c

d

Fig. 3–5. The sidearm service. (a) Ready position. (b) The backswing.
(c) The point of contact. (d) The follow-through.

the weight of the body is shifted onto the left foot. In the ensuing follow-through, the serving arm bends at the elbow to swing past the left shoulder and the right foot steps forward naturally.

In working with beginning and intermediate players, the teacher will encourage almost exclusive use of the open palm position in connection with the sidearm service. However, as the players gain more skill, she will promote experimentation with the other hand positions; with hitting the ball closer to the top half to give additional overspin; and with adjustments in power through limitation and extension of the follow-through.

OVERHEAD SERVICE

The overhead service is fast becoming one of the most spectacular plays in the game of volleyball. It provides an explosive introduction to play which seems to dare and defy the receiving team to return the ball. It must be agreed that the overhead service offers more sheer power than does the underhand and the sidearm. However, force is not its only advantage. The overhead also offers a more difficult angle of penetration. As the ball is contacted at a height above the server's head, it is directed with a whip-like action over the net and down at a sharp angle into the opponent's court. It leaves little time for the defensive team to get under the ball and to return with an overhead volley. Usually, a form of the dig must be substituted in the initial contact and consequently the receiving team is unable to take the offensive.

The volleyball teacher may rely upon similar movement patterns from other sports skills for relating the overhead service in both word pictures and basic motor coordinations. Almost all students will have had experience in throwing a baseball, softball, or just a plain childhood rubber ball; many will have had opportunity to use a one-hand overhead pass in the game of basketball; others have skills in serving and smashing in tennis as a part of their sports history; and still others may call upon what they have learned about high clears and smashes from the game of badminton. In spite of this type of previous experience, the overhead service is difficult to learn. Therefore, it is expected that instruction in it will begin, at the earliest, in intermediate levels and that the perfection and modification of the service will come only in advanced units or among competitive groups. One of the most difficult aspects of this service seems to be the toss of the ball into the air to a correct height and spot in relationship to the body. In the two previous serving techniques, the holding hand maintained possession of the ball until the serving hand made contact. In the overhead service, a preliminary toss must be perfected and this toss must be made with the nondominant hand. Consequently, in introducing this service, time spent in working with the preliminary toss of the ball will be time gained rather than time lost.

a

b

c

Fig. 3–6.   The overhead service.   (a) The backswing.   (b) Immediately after point of contact.   (c) The follow-through.

Basic Position.   The server stands at any point she desires behind the baseline. She faces the net, and the toes on her left foot, which is forward, should be several inches away from the line in order to prevent contact while she is in the act of service. The right foot is placed comfortably behind the left foot and almost at a right angle so that the toes of the right foot are pointed diagonally to the right sideline. The weight of the body is evenly divided between the two feet in the starting position. Both knees are slightly flexed. The ball is held, either in both hands or in the left hand alone, close in to the body adjacent to the right hip. The player should be taught to take a slight interval, before tossing the ball and beginning the service, to look over the positioning of the defense; to search out unprotected areas or weaker players as targets for the service; and to concentrate on the elements necessary in making the overhead service a successful one.

The Action (see Fig. 3–6).   With a slight dipping, or bending, in both knees, the player tosses the ball into the air approximately 2 feet above her own head and over the right shoulder. As the ball is tossed, the serving arm is lifted forward and upward until the upper arm is parallel with the shoulder and the forearm and hand reaches straight up into the air overhead. At this point, the weight of the body has shifted back on to the right foot, and the hips have twisted toward the right. Considerable arch develops in the back. As the ball falls from its highest point back down to a level approximately 1 foot higher than the head, the arm is brought forward in a whiplike action, which proceeds forward and downward at the same time. The hand makes contact with the ball at its center point. The weight of the body transfers on to the forward foot at the moment of contact, and the back foot may finish forward as the arm of the server finishes the swing in the follow-through.

The open palm position is the most desirable hand position for the overhead service, for it is the one in which there is the most control over the ball. In the use of the open palm position there should be a real effort to contact the ball with the heel of the hand and to use the fingers to give the final controlling touch. Later, players will want to experiment with the closed palm position so that the ball is contacted with the heel of the hand and the first knuckles of the fingers. When the ball is contacted at the center point, or slightly above, in this manner, it will have a tendency to float and becomes very deceptive to the receiving team in judging and returning it. The thumb-circle position is not appropriate for the overhead service.

ROUNDHOUSE (HOOK) SERVICE

The roundhouse, or hook, service is definitely the most difficult of the accepted serving skills to learn and even very experienced players have difficulty in developing it to a high degree of consistency and accuracy. However, it is becoming more popular in competitive play, for girls and women as well as for boys and men. When the highly skilled player is able to add the roundhouse to her repertoire of techniques, her team can claim an additional powerful offensive weapon. The major assets of the service are the tremendous force behind the ball and the top spin that accompanies it. The advanced player will find the perfecting of this service a real challenge, and it is the type of skill that should be introduced individually to each player only as she is ready, neuromuscularly and psychologically, for it.

Body Position.   The server stands behind the baseline with her feet in a modified forward-stride position, in which she is facing the side line. If the player is right-handed, the left shoulder is in toward the net. Both hands hold the ball. The weight of the body is evenly divided between the two feet, and both knees are slightly flexed.

The Action (see Fig. 3–7).   With a dipping of both knees, the server tosses the ball into the air just over the height of her head and lines up the toss with her right shoulder. As the ball moves into the air on the toss, the server bends her body sharply at the waistline to her right and swings the right arm, with the elbow only slightly bent, downward. As the ball descends to a level almost even with the head, the player bends sharply in the waistline toward her left, and the serving arm and hand continue until contact is made with the ball. The weight of the body is transferred to the forward foot. The open palm position of the hand is the accepted

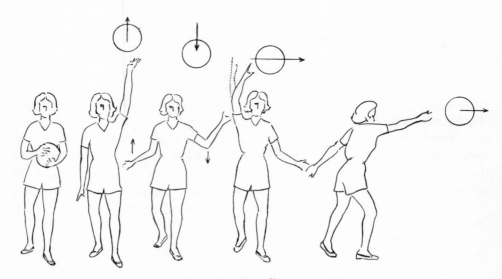

Fig. 3–7.   The roundhouse service.

pattern for use in the roundhouse service in order to have the ball contact the heel of the hand and to have the finger tips, in their firm position, add top spin. After the point of contact the serving arm should finish its arc in a complete follow-through, and the right foot steps forward.

METHODS OF PRESENTATION AND PRACTICE

Although the three basic serving skills—the underhand, sidearm, and overhead—will be separated from each other by definite intervals of time and practice, the same fundamental presentation and practice procedures are appropriate for each and are presented here in a progression that may be repeated, with modifications, for each in turn. It is assumed that at the introduction of the first serving skill, the underhand, that the student has already become familiar with the size, shape, and feel of the ball and has developed a reasonable degree of ball-handling skill.

DEMONSTRATION OF THE SERVICE

Serving skills should be demonstrated by the volleyball teacher from a proper serving position behind the baseline. Several balls should be gathered in an appropriate position for the demonstration, and a student helper should be appointed to stand on the opposite side of the net to roll the balls back under the net to the teacher as she serves them. As the teacher demonstrates the proper technique for the particular serving skill, she should be making an analysis of the major points to be remembered in executing the skill; explaining the uses of the skill in the game; outlining the particular advantages and disadvantages of the type of service; and summarizing the official rules of the game that must be observed in the service. She will also refer to other sports skills with a similar movement pattern which may be a part of the students' motor vocabulary. As each of the serving skills is introduced, it is expected that the teacher will present the open palm hand position as the most reliable and the one with which the students will have most control of the ball.

After approaching the serving technique from the whole pattern, the teacher may consider it advisable to break down the skill into its starting position, the backswing, the point of contact, and the follow-through. She should emphasize the essential points to be remembered in this step-by-step analysis and should finish the presentation by again serving the ball and stressing the whole approach. After she asks for questions and answers any that are asked, the class is ready to begin its practices.

PRACTICE FORMATIONS

The practice formations presented here begin with the most elementary of procedures and progress to those of a more complex and advanced level.

1. Using the open palm hand position and what is already known about the serving technique from the demonstration and the analysis, practice it mimetically with the students lined up in an appropriate manner behind the baseline. During this mimetic practice, use the "whole" approach by having the players follow the same speed in executing the skill as they will later when they are trying it with the ball. While observing the students in this practice, the teacher will determine if it is necessary to break down the skill into its parts and have mimetic practice in the parts: starting position, backswing, point of contact, and follow-through.

2. *Serve Against the Wall.* When the teaching station is an indoor gymnasium, the walls surrounding the playing area may be profitably used to conduct the first practices in which the students will be contacting balls. Scatter the class around the available wall space and have them assume positions approximately 20 feet away from the wall. Use as many balls as are available and have each student get in as many serving practices as possible. The teacher will visit as many players as possible; make individual corrections in performance; and whenever she feels that errors are common enough to merit the attention of the entire class, she will halt practice momentarily to make suggestions to the group as a whole.

3. *Short-Distance Serving.* Whenever there is no available wall space, as in the case of an outdoor teaching station, virtually the same type of practice can be obtained by having the students move forward of the baseline and serve from a position approximately 20 feet away from the net rather than the 30-foot distance of the official court. Such short-distance serving is especially appropriate when introducing the more difficult overhead services. In both the serve against the wall and short-distance serving the beginner is allowed to work with greater chance of success than she would in serving from a regulation distance and over a net elevated to its official height. In both practice methods the player should be gradually backed up as she meets success in the primary targets, until she is serving the full required distance.

4. *Informal Serving.* The class or group is scattered equally on all of the playing courts. Each player works, more or less, with a partner. The balls available to the group are evenly divided among the playing courts. Each player stands behind the baseline on her own side of the net and serves across in the general direction of her partner. The partner allows the ball to bounce on the court and waits for it to roll back to where she is standing. She then picks it up and returns the service to the opposite side of the net. Generally speaking, each player serves every time she gets her hands on a ball. However, when the ball supply is limited, care must be taken to see that all players have equal opportunity to practice. It is important for beginning players, from the standpoint of safety procedure, to wait for the ball to roll or bounce to them behind the baseline rather than

to step into the court to procure the ball. As little control over the ball is guaranteed in beginning efforts, the teacher must put continued emphasis on this point.

5. *Server-Target Placement* (see Fig. 3–8). In addition to power placed upon the ball, the placement of the service is the second most desirable quality. Intermediate and advanced players will learn to direct services to playing areas left unprotected by the receiving team and to predetermined weaker players on a team. However, in working on placement with beginners it is usually best to outline what is considered the best possible target areas on the opponents' court and to direct services to those areas. In most cases the extremely deep area lying adjacent to the baseline and approximately 5 feet in width is an appropriate target. The deep service is usually a strong one and has another decided advantage in making the receiving team play the ball from maximum distance and thereby definitely increasing the margin of error. In addition, a deep service will be difficult for the receivers to judge and they will often be led either into playing balls which would have gone out-of-bounds if allowed to drop or into failure in making a good return because the ball was expected to land out-of-bounds.

The sidelines of the court also provide acceptable target areas because of the necessity of making judgments on potential out-of-bounds balls and because receiving players are pulled out of normal playing positions to make the return. The sideline targets also include inside "pocket" targets

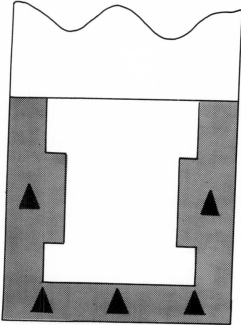

Fig. 3–8. Service-target-player placement.

between the positions normally occupied by the forwards and the backs, and services directed to these areas invoke confusion as to which player is responsible for initial contact.

Players take turn in directing their services to the targets and are given a designated number of trials for this purpose. Players standing on the target side of the court indicate the success or failure of the served ball to land in the appropriate target. As the ball is held just previous to execution of the service technique, the server should indicate to which of the target areas it is to be directed. After all the players on the serving side have finished with their trials, they exchange places with the players who have been checking on accuracy and returning balls, and the procedure is repeated with the new servers.

In server-target placement use chalk to draw the target lines on outside playing surfaces. Masking tape, chalk, or a roll of prepared marking lines (made of oil cloth or carpet binding in 1½- to 2-inch widths) is easy to put down and to take up on indoor playing surfaces.

6. *Server-Player Targets* (see Fig. 3–8). Six to eight players compose a group. One player is the server, and she may have one or two helpers on her side of the net when the group is made up of seven or eight players. The other five players are stationed at strategic points within the target areas described in server-target placement. The server is given five service trials, and beginning with the player in the right side line target, she serves one ball in turn to each of the players within the target areas. Each player "calls" the ball and makes the initial contact on it, preferably with an overhead volley. After the server has finished her five trials, she takes the place of the player occupying the right side line target and all of the others move one target position to the left. The player in the left side line target becomes the server when the group is composed of six players, or a helper when seven or eight players are involved. In addition to service practice, this formation provides excellent opportunity to work on initial contact in receiving the service, one of the most difficult plays of the game.

7. *Server-Team Return.* Seven to eight players compose a group. One player is the server, and there is a full team complement on the other side of the net. Any additional players are helpers on the server's side. The object is for the server to have practice in directing the ball to a full team stationed in one of the recommended receiving positions to defend against the service (see pages 125–27). Remembering the target areas previously outlined, and the strategy of directing the service to an unprotected court area or a weaker player, the server serves a designated number of balls in the serving technique being emphasized. The receiving team calls the ball and, utilizing its three legal contacts, returns the ball to the server's court. As soon as backing-up assignments have been introduced in defending against the service (see pages 127–28), the receiving team can practice effecting these

against the server's skill. As soon as the server has finished her designated number of services, she takes the place of the left forward in the receiving team's lineup. All of the other players rotate in the usual clockwise pattern, except the left back, who moves over to become the server in a group with seven players, or a helper in a group that numbers eight or more players.

8. *Server-Team Return Game.* In server-team return game the plan of organization is the same as for server-team return. However, this practice formation allows the server and the team to earn points under certain conditions. The server scores only when she has served an ace—that is, a service which the receiving team is unable to return legally. The team scores only when the service is illegal. When the server serves a legal service and the team makes a legal return, no point is scored. Therefore, when both the server and the team are performing correctly, the score of the game should end 0–0.

Because this practice formation provides competition and is motivating, it can be used among beginners when they are dealing with one service only, or intermediate and advanced players can use it as they attempt to vary techniques and placement, power, and penetration angle of the ball.

A designated number of services should be allowed each server, in turn, and rotation is conducted, as previously described, to secure the new server.

9. *Comic Strip Serving.* As players gain more skill in placing the ball, more difficult service targets may be arranged. Save the colored comic pages from Sunday newspapers and encourage the class or competitive group to do the same. When an ample supply is available, spread them in double-page targets in strategic target positions on the half-court. The colors will make a vivid target and the double page, some 22 by 30 inches, will be sufficiently large to challenge the skilled player and yet have her meet some success. The most satisfactory procedure is to number the targets and have the server attempt to send the ball to each number in succession. Recognize the server or the team of servers who score the highest number of points within their allotted trials.

10. *Needle-Eye Serving* (see Fig. 3–9). Needle-eye serving may be used within intermediate or advanced skill levels when the servers are able to place the ball with a high degree of accuracy. An assortment of sporting-goods objects with which the volleyball player is likely to be familiar is used for targets. These should range from a fairly large article down to one quite minute. The server serves to pick off the objects one by one, beginning with the largest and ending with the smallest. Scoring the practice should be in reverse—that is, the largest item gets only one point value and the smallest, the highest point value. Articles could include: a badminton net, outstretched near the baseline, 1 point; a bull's-eye cover from an archery target, 2 points; a black and white-striped official's pinny, 3

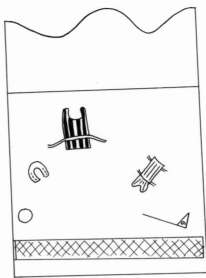

Fig. 3–9. Needle-eye serving.

points; a field hockey shin guard, 4 points; an indoor rubber horseshoe, 5 points; and a golf ball greensmarker, 6 points.

Players are given a predetermined number of trials to hit each target, and a simple score can be taken of the number of points gained. A team basis of competition can be arranged by totaling the number of points gained by each player on a team.

11. *Serve-Screening Practice.* Among intermediate and advanced students and in competitive groups, practice on serving from behind the cover of a screen (see pp. 105–11) as soon as that element of offensive strategy has been introduced. The use of the three-man and the four-man screens allowable under DGWS rules and these and the five-man screen, acceptable in USVBA play, will work quite well in the practice formations of server-player targets, server-team return, and server-team return game previously outlined.

12. *Relays.* In addition to the practice formations previously suggested which have a game element in them, many simple service practices can be oriented to competitive play. For example, in informal serving the players on one side of the net can serve as a team and their opposites as a second team. As long as a player keeps serving successfully she is still "in" the game. The object is to see which team can keep a successful server going the longest. An opposite version of this would be to have players sit, kneel, or squat as soon as they have been able to serve the emphasized service successfully. An individual or team can be recognized in this way.

Server-target placement can be modified to give points for getting the service into the suggested target areas. In fact, the service skill tests presented in Chapter 9 use this idea. Therefore, an early introduction of skill tests will provide a means of competing and will motivate the individual player to improve her own skills.

13. *Incentive Serving.* When putting a newly introduced serving skill, especially the more difficult overhead and roundhouse, into a regulation game, use some incentive to encourage students to try the new technique rather than reverting to an easier skill. One possibility is to provide a service line inside the baseline, reducing the distance, and to allow the server to station herself there as long as she is attempting the new skill. Another possibility is to provide two trials to get the service in, like the game of tennis. If the first service is good, it is played; if it is not good, it is called a "fault," and the server gets a second trial. Still another possibility is to give two game points instead of one for points earned on a service using the new technique.

NET RECOVERY

The volleyball rule that permits a team to contact the ball three times on its side of the net makes a net recovery not only legally possible, unless all three contacts have been used, but makes its usage by a team, when necessary, a brand or symbol of determined, skillful play. The basic skill used in recovering a ball from the net is underhand ball-handling technique. However, this technique must be performed with such special strategic intent that it warrants separation of net recoveries into a particular category of skills.

TWO-MAN DEFENSIVE NET RECOVERY

Two factors determine the type of net recovery which should be attempted. First and most important is the number of contacts that have been made on the ball. Second is the situation of the team, in respect to positioning and stability, at the time that the ball makes the contact with the net. When the first player who attempts to play the ball, perhaps a back in trying to pass the ball to the Key-Set, misjudges the distance and sends the ball into the net instead, two contacts remain. Therefore, one of two acceptable two-man net recoveries is a possibility and definitely preferred over a one-man recovery.

Granting that two contacts on the ball are left, the next factor which must be considered is the situation of the team at the particular moment. If the team has been pulled out of its regular playing position for any reason, or any one player is unstable, unbalanced, or off-guard, the net recovery which should be effected is the two-man defensive net recovery. The strategic intent of this particular net recovery is to provide a delaying action which will enable the team to reassume normal playing positions and each individual player to recover her stability. To accomplish this purpose, the forward playing the ball as it drops out of the net attempts to set the ball straight into the air, on her own side so that it is not legally playable by the opponents, and one of her teammates, usually a back, moves forward to volley the ball with a high, lobbing action toward the baseline of the opponents' court.

Basic Position. A forward, playing her usual position at the net, when the ball is in her own half-court, will have one shoulder or the other toward the net and will be facing a side line. It is expected that the forward designated to receive the would-be pass will be in the best position to try to execute the net recovery. Therefore, as she sees that the ball is going into the net before she can meet and control it, she should bend her knees sharply, dropping down into a crouching or kneeling position that will allow her to play the ball as it drops completely free from the net. As she moves to this position, she is getting her arms and hands ready to make contact with the ball.

The Action. The possible underhand ball-handling skills the forward can use in recovering the ball from the net are the underhand volley, the two-handed dig, and the one-handed dig. Again, it should be emphasized that the underhand volley is used only in play in beginners' units and in purely recreational situations. The intermediate, advanced, and competitive volleyball players must rely upon one of the two digging techniques. The preferable dig to use in the two-man defensive net recovery is the two-handed dig, because of its advantage in control of the ball. However, on some occasions the one-handed dig may be needed in this play.

The objective of the forward is to execute a two-handed dig from a position close to the playing surface and to set the ball straight into the air and parallel with the net on her own side, and to call out some prearranged signal, such as "Back!" indicating that the appropriate action is to have a back move forward to the net and use the momentum of her moving body behind the ball to send a high, lobbing volley to the baseline of her opponents' court.

TWO-MAN OFFENSIVE NET RECOVERY

If there are still two contacts left on the ball when it is sent into the net, and the team and its individual members are in their respective positions on the court and stabilized, it is often possible to convert what looks like a costly game error into a surprisingly effective offensive weapon. This offensive weapon is the two-man offensive net recovery. The strategic intent of this particular net recovery is to play the ball as it drops out of the net in such a way that an adjacent forward-line player can jump into the air and execute a spike. To accomplish this purpose, the player executing the net recovery waits for the ball to drop completely free of the net; sets it straight and high into the air on her own side of the court so that it is not legally playable by the forwards on the opposite side; and a spiking teammate approaches the ball on the run and executes a spike in the same manner as if she had received a regular set.

Basic Position and Action. The ball is played as it rebounds completely free of the net in much the same manner as previously described for the two-man defensive net recovery. Again, because of its advantage in control of the ball, the two-handed dig is preferred over the one-handed dig. Since the two-man offensive net recovery is an advanced skill, involving complicated timing and execution of the spike, it is not expected that instruction in it will be given to beginners. Therefore, the use of the underhand volley in its performance is virtually eliminated. The signal for attempting the spike in the two-man offensive net recovery can be "Right" or "Left," indicating the relationship of the player who should attempt to spike to the player bringing the ball out of the net.

ONE-MAN DEFENSIVE NET RECOVERY

The one-man defensive net recovery is a "last-ditch" desperation attempt to bring a ball out of the net and send it over at the same time when there is only one contact legally remaining. Admittedly, it is a very difficult technique to perform without committing a ball-handling violation or net and center-line fouls. However, players who desire to have each game point go to its fullest and are endowed with competitive spirit will play the ball until it is dead. The strategic intent of this particular net recovery is to play the ball as it drops out of the net in such a way that it will follow a high, arching flight pattern, clearing the net, and as much as possible out of the reach of the potential spikers or blockers on the opponents' side. At this point no legal assistance can come from any teammate; therefore, the forward executing the play is on her own. The play is entirely "defensive" in nature and will be deemed at least partially successful if the net is cleared. It is fully successful when the ball passes out of the reach of the opposing forwards.

Basic Position. As soon as the forward judges that she is not going to be able to handle the ball before it contacts the net and realizes that two contacts have already been made, she should immediately drop into a crouching or kneeling position facing the side line in the direction of the ball. The position is one from which either the two-handed or one-handed dig can be executed. In the one-man defensive net recovery the ball must be allowed to drop as close to the playing surface as possible.

The Action. The degree of difficulty of this net recovery makes its use by all but advanced players prohibitive. Therefore, utilization of the underhand volley is ruled out, and one of the two digging actions is appropriate. Because of the desired flight pattern of the ball, the one-handed dig is preferable. As the ball drops close to the playing surface, the player modifies the regular one-handed dig action by a sharp outward rotation of the arm and hand away from the net just previous to contacting the ball. This action will give forward and upward momentum, and when properly applied, will carry the ball over the net and out of the reach of the opposing forwards. The player involved in the one-man defensive net recovery must quickly assume her normal playing position at the net to help defend in any quick return of the ball by the opponents.

METHODS OF PRESENTATION AND PRACTICE

As the development of good net recovery technique depends largely upon skill in underhand ball-handling, the presentation and practice methods previously outlined for the underhand volley (for beginners and purely recreational groups) and the two-handed and one-handed digs (for intermediates, advanced, and competitive groups) are appropriate and should be restressed. Additional practice formations are presented here for the use of these ball-handling skills in specific reference to net recoveries.

DEMONSTRATION OF NET RECOVERIES

While it is expected that beginners should be called upon to perform in one type of net recovery, the two-man defensive, the two other varieties will be held for more advanced instructional units. However, as each is presented for the first time there should be a demonstration of the skill with the teacher performing as the player who recovers the ball from the net and selected students serving as her helpers. During the demonstration the teacher will explain the use of the particular type in the game; analyze the major points essential to correct performance in the skill; outline the advantages and disadvantages of the three possible ball-handling techniques used in connection with net recovery; and summarize some of the game rules, such as ball-handling violations and net and center-line fouls, which must be closely observed. Before proceeding to practice, she should ask for, and answer, questions arising from the class.

PRACTICE FORMATIONS

At the discretion of the teacher or coach, any portion of the practice formations presented for the digs (see pages 43–46) may be repeated. Additional practices should include:

1. *Experimentation with Ball Landing in the Net.* With nets properly elevated and in a state of tautness that permits enough rebound for the ball to be playable, let the student experiment by throwing a ball into the net and studying the types of rebounds that she gets. A ball that hits the

net near its top cable will fall quickly and in a path that is almost straight down. When the ball lands in the center of the net, the net will shudder, recoil, and push the ball out a short distance away. The bottom of the net seems to catch or hold the ball momentarily and then sends the ball gently out before it begins to drop down to the floor.

2. *Toss and Catch.* Divide the class into groups of four. Two players are opposite to two others with the net in between. On each side there is a back and a forward, with each player aware of and following through on what is her expected playing position responsibilities. The back begins the action by tossing the ball into the net, varying her tosses so that they contact the net near the top, the bottom, and the center. Her forward, studying the reaction of the ball as it hits the net, reaches out and catches it before it is allowed to hit the playing surface. The two players on the opposite side repeat the same action. On some prearranged signal have the backs and forwards exchange positions and duties.

3. *Net Toss and Dig.* The class is divided into groups of four. Two players oppose two other players on the opposite side of the net. In each twosome there is a player assuming the playing duties and position of a forward and a player who covers the responsibilities of a back. The back puts the ball into play by tossing it into the net, varying the tosses so that they contact near the top of the net, close to the bottom, and in the middle. As the ball rebounds from the net, the forward executes either a two-handed or one-handed dig. Then the ball goes to the other two players and they repeat the same procedure. After an appropriate interval of practice, the two players on each side of the net exchange positions with each other.

4. *Two-Man Defensive Net Recovery Practices* (see Fig. 3–10). One of the best ways to practice the two-man defensive net recovery is in the same formation outlined in net toss and dig. The number of players, their relative positions, and the preliminary action are the same. However, when the forward contacts the ball as it rebounds from the net, she is not merely digging it, she is playing it with intent. The two-handed dig is preferable, but the one-handed may also be used. As she plays the ball straight into the air, above her own head and on her side of the net, she calls out the prearranged signal which will bring the back to the net immediately. It becomes the duty of the back to play the ball with a high, lobbing volley so that it will go deep into the opponents' court, preferably close to the baseline. When the ball passes over the net, the two players on the opposite side stop it and execute the same procedure on their side of the net. As every player on a team is a potential figure in a net recovery, each should be given the opportunity of assuming the role of forward and back.

After the players have gained some skill in executing this particular type of net recovery, use the two players stationed on the opposite side of the net up in regular forward positions and allow them to try to block the

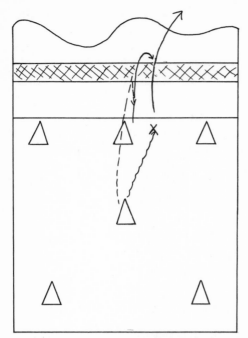

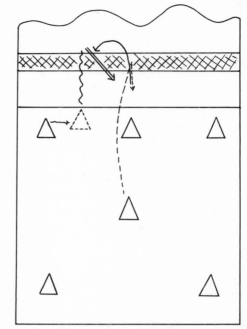

Fig. 3–10. Two-man defensive net recovery practice.

Fig. 3–11. Two-man offensive net recovery practice.

ball back to its original side. If the volley following the net recovery is out of the reach of these opposing forwards and there is no chance for any immediate return, the two-man defensive net recovery may be deemed successful.

5. *Two-Man Offensive Net Recovery Practices* (see Fig. 3–11). The class is divided into groups of six players. Three players are established in these positions on each side of the net: Two players occupy front-line positions and are forwards; one player is behind and assumes the role of a back. The back puts the ball into play by tossing it into the net. During the practice the back should vary the toss so that it approximates a ball going into the top, bottom, and middle of the net. One of the two forwards, specifically the one for whom the poorly judged pass was intended, drops to a kneeling or crouching position as the ball rebounds from the net and executes a dig. The two-handed dig is preferable, although the one-handed may also be used, and the object is to set the ball straight into the air so that it is nonplayable by the opponents but can be reached and spiked by the other forward teammate.

After the ball has been spiked over the net, the three players on the opposite side stop the ball, and repeat the same procedure. Since every player on a volleyball team may be called upon to execute this type of net recovery in the game, it is important that the teacher or coach provide enough practice time for all three players to rotate through each of the player's duties.

After the players have become fairly successful in the two-man offensive net recovery, test its effectiveness by using the two forwards on the opposite side of the net to block and the back to pick up the spike. Again, rotate all players so that they can have practice in each assignment.

6. *One-Man Defensive Net Recovery Practices* (see Fig. 3–12). The number of players in the practice group is four. Two, in forward and

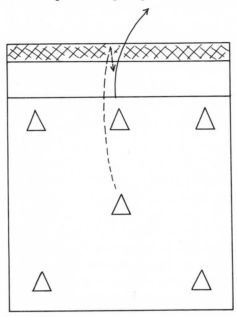

Fig. 3–12. One-man defensive net recovery practice.

back positions, are situated on either side of the net. The action begins by having a back toss the ball into the net, varying it so that practice may be gained with balls landing near the top, bottom, and middle. The forward drops very close to the floor as the ball rebounds, and executes the one-handed dig with a sharp outward swing of the arm and hand away from the net just previous to contacting the ball. There must be enough force behind the play so that the ball clears the net and goes beyond the reach of the forwards on the other side. The two players on the other side stop the ball and play it back, using the same procedure. All players should have an opportunity to serve as both forwards and backs.

The effectiveness of the one-man defensive net recovery may be tested by having the two players on the opposite side of the net serve as forwards who try to block or immediately return the ball to its original side. The players should be rotated so that there is practice opportunity in each assignment.

4

Spiking and Defending
Against the Spike

THE SPIKE

On the face of a beginning student as she sees a skilled player spike the ball for the first time is written all that one needs to know about the spectacular qualities of this phenomenon among sports skills. Yet attendance at a skilled and highly competitive match will reveal the same expression, repeated over and over again, on the faces of even the most experienced of players and spectators. The jumping ability involved, the timing, and the sheer power flowing out of a body seemingly suspended in the air combine to make the player who can perform this skill effectively one of the most outstanding and envied of all performers in the sports world.

The spike is the offensive weapon used by front line players to put away or "kill" the ball so that the opponents are either unable to return the ball or their return is so weakened that the following play is successful in the same purpose. Such a spike must be preceded by a good set, usually from another front line player, and in most instances the way is paved for the set through a good pass, most often coming from a player in a back position. The ability to spike involves ability to jump, good body balance, excellent coordination, and quick reaction and timing. While it is an accepted anatomical fact that the structure of the girl and woman is such that her center of gravity is lower, in the hip cavity, than that of the boy or man and that this factor prohibits her from being able to accomplish the same height in jumping, there is no evidence to deny that the girl and woman can be taught to use the body effectively in the jumping that is essential to good spiking.

SPIKING APPROACHES

Two approaches are possible in executing the jump for the spike. First, there is the stationary approach in which the spiker assumes a waiting position and without preliminary steps jumps into the air and makes the contact with the ball. Second, there is the running approach in which the spiker uses short, quick steps to gain position and momentum before lifting the body in the jump. Of the two, the running approach is far more effective and more widely used in competitive volleyball play.

TAKE-OFFS

In addition to the two approaches that have been developed for the jump in spiking, two take-off procedures are possible. However, one of these, the double foot, has definitely moved to the forefront and is used almost exclusively in skilled play. In the double-foot take-off, both feet are brought together just before the jump, regardless of the fact of a stationary or running approach. Then, with the ankles and knees flexed so that the extensors can be more completely used, the body is lifted into the air vertically. The one-foot take-off, which was popular originally because it helped the player to get a higher extension in the air than is possible through the double-foot take-off, involves stepping on to the left foot and jumping into the air with the right foot as the arm lifts to make contact with the overhead ball.

Body Position. In the double-foot take-off, the spiker faces the net squarely. She is standing some 12 to 24 inches away from the net when the stationary approach is to be used and is some 6 to 8 feet away when she intends to use a running approach. The body is in a state of flexion, with the knees, hips, and ankles bent and the trunk tilting forward, as she studies the approaching ball. If the running approach is to be used, the quick, short steps are interjected and the spiker's body assumes the same position just previous to the jump.

When the one-footed take-off is used, the spiker is facing the direction from which the pass is to come and is some 12 to 24 inches away from the net for a stationary approach. For a running approach, she will be standing some 6 to 8 feet away from the net and is turned in an oblique position in respect to the net and the Key-Set. Again, short quick steps are used to approach the net and the ball, with the final step coming off the left foot and the right foot lifted into the air.

The Action (see Fig. 4–1). In the double-foot take-off, complete emphasis must be on the vertical lift. From the state of flexion in the body position, there is a lift in the trunk to make it erect, and an emphatic upswing for the final lift comes from the spiking arm and hand. The purpose is to keep the jump high, but at the same time to maintain control of the body to avoid falling or stepping forward. The spiking arm is lifted behind the head and shoulders. The elbow is raised in a bent position just above the head. The spiking arm moves to meet the ball, elbow leading, as the body

How to spike

Fig. 4–1. The double-foot take-off for the spike.

reaches maximum height in the jump and just before it begins to descend. There is a feeling of hanging suspended in the air momentarily. From the elbow down through the hand the arm is brought forward to contact the ball in a whiplike action. The hand makes contact with the ball from an open palm position with the heel of the hand responsible for the primary force and the fingers touching to bring control. There is an accompanying powerful flick of the wrist as the hand makes contact so that the ball is directed downward with some top spin. The spiker lands on both feet with the balls and heels making contact with the playing surface and with the knees flexed. This type of landing will prevent the spiker from losing balance and moving forward into the net or over the center line and will also permit her to move readily if the blocking action by her opponents demands it.

In the one-footed take-off, emphasis is on use of the right foot to help draw the body up into the air. As the left foot leaves the floor to follow the right, the body turns in the air so that at the moment of contact it is facing the net squarely. The uses of the arm, elbow, wrist, and hand are the same as for the double-footed take-off. Again, the body should land facing the net squarely with the weight distributed on the balls and heels of both feet.   One disadvantage of the one-footed take-off is that the momentum of the body in this jump and turn is often forward as much as it is vertical.   Another is that landing properly so that the player can immediately return to action when the opponents make a quick play back is difficult and often impossible.

Teaching a spike

METHODS OF PRESENTATION AND PRACTICE

It is expected that skill in spiking is introduced either at the end of a beginner's unit in volleyball, or as soon as possible in an intermediate unit. The initial requirement of a teacher in presenting the spike is the teaching of good jumping technique to those students who do not already have it in their repertoire of basic movement patterns. Unfortunately, this is often the majority among girls and women.   Therefore, adequate time must be given for this purpose.

DEMONSTRATION OF THE SPIKE

It is absolutely essential that students being introduced to the spike have an opportunity to see a skilled performer in action in order to grasp all of its power and placement possibilities. If the teacher is such a skilled performer, she should conduct the demonstration. However, if she is not, an outsider should be brought into the class for this purpose. Another teacher, a student in an advanced unit, a player of competitive caliber, or a community expert are all possibilities.   In any event, the teacher will need a helper, student or otherwise, who is capable of delivering a good set so that the spiking demonstration can be successful. The demonstration should show spikes which have sheer power for their purpose and spikes which are placement-oriented to straight directions, slight angles, and sharp angles. The demonstration should also show spikes taken from a stationary and running approach and spikes taken from a double-footed and one-footed take-off. The advantages and disadvantages of each are pointed out to the students, and similarities are drawn between the spike, the overhead service, and other sports skills, such as an overhead throw in baseball or softball, clears and smashes in badminton, and services and smashes in tennis. In addition, the rules that should be especially noted when spiking the ball should be summarized by the teacher. After asking for, and answering, questions from the class, she should begin practice.

PRACTICE FORMATIONS

The following is an outline guide to methods of practice for the spike, beginning with initial practices in jumping and continuing to advanced methods used by competitive teams for developing the attack in a system of offensive strategy. In all practices involving jumping, the teacher or coach will choose the take-off she considers best and wants emphasized.

1. *Sargent Chalk Jump Test.*   The administration of this test is one of the best ways to show a student exactly what her jumping ability is. If the one-footed take-off is to be presented, have the player stand with her left shoulder toward the wall and with a piece of chalk in her right hand, reach over her head and mark a reach line on the wall. The heels of both feet should be on the floor. From a crouching position with the left foot forward, the player steps on to the left foot and lifts the right foot into the air. As she does so, the body turns to face the wall, and at the highest point of her jump, she makes a chalk line on the wall, representing her jump line. The distance of the jump is measured by using a yardstick with the 0-end even with the jump line and the number of inches jumped indicated at the reach line. Give each student an opportunity to jump at least three times and consider the highest jump her score. Use the same procedure, but different positioning and technique, as previously outlined, for the double-footed jump.

The Sargent Chalk Jump Test is another excellent individual practice which the student can engage in as she comes early for class, or the competitor, as she arrives for the practice session. It is recommended that competitive groups be allowed to leave reach lines and best jump lines on the wall to motivate them to improve jumping ability throughout the season.

2. *Jumping at the Net.*   In a teaching station where no wall space is available, jumping at the net will accomplish the same major purposes. Teachers with wall space available may want to use it to supplement the Sargent Chalk Jump Test. Each player has a partner, preferably someone approximately her own height so that early frustrations in trying to match the jump of a taller player are avoided.

STATIONARY APPROACH.   The partners face each other squarely across the net. On the signal, "Ready?" by the teacher, the players assume the best possible basic position previous to the take-off for the jump. On the signal, "Jump!" the player uses the one-footed or two-footed take-off as directed and executes the proper action for the spike. Emphasis should also be placed on landing properly. Potential spikers have some idea about the height of the jump by comparing the level reached with the height of the net and with that reached by their partners.

RUNNING APPROACH.   Using the same procedure the class can practice the jump at the net preceded by a running approach. The partners back away from the net, some 6 to 8 feet. On the signal "Ready?" by the instructor, the players become alert and ready for the run. On the signal, "Go!," they move to the net taking short, quick steps, and jump into the air, executing the proper action for the spike. Landing to avoid fouling the net and center line and to maintain balance should be emphasized. In this practice the players gain a better understanding of what the momentum coming from the run can do for their jumps, and even the shorter players will begin to get a feeling that they can be successful in getting the spiking hand and arm above the top of the net.

3. *Wall Spiking.*   Wall spiking should be used to teach proper technique in the use of the body, arm, and hand in spiking.   Many students will have false preconceived notions about what actually takes place in good spiking technique.   Two of the popular misconceptions are that the arm is propelled in a windmill fashion and that the correct hand position is a fist.

Wall spiking is a form of individual practice in which the students are scattered throughout the teaching station and are facing a solid wall surface. Emphasizing the correct use of the body, arm, and hand, the player hits the ball at approximately shoulder height.   The objective is to have the ball bounce from the playing surface on to the wall and then back down to the playing surface, where it will be contacted again.   Lines can be arranged on the floor and on the wall to encourage heights and distances in keeping with the desired standards relative to game use.   For example, a line on the floor, 5 feet away from the wall, will encourage the player to hit the ball so that it bounces at least this distance away before rebounding on the wall, and after contacting the wall, it must again bounce beyond the floor line before contact is repeated.   A line on the wall, 5 feet from the floor, will emphasize the amount of force that must be put on top of the ball to have it rebound from above that height.

4. *Spiking Handball* (see Fig. 4–2).   By using the line markings suggested in the previous formation and adding side lines to enclose an area

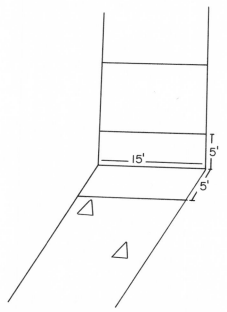

Fig. 4–2.   Spiking handball.

15 feet in width, the wall spiking procedure can be modified so that two players can compete against each other in a spiking handball game. The rules are similar to those of the game of handball. Beginning at any desired position behind the 5-foot restraining line, one player puts the ball into play by hitting it with a spiking motion downward so that contact is made before the ball passes over the 5-foot restraining line on the floor. On the wall contact the ball must clear the 5-foot level and must rebound beyond the 5-foot floor line. The second player then must make the next contact, and play alternates between the two players until a fault is declared. Scoring is the same as for a regulation game with only the player putting the ball into play having scoring privileges. Faults are failing to clear the line markings on the bounce, wall contact, or rebound; hitting the ball out-of-bounds on the bounce, wall contact, or rebound; using any kind of hand contact except a one-hand overhead spiking action; not allowing the ball to bounce on its rebound from the wall before contacting it; and interfering with the opponent's play. Interference will be called if a player, having made her contact with the ball, does not step behind and out of the way of her opponent so that she has clear access to the rebounding ball.

Spiking handball will challenge advanced players to put more force and spin behind spikes. As only two players are necessary, the game is closely akin to individual practice and is of importance to individuals who need to work on perfecting spiking skills.

5. *Harnessed Ball Practices* (see Fig. 4–3). After players who are learning to spike have had practice in the proper jumping and ball-handling techniques, as previously outlined, the two can be effectively practiced together by means of a semistationary harnessed ball. Rig up a harnessed ball by using a tether ball standard and ball with an extension at 8 feet for high school girls and at 8½ feet for college women. The extension should allow the ball to hang from a rope about 6 inches in length. Players prac-

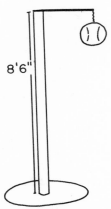

8'6"

Fig. 4–3. Harnessed ball practice.

tice jumping into the air and executing the spiking action against the ball harnessed in this position.

6. *Toss and Spike* (see Fig. 4–4).

REDUCED NET HEIGHT—STATIONARY APPROACH. Divide the class into groups of seven or nine players. The odd-numbered player is stationed on the opposite side of the net from the rest of the group to retrieve balls. The group is divided into a toss line, on the right, and a spiking line, on the left. The first player in the toss line stands about 18 inches from the net with her right shoulder turned toward the net and faces the first player in the spiking line. With an underhand toss she sends the ball 10 to 12

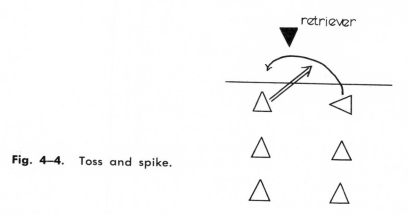

Fig. 4–4.   Toss and spike.

feet into the air and parallel with the net, approximating as closely as possible what she knows about a good set for a spike. Using a stationary approach, the first player in the spiking line executes the spike, and then each of the players goes to the end of the opposite line so that during their next turn at the net their duties will be exchanged. The reduced net height, to 6 feet for high school girls, and to 6 feet 4¼ inches for college women, and the tossed ball will ensure some early successful experiences in this difficult skill. The odd-numbered player should be rotated in to the tossing line after each player has had an initial turn in tossing and spiking, and the player who occupied first position in the tossing line becomes the retriever.

REDUCED NET HEIGHT—RUNNING APPROACH. Move the spiking line back approximately 6 to 8 feet and have the spiker advance to the net with a running approach to contact the ball. The toss remains the same as the one outlined for use with the stationary approach.

REGULATION HEIGHT NET. Elevate the net to its regulation height, and still using a toss instead of a volley-set, practice spiking from the (1) stationary approach and (2) running approach, as outlined under the reduced net height practices.

7. *Set and Spike.*

STATIONARY.   Using the same type of procedure as outlined for toss and spike, change the practice formation to have the spike follow a volley-set rather than a toss. In this practice the quality of the volley-set must be stressed as equally important as the correct technique in executing the spike. The first player in the setting line stands from 18 to 24 inches away from the net and attempts to set the ball in a parallel line with the net and 10 to 12 feet high. The ball should come to the highest point about half-way between the set and the spiker and should drop to spiking height without the spiker having to back up to play it. Rotate the odd-numbered player, who serves as a retriever, into the setting line so that each player has an equal number of practices in setting and spiking. As players become advanced and begin to function in game play as sets or spikers, this practice formation may be repeated with players finishing their turn at the net and retiring to the end of their own line.

RUNNING.   Set and spike may also be used as a practice formation with the running approach by moving the spiking line back away from the net some 6 to 8 feet. From that position the spiker advances to the net with her short, quick running steps and meets the set ball in relatively the same position as she did in the stationary approach. Again, a great deal of emphasis must be put on the quality of the set.

8. *Pass-Set-Spike (by Two's).*

STATIONARY APPROACH.   This practice formation begins to approximate very closely the 1-2-3 attack of game play. Again, there is a setting line and a spiking line, with the first player in each of the lines in the same relative positions in regard to the net. However, this time the ball begins with the spiking line. The first player puts the ball into play by executing a pass to the first person in the setting line. The set then returns the ball to the spiker, who attempts to put it away. This practice formation may be used with players moving to the end of the opposite line. However, it is expected that it will be used more often with advanced and competitive players who are identified as sets or spikers, and who will move to the end of their own lines to gain as many practices as possible in the play they will most often be called upon to perform in the game.

RUNNING APPROACH (see Fig. 4–5).   The pass-set-spike formation provides excellent practice for running approaches to spiking as performed by skilled teams in good volleyball play. The spiking line is moved some 6 to 8 feet back away from the net, and from that longer distance, the first player is required to make a longer pass to the set, with the distance closely approximating actual game play conditions. The set, in turn, sets the ball high and parallel with the net, and the spiker, using short, quick, running

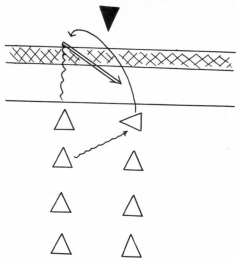

Fig. 4–5. Pass-set-spike by two's.

steps, approaches to contact the ball in almost the same position as she did for the stationary approach.

9. *Pass-Set-Spike (by Three's).*

STATIONARY APPROACH. Pass-set-spike by three's offers another game like opportunity to practice the 1-2-3 attack. In this formation a third line, a passing line, is added (see Fig. 4–6). No more than four players should occupy each line. The first player in the passing line functions as the back does in game play. Her duty is to make an excellent overhead volley-pass

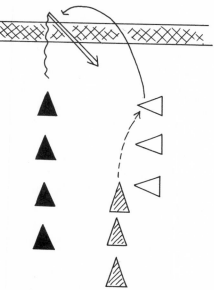

Fig. 4–6. Pass-set-spike by three's.

to the first player in the setting line. The set, in turn, sets the ball to the first player in the spiking line, who attempts to "kill" the ball. Much of the value of this practice formation lies in the fact that three different players are called upon to handle the ball, as in the usual pattern of game play. This practice formation may be used when introducing the 1-2-3 attack, and when this is the case, the teacher will organize rotation from one line to another. The first player in the passing line rotates to the end of the setting line; the first player in the setting line becomes the back player of the spiking line; and the spiker moves to the end of the passing line. It is also recommended practice when players are identified as sets or spikers. Use sets exclusively in the setting line, spikers in the spiking line, and have the passing line composed of half and half. The passing line players should then have practice in the appropriate setting or spiking line.

RUNNING APPROACH. The pass-set-spike (by three's) can be modified for a running approach by having the spiking line stationed 6 to 8 feet away from the net and the first player moving forward on the run to jump into the air at the net and execute the spike.

10. *Volleyball Doubles.* The lead-up game, Volleyball Doubles (see page 155), provides excellent opportunity to practice the spike and to work on the 1-2-3 attack involved in all patterns of offensive strategy. It further provides incentive to the players, especially in the Pair-Partner (3-3) system of play, to develop their combined efforts to the highest possible level of competitive play.

11. *Trio Volleyball.* Another game, which can be used effectively in the development of the spike, as well as the pass and set preliminary to it, is Trio Volleyball. Instead of two players, as in Volleyball Doubles, a team is composed of a trio of players. The game is played on one half-court, splitting it down the middle from end line to end line. The rules of the game and the scoring are exactly the same as in regulation play. Trio Volleyball allows one player, the server, to play fairly deep in the court as a defensive player. The other two players assume offensive roles by serving as the set and the spiker in the attack and as defensive players by serving as blockers against the opposing team. Another advantage of this game is that three players contact the ball on one side of the net as is usually the case in actual game play. In addition, Trio Volleyball lends itself to the use of running and stationary approaches for the spike.

Trio Volleyball provides excellent opportunity to practice the 1-2-3 attack through the Two-for-One (4 to 2) team offensive pattern (see pages 117–21) and the Two-for-One Interchange (see pages 121–22). It may also be used for development of the Pair-Partner (see pages 113–17) and the Five-to-One Interchange (see pages 122–23) systems.

12. *Reverse Set-Spike.* The reverse set-spike formation provides structured practice for game play when the initial pass is to go to the Key-Set

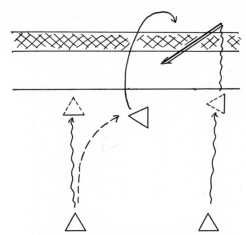

Fig. 4–7. Reverse set-spike.

in the center forward position and she sets the ball over her own head to the spiker in the right forward position instead of to the Key-Spiker, playing in the left forward position. This play is of significant value in the Pair-Partner system each time a Key-Set occupies a position of center forward and has spikers on either side of her; in the Two-for-One and Two-for-One Interchange, when the Key-Set is in the center forward position, or when an interchange is made to get her there; and in the Five-to-One Interchange under the same conditions.

Have the group or class divided into groups of three. A player, in the role of the Key-Set, maintains her position at the net and is facing in the direction of the left forward. The two spikers are stationed some 6 to 8 feet away from the net as for a running approach. One of them begins the action by passing the ball to the Key-Set, who reverse sets the ball to the right forward spiker, who spikes the ball (see Fig. 4–7). The effectiveness of the play depends upon the quality of the reverse set and the faking action of the spiker who is not to handle the ball. The offensive team should be able to keep the defensive team from knowing until the last moment who is actually going to spike the ball and from being able to throw up an effective block at the net.

Vary the practice by having the spikers mix up who is making the original pass and by having the Key-Set face the right forward position and reverse over her head to the Key-Spiker in the left forward position. In each instance, both spikers approach the net with the preliminary running steps and the jump so that the faking action is practiced right along with the actual play.

13. *Cross Set-Spike.* The cross set-spike formation provides practice for game play when the initial pass is to go to the Key-Set occupying the left forward or center forward position and her objective is to set the ball to a

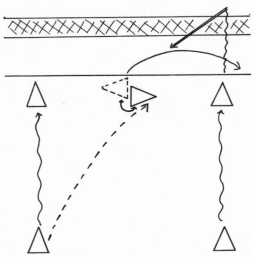

Fig. 4–8. Cross set-spike.

right-handed spiker playing to her immediate right. This play has significant value in the Pair-Partner pattern when the Key-Set is playing center
forward and wants to set the ball to the right forward spiker to be spiked
or on an occasional play when the pass is directed to a set player who has
rotated into the left forward position, and the Key-Spiker and the Key-Set
are playing center forward and right forward, respectively.

In the Two-for-One, Two-for-One Interchange, and Five-to-One Interchange, the cross set is of significant value when the ball is passed to the
Key-Set playing left forward or center forward, or to the Key-Set when she
interchanges to that position, and sets the ball to a right-handed spiker on
her immediate right-hand side.

In setting up the practice formation, have the players again work in
groups of three. The Key-Set maintains her position at the net as center
forward or as left forward. The two spikers are away in their positions for
a running approach, as left and right forwards when the Key-Set is the
center forward (see Fig. 4–8), or as center and right forwards when the
Key-Set is the left forward. In either situation begin the ball with one of
the spikers, who passes to the Key-Set, who, in turn, cross sets the ball to
the spiker on her immediate right. Again, both spikers move to the net
with the running approach as if to spike the ball. Consequently, the blockers will be unable to detect who is to spike the ball until the last moment,
and the defense will be considerably weakened. Vary the practice by having the Key-Set occupy the different front line positions open to her for a
cross set play and by having the spikers alternate beginning the ball from
their varied position possibilities.

14. *Over Set-Spike.* The over set-spike formation provides practice for game play when the initial pass is to go to the Key-Set in the left forward position and she wants to set the ball over the head of a spiker occupying the center forward position to a spiker playing the right forward position. It is also appropriate when the Key-Set is playing right forward and she wishes to set the ball over the head of a spiker playing center forward to a spiker occupying the left forward position. Since sets and spikers always alternate with each other in the Pair-Partner pattern of play, this practice is not appropriate for teams using that system. However, it of significant value in the Two-for-One, Two-for-One Interchange, and the Five-to-One Interchange patterns of offensive strategy.

In the practice formation groups of three work together. One player, the Key-Set, plays either left forward or right forward and maintains her same relative position in regard to the net. The spikers, as center and right forwards or as center and left forwards, respectively, assume positions for running approaches. Either spiker may begin the ball by making the initial pass to the Key-Set, who, in turn, sets the ball to the appropriate right or left forward over the head of the center forward (see Fig. 4–9). The effectiveness of the play depends upon the quality of the over set and the ability of the spikers, including faking action, to keep the defense guessing as to whom the set will actually go to be spiked.

Vary the practice by having the two spikers interchange in making the initial pass and by using the Key-Set in both the left forward and right forward positions.

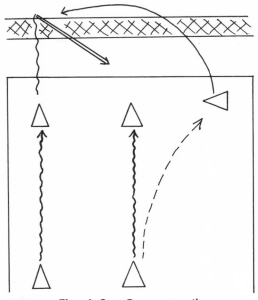

Fig. 4–9. Over set-spike.

15. *Jumping Wall Spiking.* The advanced and experienced player can gain additional spiking skill by practicing the spike individually against the wall. However, this practice differs from the one used by the beginning spiker in that after the initial contact the ball is not allowed to bounce on the floor after rebounding from the wall. Consequently, the player must jump into the air to execute the spiking motion at an appropriate height level as the ball leaves the wall. The line marker on the wall for this practice should equal the height of the net.

16. *Variation of Spiking Practices through Additional Game Elements.* Beginning with spiking practice Number 7 and continuing through Number 14, the formations may be modified to contain additional meaningful game elements:

MODIFYING THE SPIKE SO THAT DIRECTION, AS WELL AS FORCE IS PRACTICED. The spiker who is practicing spiking from a left forward position will attempt to direct spikes straight down the left side line, diagonally to her right, and sharply to her right. A spiking center forward will practice spiking sharply to the left, straight down the center of the court, and sharply to the right. A spiker in the position of right forward will aim for spikes moving straight down the right side line, diagonally left, and sharply to the left.

ADDING DEFENSIVE PLAYERS TO COUNTERACT THE SPIKE. In order to execute an effective spike, the offense must maneuver the ball out of the reach of the defensive players. Therefore, blockers, one, two, or three in number, and backs with designated picking-up or "saving" assignments should be added to the spiking formations. These will be covered more fully in practices outlined with the block and pick-up (see pages 92–96).

USE OF A DINK OR TIP. The dink or tip is a play made by the spiker in which she uses the hand behind, rather than on top of, the ball, and with a flick of the wrist taps it just over and out of the reach of the players involved in the block. The dink, to be effective in the game, must be used sparingly and must come as a surprise to the defending team. Therefore, the spiker executing the dink must use all of her resources to make the defensive team think that the action she is taking is a spike. Practices using the dink or tip are most profitable when they are undertaken with the blockers and pick-up defensive backs at work.

USE OF VOLLEY AS A LOB. Practice having the spiker execute a high, deep lobbing volley, instead of a spike, over the hands and out of reach of the opposing blockers. This action is very useful as a surprise attack in the game, especially when the backs of the opposing team begin to pull in toward the net to assist the blockers or to execute a save. Again, the spiker must make all of her preliminary movements indicate that a spike is forthcoming.

BLOCKING

Throwing up an adequate defense against the 1-2-3 attack, which culminates in a forceful and well-directed spike, indicates the use of two kinds of skills. The first is the block, or the front-line defense, against the spike. The second is the pick-up, or save. Blocking involves a separate individual skill, but picking up, or saving, usually calls for use of the two-handed or one-handed dig, which has already been presented in Chapter 2.

Although blocking is an individual skill, the use of blocking in the game is moving from the one-man block, which is effective only against weaker spikers, to two-man and three-man blocks on the most highly skilled competitive levels.

Some of the same requirements of being a good spiker are essential to performance as a blocker. First of all, the player must develop jumping ability so that both hands and the forearms near the wrist can clear the top of the net. In addition, the blocker must have excellent reactions to game play and must have finely developed coordinations and timing. The blocker, or blockers, never takes anything for granted. The job to be performed is to anticipate, meet, and, whenever possible, outplay the opposing spiker. The blocker, or blockers, must hold off the move to block until the offensive team is committed beyond threat of recall. After the ball has been contacted by the Key-Set, usually the second play by the offensive team, and the ball is moving in the direction of the third player, the spiker, it is safe for the blocker, or blockers, to converge to a point along the net directly opposite the attacking player.

Basic Position.   The basic position for the player executing the one-man block is to face the net squarely, some 15 to 20 inches away, directly opposite the spiking player. Beginning with the weight of the body evenly distributed on the balls of both feet, the knees flexed so that the extensors can be used in the vertical lift, and the arms at the side of the body, the blocker concentrates on the position of the spiker in order to learn from the direction she is facing and her preliminary movements what she can about the ball to be spiked.

The Action.   Using a double-foot take-off in which the effort of the jump is geared toward a vertical lift, the blocker times her action pattern to coincide with that of the spiker. As she jumps into the air, both arms are vigorously lifted overhead so that each is elevated almost directly over the shoulder. The hands come together with the thumbs contacting each other. The fingers are somewhat spread, slightly flexed, and held in a firmed, but not rigid, position. From the wrists the hands are tilted back, and as the spiker contacts the ball from slightly above, the hands move forward to become aligned with the wrists, and in this motion, the spiked ball is contacted in the block. The contact occurs 4 or 5 inches away from the net. Two kinds of objectives may be met through a block executed in this manner. The first objective may be to have the ball played immediately back down on the opponents' side of the net, just between the spiker and the net. In this kind of play, the block becomes an offensive as well as defensive action, and is quite successful when the spiker is unable to gain momentum in time to play the ball again. The second objective may be to have the spike deflected in such a manner that it can be played by members of the blocker's team. In this kind of play, the block is used to take the force from the spiked ball and to make it playable in an offensive manner by the teammates of the blocker.

The blocker, or blockers, must learn to land facing the net squarely, with the weight evenly distributed between both feet, and in a position to get back into the next play should the blocked ball be quickly returned by the original spiker or one of her teammates.

The players whose duties it is to back up the blocker, or blockers, in picking-up assignments should be coached to listen intently for the sound of a blocked ball. If the block has only partially deflected the ball, the pick-up may become more difficult due to the demands of quick judgment and reaction. If competitive teams are likely to play with large audiences in attendance, a verbal signal, such as "Touch!" sounded by the blockers, will help the pick-ups in determining the specifics of their responsibilities.

ONE-MAN BLOCKS

In blocking against a team with limited spiking ability, the one-man block is all that is needed to throw up an adequate barrier. The player receiving a one-man blocking assignment is the player on the defensive team immediately opposite to the spiking player. In other words, in a one-man block a right forward covers the left forward, the center forward the opposing center forward, and the left forward an opposing right forward.

TWO-MAN BLOCK (SEE FIG. 4–10)

Better girls' and women's teams call for use of a two-man, or four-handed, block in combating the skill of a good spiker. The two-man block is executed by two front line players, with the center forward always involved. When the opposing left forward is the attacking player, the right forward and the center forward of the defensive team have the responsibility for throwing up a two-man block. Waiting until the offensive team is totally committed to running the attack through the left forward, the two players

Fig. 4—10.   The two-man block.

converge to a point directly opposite her and assume the basic position for the block. As they jump into the air, the inside shoulders of the two blockers should be slightly inclined toward the net to prevent the ball from being directed out of bounds on contact. The four hands and forearms of the two blockers should prevent a solid barrier above the net.

If the center forward or the right forward is the spiker on the offensive team, the two defending players involved in the block are the center forward and the left forward. They follow the same procedure as did the right forward and the center forward in blocking against the left forward.

THREE-MAN BLOCK

As the better girls' and women's teams have demanded use of a two-man block in defensive play against a spiker, the best teams have moved to use of a three-man block. In a three-man block the assignments go to two front line players and the center back. Again, the defending team must wait until the attacking team has totally committed itself to use of a particular spiker, and then the three players with the blocking assignments move to a position with the center blocker directly opposite the spiker. From a position some 15 to 20 inches from the net they wait until the spiker makes her take-off for the spike and move into the .air to meet, match, and overcome her efforts. As the blockers jump into the air, the center blocker should be facing the net and the opposing spiker squarely. Her two teammates should have their inside shoulders slightly in contact with her, but the outside shoulders should be slightly inclined toward the net to prevent the ball, once contacted on the block, from being directed out of bounds. In the three-man block, six hands and forearms are elevated side-by-side to meet the attacker's onslaught.

When the opposing left forward is the spiker, the three-man blocking assignment is given to the defending right forward, center forward, and center back. The center back moves up to take the center blocking position. When either the center forward or the right forward of the offensive team is the spiker, the three-man blocking assignment is given the defending left forward, center forward, and center back. The center back again assumes the center blocking position. In all multiple blocking assignments the right or left forward not involved falls back away from the net to assist the backs in establishing a second-line defense against the spike.

THE PICK-UP

A second-line defense must be established to meet the spikes that blockers miss at the net or to assist in returning those spikes only partially deflected by the blockers. Picking-up, or saving, assignments are most often in the hands of the defensive backs. However, they may also be the responsibility of the forward who is not involved in a multiple block. This is often the case when the spiker is able to spike at sharp angles to her playing position.

To say that the ideal way to play the ball on a pick-up is through an overhead volley is accurate, but it is also highly impractical. Working against a skilled, forceful, and well-directed spike, allows little, if any, time to get in the ready and waiting position that is desirable in the execution of a good overhead volley. Therefore, the two-handed and one-handed digs are most often used in skilled play for this purpose. The two-handed dig is preferred when it is possible to get both hands and forearms into the action because it provides most control. However, in competitive volleyball, players must be skilled in the performance of the one-handed dig, for they will be using it often against the skilled spiker.

Players with picking-up assignments listen for the sound of the block or the signal of the blockers, and then go into action. The object of the pick-up is to get the ball back into the air so that it is playable by a team-mate, and, whenever possible, to give the ball forward momentum, as in a regular pass, so that it may be handled next by a front line player who would attempt to set it to be spiked.

METHODS OF PRESENTATION AND PRACTICE

It is expected that blocking and picking-up will be introduced to volleyball classes in intermediate or advanced units after the students have had some experience with spiking and with digging. Therefore, part of the teacher's work in teaching these two defensive skills will have been accomplished. For example, the student will have learned something about the mechanics of effective jumping and how to propel the body in a vertical lift in spiking, which is, in essence, the same as use of the body in blocking. While learning something about underhand ball-handling techniques, the student will have learned about the type of skill that is used in picking up the spiked ball.

DEMONSTRATION OF THE BLOCK

The demonstration of a block requires performance by more than one person. In fact, to be effective and realistic, the demonstration of a block requires at least a set, a spiker, and one blocker. Preferably, a player given the responsibility of passing the ball is added to the offensive side of the lineup and the blockers are increased to two or three when it is deemed desirable to show the increased efficiency of the two- and three-man blocks over the one-man block. Consequently, the teacher presenting blocking skills must be prepared and practiced ahead of class time to make the demonstration worthwhile. She may have to call on personnel outside the class itself, such as other teachers, students from advanced units, competitive programs, or some community experts. The demonstration should show blocks which have as their objective the immediate replay of the spiked ball back into the spiker's court and some which are merely deflected so that teammates of the blockers can next handle the ball. The major points of blocking skill should be emphasized, along with the game rules which have a special bearing upon blocking. After questions from the class are asked and answered, practices should begin.

PRACTICE METHODS

Since blocking alone is not an adequate defense against the spike, practice in picking up, using the digging techniques, should be added to every blocking practice. Therefore, these two defensive skills have common practice methods and are presented together.

1. *Sargent Chalk Jumping Test.* The same test administered in connection with teaching the spike is appropriate in practicing the block provided that only a double-foot take-off be allowed.

2. *Jumping at the Net.* Use the same procedure as outlined for spiking to work on the jump for blocking opposite a partner at the net.

3. *Harnessed Ball Blocking.* The same rig that was arranged to practice spiking technique can be used to practice blocking technique against a harnessed ball. The blocker will have an opportunity to learn a great deal about timing her jump and the use of her hands and forearms in the block if she practices simultaneously with a spiker on the harnessed ball.

4. *Blocking and Picking Up (One and One).* The most practical and effective way to practice the defensive skills of blocking and picking up is to have them pitted against the spike and its preliminary offensive ball-handling skills of passing and setting. Therefore, the same practice formations which were used to drill upon offensive patterns may later be modified to take care of defensive play. It is highly recommended that the defensive units, as outlined here, be tried step-by-step against the spiking practice formations of set-spike, pass-set-spike (by two's), pass-set-spike (by three's), reverse set-spike, cross set-spike, and over set-spike (see pages 80–85).

The first defensive alignment against these offensive practice formations should consist of one blocker and one pick-up. The blocker assumes the position at the net opposite the line of spikers. The pick-up plays deep in the court. After defensive practice in these positions, these two players can easily rotate as a unit into the partner-type of procedures called for in both the set-spike and pass-set-spike (by two's) offensive formations.

5. *Blocking and Picking Up (Two and One).* Using the same offensive patterns as the bases, practice the two-man block and single pick-up by utilizing three defensive players. The two blockers assume positions opposite the known spikers in set-spike, pass-set-spike (by two's), and pass-set-spike (by three's). The pick-up player maintains her position and assumes her duties deep in her own court. The three defensive players can easily rotate, as an offensive unit, into pass-set-spike (by three's) when they have finished a satisfactory number of trials as the defensive unit.

6. *Blocking and Picking Up (Two and Two).* A fourth player, assuming the position and duties of a back who is assigned to serve as a pick-up, is added to the defensive unit. Still concentrating on a two-man block, the blockers assume their net stations and this defensive unit can practice in a realistic manner against set-spike, pass-set-spike (by two's) (see Fig. 4–11), and pass-set-spike (by three's). In the first two formations, where there is a partner-type of arrangement on the offensive, rotation of players from

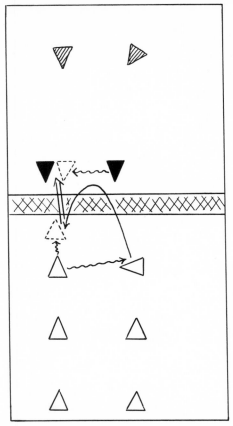

Fig. 4–11. Blocking and picking up (two and two).

the partner-type of defense may be easily effected to provide both offensive and defensive practice.

7. *Blocking and Picking Up (Three and Two).* Reverse set-spike, cross set-spike, and over set-spike are offensive practice formations which keep the identity of the spiker concealed until the last possible moment. Their strategic orientation makes them quite valuable when there is need to gain defensive practice against a surprise attack. In fact, to defend against either formation effectively, the defensive unit will need to be of full, or almost full, force. In defending against either formation, experiment with two variations of the three and two defensive units. If the team is still concentrating on a two-man block, use two blockers at the net, shifting where they are needed, to protect against the spiker. Use a third player in the relative position of a center back and as a pick-up to assist the right and left backs who are stationed deep in their own court and have the picking-up assignments.

If the team is beginning to work on three-man blocks, arrange for the beginning position to be the same as that just outlined, but as the offensive unit sets the ball to the spiker, have the center back move to the front line and become the third blocker. The teacher or coach may find that it is quite profitable to have the three-two blocking and picking-up defensive unit work out against the easier set-spike, pass-set-spike (by two's), and pass-set-spike (by three's) before operating against the more complicated offensive formations.

8. *Blocking and Picking Up (Full Team Complement).* A team should have opportunity to practice its total team defense against the various of-

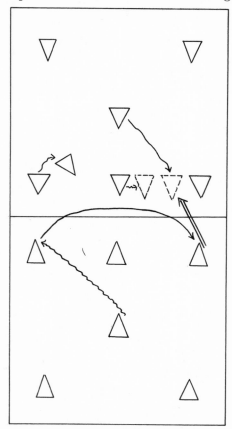

Fig. 4–12.   Three-man block and pick-up against over set-spike.

fensive formations. Therefore, set up a defending team on one side of the court and using a two-man block have them function as a total unit against each of the offensive practice formations in turn. In addition, when the team is ready to work on effecting a three-man block, concentrate on this effort within the total team framework (see Fig. 4–12).

9. *Volleyball Doubles (Blocking).* Use the game of Volleyball Doubles to get in some concentrated practice of the one-man block. As it is advis-

able in this game to leave one player deep in the court to defend against well-placed spikes, dinks, and high, lobbing volleys, only one player is available to try to stop the spiking action at the net.

10. *Trio Volleyball (Blocking)*. Since Trio Volleyball provides each team with a third player, she can be stationed near the baseline, after serving or after receiving the service, and the other two players are relatively free to try to stop the spiker at the net. Therefore, Trio Volleyball allows concentrated opportunity to develop the two-man block.

The uses of individual defensive skills in building team defensive patterns of play are presented in Chapter 6.

TEAM PATTERNS
OF PLAY

5

The Offense

In the game of volleyball there are no so-called "secret plays" or "hidden weapons" to be masterminded by the coach or teacher and dictated from the side line. Neither is there a highly developed player-specialist in one skill, sitting hopefully by the coach and waiting an opportunity to enter the game, however briefly, just to perform her particular art. For these reasons, some unknowing persons in the sports world have had a tendency to look down upon volleyball as a less than major sports activity.

On the other hand, the fact that all well-coached and well-skilled teams strive to play the same basic offensive pattern is one of the most exciting and most demanding aspects of the game. With every good team working its offense around the basic 1-2-3 attack, the team that has best individually and collectively mastered and perfected the individual skills and molded them into a polished system that is able to surprise and catch offguard the strongest of defensive teams is sure to be a winning team. Not only will they be a winning team, but they also will be a winning team in a game that is able to capture the heart, imagination, and adventuring spirit of athletes and sports fans, men and women alike, all over the world.

THE SERVICE

Since volleyball rules give the privilege of scoring to the serving team only, each team must develop serving skills to the highest possible degree and look upon the service as the number one offensive weapon available to them. To realize the potential of serving skills as a major offensive weapon, the volleyball team must be ready to take full advantage of variations, power, and placement.

VARIATIONS

The types of serving skills: the underhand, sidearm, overhead, and roundhouse; their special uses and advantages; and detailed practice methods for their development were presented in Chapter 3. As noted in assessing their particular strengths and weaknesses, the interchanging of these skills in game play provides variation in the amount of speed and force behind the ball; the angle of penetration in which a served ball enters the opponents' court; the amount and type of spin on the ball; and the degree of control or placement. Through these variations the players who can interchange serving skills during the game, or even during a single term of service, may assist their team in reaching an offensive advantage over the opponents.

In the interchanging of serving technique a good guide for the teacher and coach to follow is:

1. Expect beginning skill level players to be able to perform one serving skill, usually the underhand, with accuracy and with some placement control.

2. Expect intermediate skill level players to be able to use interchangeably and effectively two out of the four serving skills. Having been introduced to the sidearm service technique during a beginner's unit, they will have a chance to develop it fully in an intermediate unit. Thus, the sidearm service with its greater advantages in power, spin, and angle of penetration, but lessening in the degree of placement control, joins the intermediate's underhand as an interchangeable service skill.

3. Expect the advanced skill level players to be able to use interchangeably and effectively the underhand, sidearm, and overhead serving techniques. It is expected that the volleyball player will be introduced to the overhead service during her intermediate unit or experience in volleyball, but her perfection of this skill will most likely occur during an advanced unit. The additional advantages to be gained through the power, spin, and resultant more difficult angle of penetration make the adding of this technique to the repertoire of serving skills of high importance. However, the performance complexity of this skill also reduces its accuracy and increases the amount of difficulty in placement. Therefore, only players who have developed this service to the highest degree of accuracy and control should be called upon to use it in the game.

4. Expect only the most advanced and competitive players to be able to use the roundhouse, or hook, service as an interchangeable skill. As a highly complex skill requiring the greatest of neuromuscular coordinations, the advanced player should be allowed to work to develop this technique when all three others are perfected and when it serves as a particular challenge to her.

POWER AND PLACEMENT

Power, or sheer force, is a quality of the service which can be developed to the extent that it makes a return of the service by the receiving team either completely impossible or else definitely weakens the return by forcing the use of two, or even three, contacts to bring the ball under control and to make a return to the serving team's court. When the contacts of the receiving team must be used in this way, they are unable to return the ball in an offensive pattern and the serving team is in a better position to effect a point-winning 1-2-3 attack. The relative value of the types of service in producing this kind of force, in order, is: the roundhouse, the overhead, the sidearm, and the underhand.

Accuracy. The first concern of a team in placement of the service to produce a major offensive weapon is simply that of accuracy. Accuracy, in this case, means serving a ball that is over the net and inbounds. No team can possibly develop into a successful one before every player thoroughly understands and accepts the principle that "keeping the service" is an absolute essential. As a player rotates to serving position, it is her responsibility to give her act of service her undivided attention and to take the time that is needed to plot the service as an offensive weapon.

Placement. Plotting the service as an offensive weapon, from the placement point of view, means that the server will take full advantage of what she knows about the individual players on the opposing team, what she can detect about her opponents' receiving position as she moves into her own serving position, and what she has already practiced and developed in serving the ball to particular targets on the playing court. The server should direct her services to known weaker players, causing them to err in handling the ball or to make a poor pass. Usually, a member of the receiving team will move to help the weaker player cover her court area. As a receiving player makes this move, she often does it prematurely, leaving an unprotected area on the court as a very desirable target for placement of the service. Aiming a served ball to a point just between two players waiting to receive the service is also strategically sound. If the served ball is one that is approaching with a great deal of speed, the two players may become confused as to who has the responsibility for the initial contact and the quality of the pass under these conditions suffers. In addition, the baseline area of the opponents, the side line area, and the inside pockets between the receiving backs and forwards (see Fig. 3–8, page 62), are desirable targets for placement of the service because services directed toward these areas require that one or more receiving players move out of basic positions maintained as most advantageous for an offensive return to the serving team's court. Baseline services are also strategic because they force the opposing teams to play the ball the full distance of their half-court and increase the probable margin of error.

Correction of Serving Errors. In order to master and perfect the service as an offensive weapon, errors in serving form should be detected and corrected as soon as possible. Repetition and drill in serving technique are required for the observation and analysis essential in adequate error correction. The practice formations outlined for concentration in the development of serving skills, presented on pages 60–66, provide this opportunity. The player, the teacher, and the coach should become aware of and correct these probable common errors:

1. Underhand service.
   a. Poor stance. Correct by separating the feet and keeping the left one forward when the server is a right-handed player. Check to see that the weight of the body is being carried between the two feet before the player shifts into the backswing.
   b. Shifting of holding arm and hand with serving arm and hand. There is a natural tendency to allow the holding arm and hand to move forward gradually as the serving arm and hand are moved in the backswing. The player must be coached to "anchor" the holding hand and arm into proper position, which is close to the knee of the forward leg.
   c. Failure to keep the swing of the serving arm forward. Correct any sideward motion of the swinging arm by aligning the swing foward from the backswing to pass the feet in stationary position on the playing surface straight through toward the net.
   d. Elbow bend or premature body lift. The full arm extension should be used. Therefore, any bend in the elbow before the ball is contacted results in hitting the ball too close to the top rather than in its center, and the served ball will fail to clear the net. With a full arm extension at contact the body must be left in its crouched position to prevent hitting too close to the top of the ball.
   e. Tossing the ball. The underhand service involves hitting the ball directly off the holding hand without any preliminary toss. Such a toss often results in a ball hit on the underneath side, which makes the flight pattern too high and too easy for the opponents to get under in time to make an effective return. Tossing the ball on the underhand service also limits the amount of control or placement possible, and since this is probably the most valuable asset of this type, it should not be sacrificed through this kind of error.
   f. Failure to keep eyes on the ball. Looking away from the ball during the act of service often causes the server to make mistakes in accurate contact of the ball. The use of the eyes to evaluate strategic placement of the service should occur before the player moves into her backswing.
   g. Inadequate follow-through. Although the follow-through may be used to control the height of the flight pattern and the force behind the underhand service, each follow-through must be adequate to accomplish the desired effect. In balls failing to clear the net, look for failure of the serving hand to approach shoulder level at completion.
2. Sidearm service.
   a. Poor stance. Correct the stance by having the player face the side line

toward her right with her left shoulder in toward the net and her left foot slightly forward of the right. Check to see that the weight of the body is evenly distributed between the two feet before the player shifts into the backswing.

b. Allowing the holding arm and hand to shift forward. As the serving arm and hand shift into the backswing, there is a natural tendency to allow the holding arm and hand to shift forward. The player must be coached to leave the ball "anchored" in alignment with the left shoulder as the right arm moves into the backswing.

c. Dipping or climbing arm swing. A dipping arm swing will allow the serving hand to contact underneath the ball and give it too much height in its flight pattern. A climbing arm swing will result in hitting on top of the ball and the served ball will fail to clear the net. Correct these errors by swinging the arm forward at shoulder height to meet the ball held in the holding hand at shoulder height.

d. Bent elbows. At the point of contact both the holding and serving arms should be fully extended. A bent holding elbow will cause the serving arm to overreach its objective and the ball will be hit on the side and will move in a direction to the left sharply and without control. A bent serving elbow will cause an underreach of the held ball and it will move to the right sharply and without control.

e. Tossing the ball. The sidearm service involves hitting the ball off the stationary holding hand without any preliminary toss. If the ball is tossed before it is contacted, it is likely that it will be hit from a point below its center and will result in a high flight pattern. In addition, the tossed ball presents too many variables, making control of it more difficult.

f. Failure to keep eyes on the ball. During the act of serving the eyes should keep in continual contact with the ball. Therefore, any survey of the opposing team with strategic intent must be made preliminary to the actual performance of the serving skill.

g. Insufficient follow-through. One of the main objectives in use of the sidearm service is to obtain power. The forceful sidearm service is accomplished with a full, high speed swing of the serving arm from its backswing all the way into a complete follow-through.

3. Overhead service.

a. Poor stance. Correct the stance by having the server stand facing the net squarely with the left foot forward and the right foot at almost a right angle. Check to see that the weight of the body is evenly distributed between the two feet before the player tosses the ball and begins her backswing.

b. Poor tosses. Faulty overhead services are frequently the result of poor tossing by the holding hand. A toss that is made too far forward of the server's body results in failure to hit the ball solidly and often below its center, and the ball fails to carry far enough to clear the net. A toss that is too far behind the server's head will result in an abnormal twisting of the server's body and the ball is often hit from underneath and up into the air rather than from behind its center and forward. Tosses that are too far to one side or the other will result in contacts of the ball off-center and sharp directions sideward, frequently ending with an out-of-bounds service. Tosses that are too low result in a forced and often incomplete serving motion. Tosses that are too high become more difficult to time and hit. As previously suggested, the toss for the overhead service should be practiced separately until the server can control it for her own purposes.

   c. Straight arm swing. The arm executing the overhead service is used in a bent arm action until the actual contact with the ball is made. Coach players to avoid trying to swing the arm straight into the backswing, and instead emphasize the point that the elbow should be leading in this technique.

   d. Poorly aligned arm swing. If the serving arm is allowed to veer to the right or left of the server's body, the consequence will be a ball that is contacted on the sides; the direction will be toward the sidelines; and often an out-of-bounds ball will result. Coach the player to swing the serving arm directly forward toward the net.

   e. Failure to keep eyes on the ball. The tossed ball preliminary to serving overhead requires absolute concentration on the ball and its position in order to adjust the timing of the swing and the point of contact. Any viewing of the opponents' positioning for strategic intent must be accomplished previous to the act of serving.

   f. Inadequate follow-through. An adequate follow-through is essential in providing the power which is the particular asset of this type of serving skill. The player should be helped to get the feel of the forceful action of the swing from its beginning complete to a full follow-through. In order to prevent foot fault and to ensure contacting the ball solidly, coach the server to begin with the forward foot 6 to 8 inches behind the baseline; to keep her feet stationary until the point of contact; and then to step forward in her follow-through.

4. Roundhouse (hook) service.

   a. Poor stance. Correct the stance by having the server face the sideline with the left foot forward and the right foot at almost a right angle. Check to see that the weight of the body is evenly divided between the two feet before the player tosses the ball to begin her backswing.

   b. Poor tosses. The errors made in tossing the ball in the regular overhead service are likely to be repeated in the roundhouse service and they should be corrected in the same manner.

   c. Bent arm swing. Because of the rotation of the body during the roundhouse service, the serving arm should be held in full extension as it swings to make contact with the ball. The movement pattern of this service is essentially the same as that used by the basketball player in executing a hook pass or shot. In fact, it is appropriate practice while learning this skill for the volleyball player to hold a ball in her serving hand and let it "ride" throughout the complete swing required by this technique.

d. Poorly aligned swing. Again, the server must avoid allowing the serving arm to veer to either side. Instead, she must concentrate on swinging the serving arm directly toward the net.

e. Failure to keep eyes on the ball. The complicated nature of the toss and timing of the roundhouse service necessitates keeping an eye contact with the ball through the execution of the roundhouse service. The strategic intent to be gained through looking for unprotected areas and weak players on the opponents' court must be accomplished before the act of service begins.

f. Insufficient follow-through. The increased velocity behind the ball, one of the prime objectives in the use of this service, is gained only through use of a complete follow-through. Coach the player to get the feel of the increased power that accrues when there is a full, unified swing, beginning with the backswing and ending with the follow-through.

SCREENING

Contrary to popular belief, screening is possible within the intent and spirit of the DGWS volleyball rules, as well as the rules of the USVBA. As an aid to the serving team, screening should be introduced at the intermediate skill level and should be a highly developed offensive weapon for advanced and competitive players.

A screen is the use of three or more players operating in a preplanned floor arrangement which enables them to conceal the server from the easy discernment of the receiving team. Thus, the server is able to assume stances and interchange types of serving skills without the receivers being able to view her actions easily. The screen also allows the server protection for mannerisms which might betray the intended direction of her service, the amount of force to be put behind the served ball, and the possible penetration angle of the served ball. Through use of a screen, the sidearm, overhead, and roundhouse services, which come into the receiving court close to the net, are impossible to locate and to judge accurately until the last possible moment. Thus, the return of the receiving team is often weakened.

Two additional values of the screen are deserving of some attention. First, in highly competitive play the tensions and pressures upon the individual player are often heightened by the fact that she is expected to stand in a stationary or fixed position while her own teammate is serving the ball. Then, she is required to move effectively to meet the receiving team's return and turn the pattern into an attacking play. The setting up and breaking out of a screen promotes preball-handling activity, which is effective in the relaxation of the tense player. Second, the operation of an effective screen does much to encourage a spirit of team unity and effort, so highly desirable in volleyball, as in all team activities.

Within the framework of the DGWS rules two types of screens are permissible and effective. They are the Three-Man Screen and the Four-Man Screen. Under the USVBA rules up to five players may be used in the formation of a serving screen.

SCREENS FOR DGWS PLAY

In understanding the formation of the two screens possible within DGWS play, it is essential to review two pertinent rules. First, it is permissible for the server to stand behind the baseline at any point from one imaginary extension of the side line to the other. Second, the rules clearly state that each player must be in her own respective position and playing area of the court when the ball is put into play on the service.

Three-Man Screen. The Three-Man Screen (see Fig. 5–1) can be employed when the server moves to a point behind the baseline and ten feet in from the right sideline to execute the service. The three teammates involved in forming this screen are the center forward, the right forward, and the center back. All three players converge at the point on the playing court where their respective areas lie adjacent to each other. The two forwards stand with their backs turned toward the net and face in the direction of the server. The center back faces the center forward and the net squarely.

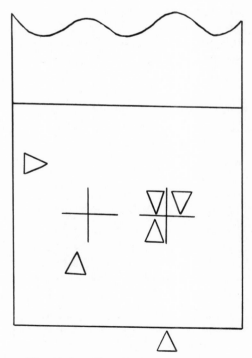

Fig. 5–1. The three-man screen.

The individual stance of all three players is with the feet parallel and some 12 to 15 inches apart. The weight of the body is balanced forward on the balls of both feet. The knees are kept slightly flexed. This positioning will enable quick movement once the ball has been contacted on the service and the duty of all three players is to return to regular playing positions as soon as possible.

Four-Man Screen. The Four-Man Screen (see Fig. 5–2) is permissible and effective when the server moves to a point behind the baseline 10 feet in from the left, or 20 feet in from the right, side line. The players eligible to participate in this screen are the left forward, the center forward, the left back, and the center back. All four players converge at the point on the playing court where their respective areas lie adjacent to each other. The positioning of the feet, the weight of the body, and the flexing of the knees remain the same as that outlined for the Three-Man Screen. Again, the two forwards face the server and have their backs turned toward the net. The left back joins the center back in facing the net and in turning her back to the server. The left back is in direct alignment with the left forward, and the center back follows suit with the center forward.

Fig. 5–2. The four-man screen protecting a roundhouse service.

Hands and Arms in the Screen.   Three systems of use of the hands and arms have been tried and found successful in setting up a screen.   In the first system, the forwards involved elevate their hands to a position in front of the forehead and the backs lift theirs to a position behind the head and at the base of the skull (see Fig. 5–3).   As a result, the elbows of the three, or four, players protrude to the side of the head and provide density and width to the screen.   In addition, the hands of the back, or backs, held behind the head serve as an added safety precaution in the event of a poor service which goes wild into the screen.

Fig. 5–3.   Hands shielding base of skull in screening.

In the second system, the three, or four, players involved extend their arms to full height above their heads and spread their fingers wide.   This type of arms and hands position gives additional height to the screen, and the players may add to the coverage by waving their hands in the air as the server prepares to execute the service.   An additional advantage lies in the fact that this position is closely related to the use of the hands and arms in the basic receiving stance.   A disadvantage lies in the fact that there is no protection of the heads of the back or backs who stand immediately in front of the server and with their backs turned toward her.

The third system is any combination of the other two.   For example, the forwards might use the fully extended arm and hand position to give additional height to the screen and the involved back, or backs, might use the hands behind the head with elbows protruding to give density to the screen and to protect their heads against a wild service.   Another possibility, as illustrated in Fig. 5–2, page 107, is for the forwards to use the fully extended arm and hand position while the back or backs use one hand, preferably the inside one, behind the head for protection and the other fully extended to aid the forwards in giving additional height to the screen. The third system provides some of the advantageous qualities of the first and second systems and eliminates the safety hazard of the second.

Teams should experiment with all three systems and make a choice on the basis of the one that is most appropriate for their style of play.

Breaking Out of the Screen.   Unless there is quick and efficient breaking out, or away, from the screen to regular playing positions at the exact moment the server contacts the ball, the formation may become a liability rather than an asset. To the center forward goes the assignment of giving the verbal signal to her teammates to break out of the screen. The center forward not only is involved in both the Three-Man and Four-Man Screens, but is also in a position facing the server. At the exact moment the hand of the server comes in contact with the ball she should call out, "Break!" or some other brief command, which will immediately start in motion the return of all players involved in the screen to their regular positions on the court. When the back or backs hear the signal, they execute short, swift sliding steps back to their positions of individual and team readiness. In order to prevent running together and confusion, the forwards should be coached to turn toward their outside shoulders by pivoting on the outside foot and to step onto the inside foot when they are facing the net.

Practicing the Screen.   In order to ensure the fulfillment of the DGWS rule that all players be within their respective playing areas when the ball is served, it is best to divide the court into six equal parts. This can be accomplished by marking a spot down each side line 15 feet from the center line. A metal tape measurer can then be stretched from the mark on one side line to the mark on the other. Cross marks of 15- to 18-inch strips, easily distinguishable by players and officials, are then drawn on the playing surface at the 10- and 20-foot intervals of the outstretched tape. The cross marks represent the two points where the previously named players can converge to form one or the other of the two screens. Chalk can be used to put down temporary cross marks on the surface of outdoor courts. However, time and effort will be saved in the long run if paint is used. If indoor surfaces are already heavily marked for other games and sports, masking tape or pressure sensitive tape in a contrasting color can be used rather than paint. An additional advantage is that the tapes are easily removed.

To obtain full benefit from use of a screen, the server and the screen must have extended time during practice sessions to work together. A full team complement is advisable, with a player or assistant on the other side of the net to return the balls. Each player in turn takes her serving practices and calls out the screen "Three" or "Four" she desires as she rotates into serving position.

SCREENS FOR USVBA PLAY

The rules of the USVBA provide more leniency in establishing screens through provision that players be in respective positions, rather than playing areas, as the ball is put into play on the service. Certainly, both the Three-Man and Four-Man Screens are permissible, but the Five-Man Screen is rapidly increasing in popularity among girls' and women's teams functioning under the jurisdiction of the USVBA. All five players, other than the server, may form a screen at any point on the playing court provided that the formation they take does not violate the established rotating order of the players and that players currently designated as forwards stand closer to the net than the backs (see Fig. 5–4).

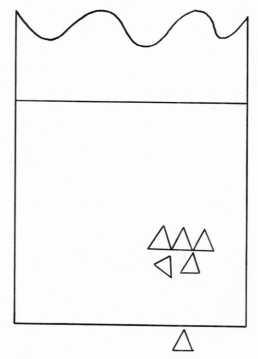

Fig. 5–4. The five-man screen.

The forwards stand close to each other and are facing the net. The two backs involved in the screen stand so that they are staggered in between the forwards and provide additional density in covering the server. One back faces the net. The other back stands so that she is facing the server, and it becomes her responsibility to give the verbal signal which will get the players out of the screen and to their regular playing positions. The choice of the left back or the center back as the player to face the server and to give the breaking-out signal will be determined by the team's style of play and the preference of the server in taking a position from which to execute the service. Obviously, the back having the best possible view of the server should receive the assignment so that the break can come at the exact moment of contact with the ball in the service.

All three arm and hand positions, as outlined for use in the Three-Man and Four-Man Screens, are appropriate for the Five-Man Screen. Each should be used on an experimental basis until the team comes up with the type that best fits their particular style of play. Then, the system adopted should be practiced in detail with each player on the team taking her service practices behind the Five-Man Screen. The position of the screen may be moved to any point on the floor, and the preference of the server, her skill in interchanging and placing services, and knowledge of the receiving team should be determining factors.

THE ONE-TWO-THREE ATTACK

Regardless of the pattern chosen by a team as a framework for its offensive play, the 1-2-3 attack is basic to all sound volleyball play. The One refers to the initial Pass. The Pass is the first play or contact with the ball that is made by a team as it comes into their own court. The Pass is a play with a purpose. The purpose is to take all speed and force out of the ball and to start it back on its way into the opponent's court. Preferably, the Pass is an overhead volley. However, among the less skilled and purely recreational groups it may be an underhand volley. Often among the highly skilled and in competitive play, where services and spiking are of excellent caliber, the Pass is a two-handed, or even one-handed dig. In any case, there is an attempt to make the Pass to the player on the front line who is functioning as the Key-Set in the offensive lineup.

The Two refers to the Set. The Set, or second contact on the ball, is a volley with another purpose. The Set must be an extremely well-timed, well-placed, and beautifully controlled volley directed to the Key-Spiker for spiking purposes. Detailed information as to the desired qualities in the Pass and Set has been presented in Chapter 2, along with many formations offering concentrated practice on these skills. In coaching the player for mastery of these skills and the way they are to be used in the attack, emphasize the following points (see Fig. 2–3, page 25):

1. *Avoid "low elbow."* Watch the player to see that she keeps her elbows elevated. When she allows them to drop, the heels of the hands have a tendency to make first contact with the ball.

2. *"Click-click" or "putt-putt."* Listen to the sound made when the player comes in contact with the ball. If the ball has been handled properly, with all ten finger pads hitting simultaneously, there is a distinct "clicking" or "putting" sound.

3. *"High, not low: Give, then go!"*   If the player is failing to get the desired distance or height in her volley Passes and Sets, check her out first on her "Give" position. Is her body in a complete state of flexed readiness? Does she continue her action to meet the ball with arms fully extended? Finally, does she finish with her entire body and the arms involved in the follow-through?

4. *"Front-face!"*   Watch the player to see that she plays the high ball with her elbows raised above the shoulders and with quite an arch in her back. Coach her to handle the ball just over and in front of her face.

5. *"Every lass must make a good pass!"*   Every player on the team must have a good volley to be used as a Pass or a Set. This type of volley should emphasize a height ranging between 10 and 12 feet. The Pass requires this height and control so that the Key-Set has ample time to get in the best possible position to receive it and be ready to make her play to the Key-Spiker. The Set requires this type of volley so that the Key-Spiker can adequately time her jump and spiking action to hit the ball from above the height of the net while it is on its descent.

6. *"Position-plus."*   Give your players a checkup and a "plus" when they observe these essentials in fundamental positioning:

1. Feet in a forward stride position for a comfortable stance
2. Knees slightly bent and the body tilted forward
3. Elbows raised sideward to a point just below the line of the shoulders
4. Wrists extended in line with the forearms
5. Wrists and hands rotated inward toward each other
6. Hands held at shoulder height
7. Thumbs turn inward and downward

The Three refers to the Spike. The Spike, with its possible variations, joins the service as a major offensive weapon in the game of volleyball. The Spike, also like the service, emphasizes the use of power and placement for strategic purposes. However, the spectacular qualities and the coordinated beauty of a well-timed and well-executed spike place it far ahead of the service in its appeal to both spectators and participants in the game. A Spike usually comes on the third play of the ball on a side of the court, and it is the end result of the Pass-Set-Spike sequence. The Key-Spiker attempts to "kill" or "put away" the ball so that a return by the defensive team, if any, is irreparably weakened. Detailed information and practice formations have previously been outlined (see pages 76–86). When coaching the spiker, emphasize the following points:

1. The spiker must master both the stationary and running approaches.
2. The spiker must time her jump and her arm motion to meet that of a moving ball.
3. The spiker must learn to swing both arms upward to get additional lift from her jump.

4. The spiker must learn to use the arm from the elbow down as a whip.
5. The spiker must learn to make contact on the ball with the hand held in a cupped position and fingers tight.
6. The spiker must learn to hit behind and on top of the ball at the same time.
7. The spiker must learn to withdraw the hand and arm immediately after the follow-through in order to avoid fouling the net.
8. The spiker must learn to land properly on the balls of both feet and facing the net to avoid net and center line fouls and to be in position to spring back into the air as soon as possible when her services are immediately needed in the replay of a blocked ball.
9. The spiker must not only be capable of spiking with power and placement, she must also be prepared to put into practice the possible variations of the spike at the net: the "dink" or "tip" and the high, lobbing volley out of the reach of opponents who have been successfully blocking.

PAIR-PARTNER (THREE-THREE) PATTERN

Until recent years, skilled teams in girls' and women's play used the Partner-Pair pattern of offensive strategy almost exclusively. In this pattern the six players comprising the team are actually three separate two-player units, each including a player whose function is to set the ball for the second player, a spiker. As the team rotates in its serving order, each pair has its turn on the forward line in the role of the Key-Set and the Key-Spiker. The Key-Set precedes her Key-Spiker in the rotating order, and as long as they remain on the forward line together, they are the pair through which the 1-2-3 attack is directed.

KEY-SPIKER AS THE LEFT FORWARD

At the beginning of each game, it is usual procedure to start the strongest spiker in the left forward position, making her the initial Key-Spiker. The player setting for her becomes the Key-Set and occupies the position of center forward. The pass from any teammate should be directed to the Key-Set, who is the "field marshal" of the offense. The Key-Set maintains her position near the net and is ready to set the ball so that it descends according to the practiced wishes of the Key-Spiker. The most desirable qualification of the set while the spiker is learning is consistency. Initially, the Key-Set will attempt to place the set some 10 to 12 feet into the air and some 18 to 20 inches away from the net for taller, and 24 to 30 inches away for shorter, spikers. Later, the Key-Set will vary the height of the set so that blockers cannot anticipate the point at which the spiker will contact the ball. The duty of the Key-Spiker is to "kill" the ball or to make her play so effective that the opponents' return, if any, is weakened. The pass-set-spike sequence in the Pair-Partner offensive pattern with the Key-Spiker in the left forward position is shown in Fig. 5–5.

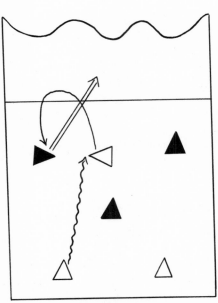

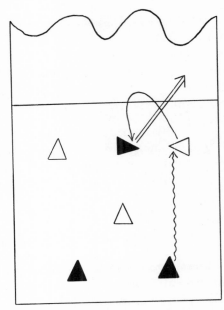

Fig. 5–5. The key-spiker as the left forward.

Fig. 5–6. The key-spiker as the center forward.

KEY-SPIKER AS THE CENTER FORWARD

After rotation has occurred, the player acting as the Key-Spiker has moved to the center forward position. Her Key-Set now occupies the position of right forward. Fig. 5–6 illustrates the pass-set-spike sequence for the new positions. When the players have rotated again, a new unit of partners occupies the front line positions, and they become the pair through which the attack is centered.

VARIATIONS OF THE PAIR-PARTNER PATTERN

After a team has mastered the basic Pair-Partner pattern, they should begin to practice variations designed to surprise and catch off-guard the defense of the opposing team. These variations should be used sparingly and at opportune times so that they do not lose their effectiveness and so that the defending team can never feel secure in establishing any one defensive maneuver.

Key-Set Spikes. An occasional spike from a player obviously tabbed by the defense as a Key-Set will do much to throw a defensive team off balance. Such a spike will be most effective immediately after the initial contact of the ball. In spiking a pass the Key-Set must quickly determine that the volley is adequately high and placed so that she can time her jump and the appropriate arm and hand motion with the arrival of the ball at the net.

Left-Handed or Ambidexterous Player. The use of a left-handed or ambidexterous player in the right forward position at the same time the Key-Spiker is in the left forward position is an invaluable asset in varying the basic offensive pattern. Instead of setting to her usual partner, the Key-Set, at the last moment, can turn and direct her set to the player in the right forward position. Often this player can get off a left-handed spike before the surprised blockers can move over to defend against her.

Reverse (Back) Set. A spike from a player in the right forward position is doubly effective when the Key-Set does not have to turn to make the set. Instead, she faces her usual partner and reverse volleys the ball over her own head to the left-handed or ambidexterous spiker (see Fig. 2–4, page 26). Again, defending players may be caught off-guard, especially if they have converged to a point directly opposite the Key-Spiker to block.

Cross Set. With the attainment of additional skill, the Key-Set can set the ball in such a way that it crosses in front of the spiker in the right forward position, and this player attempts to "kill" the ball using her usual right hand. In this maneuver the spiker establishes a stationary approach, approximately 3 feet from the net, or a running approach distance, some 8 to 10 feet away. She allows the ball to pass between her and the net and then advances to hit it on its descent from her natural (right-handed) side.

"Dinks." A faked spike, called a "dink," or "tip," may be used effectively by the Key-Spiker against the defensive team which is realizing some success in blocking against her. The execution of the "dink" must resemble in every respect the movement pattern of the spike in order to be successful. Only the final hand contact of the ball differs as the skilled spiker tips the ball just above and beyond the outstretched hands of the defensive players who have jumped into the air to block the spike.

Lobs. Another feigning action of the Key-Spiker may be use of the "lob." In "lobbing" the Key-Spiker will jump into the air as if to execute her usual spiking attack and instead will direct a high, lobbing volley toward the baseline, or some unprotected area, of the opponents' court.

PRACTICING THE PAIR-PARTNER PATTERN

All good offensive play begins with the "call" of the ball as it passes over the net from the opponents' court. Assuming this initial responsibility gives the Key-Set information as to the direction from which the pass will be coming and enables her to get in the best possible position to receive the ball and to make her own set to the Key-Spiker. Verbal calls of "Ball!" or "Mine!" are productive while learning, practicing, and playing the pattern.

Becoming a Unit. Pairs and partners who represent a good working combination should be kept together whenever possible. In all setting and spiking formations (see Chapter 4), keep the pair of players who will be playing as a unit together for practice. Real dividends will be reaped through improved timing and masterful coordinations which cannot be gained in any other way. In school and college programs, it is wise planning on the part of the teacher or coach to discover those pairs or partners who work well together during their first seasons and to keep them together through their playing careers.

Color Combinations. In beginning the development of the Pair-Partner pattern of offensive play, the use of colors to designate the three separate units will be helpful to the team. For example, have the Key-Spiker and the Key-Set wear red pinnies; the set player in the left back position and the spiker in the center back position, which will be the second attacking

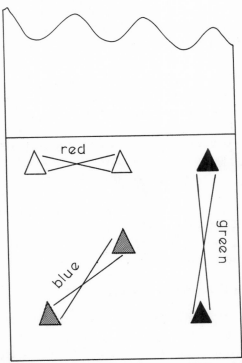

Fig. 5–7. Using color combinations to practice the Pair-Partner pattern.

unit to rotate to the forward line, in blue pinnies; and the set player in the right back position and the spiker in the right forward position in green pinnies (see Fig. 5–7). Using the color combinations to guide themselves, teammates can quickly discern the two players in the same color on the front line and can press the attack through them.

Key-Set Signal.   Until the pattern has been thoroughly learned, the Key-Set should be coached to signal to her teammates that she is the player to whom the initial pass should be directed. A verbal signal, or a visual signal with the hand, or hands, can be used. The Key-Set turns to face her team just before the ball is put into play on the service and delivers her signal.

Additional Responsibilities.   The Key-Set avoids being the receiver of a service. It is her duty to step into her regular playing position near the net and to receive the pass from which to begin the attack. All team members must accept the fact that the Key-Set is to be the second player to contact the ball if at all possible. Therefore, they must be coached to move out of the way and allow her to receive the pass. Only when there is no chance for the Key-Set to get the pass converted into a set does another player call and make the second contact on the ball. The importance of this principle cannot be overemphasized. Otherwise, the Key-Set will be handicapped by interference, however wholly unintended, and the resulting confusion cannot help but weaken the strength of the attack. In starting the team's most outstanding spiker in the left forward position, two important purposes may be accomplished. First, the psychological implications of getting ahead of the opponents in the game are of great importance. Not only does it instill a sense of security in the leading team, it builds pressures in the trailing team, often to the extent that costly playing mistakes are made. Second, there is no rotation required until a team has participated in its first term of service, and the outstanding spiker will be kept on the front line, from this position, for a maximum amount of playing time.

TWO-FOR-ONE (FOUR-TWO) PATTERN

Another bona fide and proved basic offensive system of play, and one that is receiving increasing attention among skilled girls' and women's teams, is the Two-for-One, or Four-Two, pattern. This pattern provides two Key-Spikers for each of the two Key-Sets. It does not require an interchange of players, and is, therefore, legal in both DGWS and USVBA rules.

KEY-SET AS CENTER FORWARD

In the Two-for-One pattern there are always two Key-Spikers on the front line, and the Key-Set is stationed between the two of them (see Fig.

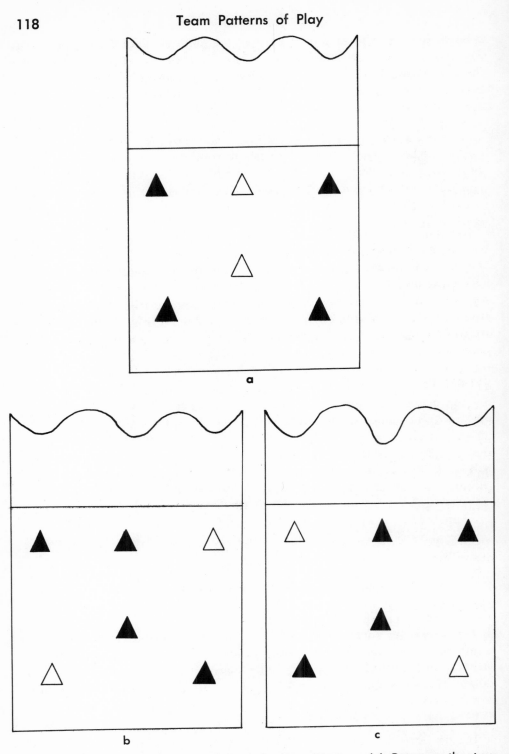

Fig. 5–8. The Key-Set for the Two-for-One Pattern. (a) Between the two spikers. (b) Preceding the two spikers. (c) Trailing the two spikers.

5–8a); precedes both of them (see Fig. 5–8b); or follows both of them (see Fig. 5–8c). When the Key-Set is in the center forward position, she sets the ball to the Key-Spiker in the left forward position or she cross sets or back sets the ball to the Key-Spiker in the right forward position. Left-handed or ambidexterous spikers are excellent choices for game beginning positions as right forward. They provide natural opportunities for variation of the 1-2-3 attack. Other variations include the Key-Set occasionally spiking a good pass and surprise uses of the dink and high, lobbing volley by the Key-Spiker, who is playing either the left forward or right forward position.

KEY-SET AS RIGHT FORWARD

When the Key-Set is in the right forward position, the Key-Spiker in the center forward position is the usual player to whom the set goes to be spiked. However, an occasional long, high set over the head of the center forward, known as an over set, to the Key-Spiker in the left forward position is strategically sound (see Fig. 4–9, page 85) and will keep the defense from assuming and maintaining blocking positions directly opposite the usual spiker.

KEY-SET AS LEFT FORWARD

When a Key-Set is in the left forward position, the Key-Spikers will occupy both the center forward and right forward positions. At this point in the offense cross sets will become quite important to the attack, with the Key-Set volleying the ball parallel with the net and in front of the Key-Spiker so that she can spike with her natural (right) hand. It is also possible for the Key-Set to set the ball over the head of the Key-Spiker in the center forward position to the Key-Spiker who is the right forward. Thus, the volley is an over set as well as a cross set. Other variations include: the Key-Set occasionally spiking, the employment of left-handed and ambidexterous spikers, and uses of the dink and high, lobbing volleys by the spikers at opportune moments.

KEY-SPIKER AS A SET

Just as the use of the Key-Set in the occasional spike of a pass serves as a valuable variation in the Two-for-One offensive pattern, the Key-Spikers can become additional team assets when they have developed ball-handling capabilities to the extent that they can set for each other to spike. The employment of this point of strategy is of most importance when the two Key-Spikers on the forward line are preceded by the Key-Set. The Key-Spiker occupying the center forward position, by prearranged signal, can call for the pass to be made to her and then can set the ball for the Key-Spiker in the left forward position to spike.

PRACTICING THE TWO-FOR-ONE PATTERN

In the Two-for-One pattern, as well as the Pair-Partner system, the play begins with the "call" of the ball as it passes over the net from the opponents' court. As the ball is spoken for by some player other than the Key-Set on the front line, the Key-Set knows from what direction the pass will be coming; can get in the best possible position to receive the ball; and can direct her set to either of the Key-Spikers who occupy forward positions with her. Skilled teams continue the use of such a verbal signal to avoid confusion in assuming the responsibility for the initial play of the ball on their own side of the net.

Building the Units. Building the units through which the 1-2-3 attack is to be centered is considerably more difficult in the Two-for-One, than in the Pair-Partner, pattern of play. The difficulty lies in the fact that each of the two Key-Sets, under the system of rotation, will eventually set the ball for all four spikers as they move across the front line from left to center to right forward. Therefore, it is absolutely essential that the two sets have every opportunity to practice with all four spikers within the framework of the relative positions they will be holding. Practice formations 8 through 14 (see pages 80–86) offer opportunity for this kind of practice.

Color Combinations. The Two-for-One pattern, admittedly more complex than the Pair-Partner system, can be somewhat simplified for teams beginning its development through use of color combinations. For example, the two Key-Sets should be distinguishable from the four spikers on the team, and this purpose can be easily accomplished by having the sets wear red pinnies and the spikers wearing blue or none at all. Teammates can easily discern the player on the front line wearing the red pinny and can direct the pass to that player. As a Key-Set that player directs the attack by sending the set to the Key-Spiker who is in the best position strategically to enforce the attack at that moment.

Signals and Other Responsibilities. Until the pattern possibilities have been thoroughly investigated and learned, it is important to have the Key-Set make the other members of her team aware of her role in receiving the pass. A signal, verbal or visual, should be given just before the ball is put into play on the service. If the team is competitive and matches are likely to be attended by large numbers of spectators, a visual signal will prove more satisfactory as it does not have to compete with the usual noises of a sports audience. In the Two-for-One pattern the Key-Set avoids being the receiver of the service or the first player to contact the ball on her side of the net. All other players function to get a good pass to the Key-Set, and none other plays the ball as the second player unless it becomes an absolute necessity. As in the Pair-Partner pattern, an excellent spiker should be started in the left forward position with emphasis on getting started in the game with points ahead of the opponents and on adding pressures to their play. If the team has a left-handed or an ambidexterous spiker, she is natural material to begin the game in the position of right forward.

TWO-FOR-ONE INTERCHANGE PATTERN

The interchanging of players after the ball has been put into play on the service is permissible under the rules of the USVBA. Many skilled teams of girls and women use the interchange privilege very effectively within the basic Two-for-One pattern. The principal use of the interchange occurs so that the Key-Set can set the ball from the center forward position. As the basic pattern calls for a Key-Set on the front line at all times and occupying a position between the two Key-Spikers, or preceding, or trailing them, the interchange will occur when the Key-Set is playing right forward, and preceding (see Fig. 5–9), or when she is playing left forward, and trailing. In gaining the center forward position in the interchange, the Key-Set is ready to effect regular sets, cross sets, and reverse sets with every advantage in mixing up the attack. Thus, the defensive team cannot afford to aggregate for a multiple block.

In addition to all of the other variations previously outlined for the Two-for-One pattern, a feigned interchange also becomes a possibility.

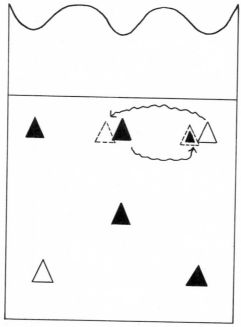

Fig. 5–9. Two-for-One Interchange pattern.

A feigned interchange is most effective when used as the ball is put into play on the service. On the feigned interchange the Key-Set and the spiker occupying the position of center forward make preliminary movements toward a change of positions and quickly return to their original ones where the Key-Set waits for the pass and puts into effect appropriate regular sets, cross sets, and over sets.

When the Key-Set occupies the center forward position on a team which uses the interchange privilege, it is unusual for a changing of positions to take place. However, there are two effective exceptions. First, it can be used as a surprise variation of the attack to prevent defensive players from converging for multiple blocks; and second, when the stronger of the two spikers on the front line is in the right forward position and her strength in spiking with the left hand or receiving a cross set for a right-handed spike is not as great.

Practicing the Interchange. Generally, the same principles outlined for practicing the basic Two-for-One pattern will be useful when the privilege of interchange is to be used. The "call" of the ball; building the attacking units; use of practice formations; color combinations; determination of initial contact and second contact responsibilities; and alignment of players by special strengths are extremely important. However, it is in the area of signal play that much more emphasis is necessary when the interchange privilege is to be used. To avoid confusion, to keep the attack running smoothly, and to keep the defense guessing will demand a system of visual or verbal signals thoroughly rehearsed and learned by the offensive team.

ADVANCED PATTERNS

THE FIVE-TO-ONE INTERCHANGE PATTERN

Admittedly a pattern requiring the highest quality of individual skills and team finesse, the Five-to-One system of offensive play is beginning to make some headway among highly competitive women's teams. In this pattern only one player is a Key-Set, and she is given the responsibility of servicing the other five players, who are all spikers. The Key-Set player exchanges places with the player currently occupying the position of center forward, and from this position she receives the pass and makes the set to either spiker on the front line. For example, a typical use of the interchange privilege occurs when the Key-Set is playing left back. When the ball is served by her own teammates, or the opponents, she exchanges positions immediately with the center forward and sets for either spiker from that vantage point (see Fig. 5–10). As soon as point or side-out is called, she must return to the left back position in the rotating order.

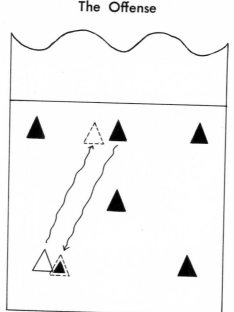

Fig. 5—10. The Five-to-One Interchange pattern.

The simplicity of the Five-to-One Interchange is somewhat negated with the necessity of finding the *one* player whose ball-handling techniques are such that she can be consistently entrusted with setting for her team's attack; with the finding of a set player who is capable of completely masterminding her team's offense; with the development of five evenly matched spikers; and with the almost overwhelming task of practicing all of the possible combinations of interchanges and strategic variations of the 1-2-3 attack. On the other hand, competitive teams which keep relatively the same personnel through several seasons of play will find the development of such a pattern of strategy both challenging and rewarding.

ALL-SET-SPIKE

Little seen, even in the men's game, is the pattern in which every player on the team is both a potential Key-Set and a potential Key-Spiker. In this type of pattern all players must be equally skilled in both ball-handling and spiking techniques.

The primary objective of this pattern is to pass the ball to the player currently occupying the center forward position. This player, in turn, sets the ball to either the left or right forward to be spiked. While this system of offensive play eliminates any need for interchanging of positions, its development to a finesse would require such unlimited skill and such tedious practice to make it prohibitive for most amateur teams. Rather, it should be reserved for use by those teams whose interests and motives in volleyball carry them into more than the usual competitive experience.

6

The Defense

Often the beautiful simplicity and mastered ease of the volleyball attack, coming from within the framework of an often practiced and smoothly polished offensive pattern, is quite deceptive to inexperienced players and spectators. However, the skilled and gamewise know that a team must be well rehearsed in all aspects of defensive play in order to compete with the team that recognizes and utilizes every potential scoring weapon.

DEFENDING AGAINST THE SERVICE

If the skill of serving, with all its possible modifications and variations of power, placement, and penetration, is accepted as a prime offensive weapon in the game, every team must be prepared to defend against the service in such a way that the ball is not only legally returned but is played in such a manner that a subsequent attack can be effected.

INDIVIDUAL READINESS

Every player on the team defending against the service is a potential receiver of the ball. In the matter of individual mental readiness, alertness and the complete attention of every team member are requisite. As the potential receiver studies the server, she should watch for any preliminary movements or mannerisms which might serve as clues as to the type of service to be used, the direction and angle of penetration, and the amount of power and spin on the ball. She must also have a complete sense of awareness as to the position she is currently holding and her exact duties in player performance from that particular position.

Physical Readiness. In addition to mental readiness, the receiver must have her body in a state of physical readiness. Basically, this involves standing with one foot or the other forward in a forward-stride position. Both knees should be flexed and the body weight should be carried forward on the balls of both feet. From this position the player can easily shift directions forward, backward, or to either side and can move by means of running steps or slides. The rest of the body should be in a state of flexion, or in what has been previously described as the "give" position. The hands are held overhead with the fingers spread and curved. Some players prefer to wave the hands slightly for purposes of relaxation. The elbows are bent so that they extend slightly above shoulder height.

TEAM POSITIONING

With every player following the principles of mental and physical readiness, the team assumes positions that will allow them to cover their own half-court and, if at all possible, to return the service in a manner conducive to attack. Two such basic defensive positions are possible.

"Fadeaway" Positions. In the first, all three forwards back away some 8 to 10 feet from the net in what is known as "fadeaway" positions (see Fig. 6–1). The "fadeaway" receiving positions are most profitable against teams recognizably strong in dropping the ball in between the forward and back lines with "floating" underhand, overhead, and roundhouse services. The center back plays almost directly behind the center forward and almost in the exact center of her half-court. The right and left backs station themselves deep within their court and stagger themselves in such

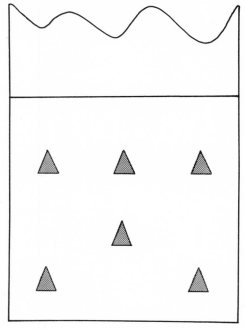

Fig. 6–1.   Team positioning to defend against the service: Fadeaway.

a way to have a clear line of vision between the forwards playing in front of them. In this defensive formation, the player functioning as the Key-Set, regardless of the offensive pattern in effect, avoids making the initial contact, or the pass. As the ball is served, she immediately steps back into her regular playing position at the net, where she gets stationed to receive the pass and to set the ball to the Key-Spiker.

The backs are usually given the responsibility of receiving services. The forwards, except the Key-Set, are responsible for receiving only those services which drop between the net and where they are standing in their "fadeaway" positions. Forwards never back up to play the served ball. A judgment must be made as soon as the ball is in flight as to its direction and power, and the player who determines that it is moving into her defensive area is responsible for "calling" its play as hers. If the forwards determine that the ball is going above their heads and out of their reach, they return to regular playing positions at the net and clear the area for the backs to handle the ball.

The Double-V. The second basic team position for receiving the service is the double-V in which both the forwards and backs are stationed in an inverted-V position in relation to the net (see Fig. 6–2). This pattern is most widely used against teams which depend on very strong services aimed toward the baseline and extreme rear side lines. In this pattern the center forward, especially when she is the Key-Set, maintains her position close

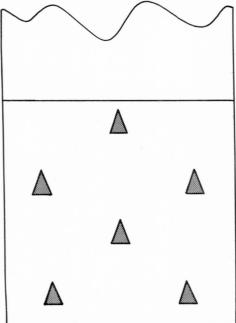

Fig. 6–2. Team positioning to defend against the service: Double-V.

to the net so that she is ready to receive the pass and get the attack started. The center back is directly behind the center forward, at approximately the center point of the court. Under DGWS rules she will need to be a half-step back from this point so that she does not violate the rule that all players must be in their respective positions and areas when the ball is served.

The right and left forwards and the right and left backs station themselves in a lineup that approximates an inverted double-V. They must be in position to watch the server. Again, it is expected that the backs will be making most of the initial contacts with the served ball. Whenever the forwards see the ball going over their heads and beyond their reach, they immediately return to regular positions at the net to give the backs ample space and a clear path in getting the pass made to the Key-Set.

BACKING-UP ASSIGNMENTS (SEE FIGS. 6–3a AND 6–3b)

With each team member in a state of individual readiness and the team in a practiced receiving formation appropriate for the type of service expected from the opponents, there is one additional defensive maneuver that will help in the defense against the service. This maneuver is the backing up or "covering" of teammates. With the force and spin that can be developed in serving techniques, it is to be expected that each initial

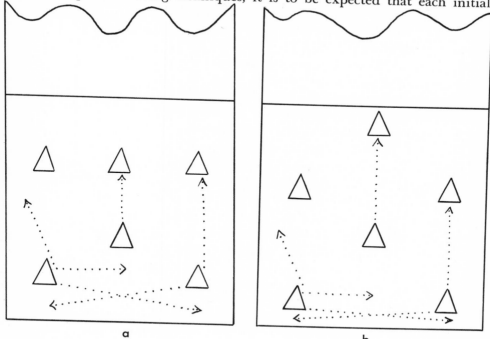

a
b

Fig. 6–3. Backing-up assignments. (a) In Fadeaway position. (b) In Double-V position.

contact of the service will not be completely successful. Instead, the ball will often deflect at random off the hands of the receiving player, and before it can be brought under control and directed back across the net, another player must come in to assist the player who made the initial contact.

The forwards, because of their positions close to the net and their duties in carrying the weight of the offense, have no backing-up assignments. The center back, due to her inside position on the court, covers only for the center forward. The right back backs up the right forward and the left back. The left back covers for the left forward, the center back, and the right forward.

The backs do not wait until a teammate is in trouble in receiving the service before they make a move to help. Instead, as soon as the ball has been "called" by any player, the appropriate back immediately moves into position for her backing-up assignment. As soon as she has helped with the assist or discovered that one is unnecessary, the back returns to her regular position.

PRACTICING SERVICE DEFENSE

Teams should begin to develop an adequate defense against the service as soon as they begin to develop serving technique as an offensive weapon. In Chapter 3 many drill formations for practice of the service were presented. Most of them lend opportunities to practice service defense simultaneously. For example, the Server-to-Player-Targets drill on page 61 can be used to improve individual readiness on the part of the receivers. Continuing, Server-Team Return and Server-Team Game can provide thorough practice of individual readiness, both styles of team positioning, and backing-up assignments.

In introducing backing-up assignments, help the three backs to discover their spatial relationships to the players they are supposed to cover. Have the center back walk forward; touch the shoulder of her center forward; and then return to her original position. The right back, in turn, should tap the shoulder of the right forward and the left back and each time return to her original position. The left back, who draws the most backing-up assignments, should practice moving to touch the shoulder of the left forward, the center back, and the right back. It will be helpful to the left back if she can establish in her thinking and reactions that the three players whom she must cover fall into a diagonal pattern beginning on the left side at the net and running to the right side adjacent to the baseline.

DEFENDING AGAINST THE SPIKE

Since the end result of the 1-2-3 attack is the spike, or the attempted "kill" of the ball, regardless of the offensive pattern adopted by the team, the defense against this weapon must consist of blocking and picking up or "saves."

BLOCKING AND PICKING UP

Blocking as an individual skill has been presented in Chapter 4, along with many suggestions for practice. The major coaching points in executing a successful block are:

1. Begin the jump from a position approximately 18 inches from the net.
2. Begin the jump off of both feet at the same time.
3. Begin the jump with the body held in a low, crouching position.
4. Begin the jump with the body facing the net squarely.
5. Begin the jump so that it is timed immediately after the spiker begins her jump.
6. At the top of the jump the hands and forearms of the blocker must be above the top of the net.
7. At the top of the jump the blocker's body should be extended in a vertical line from her feet to her elbows.
8. At the top of the jump the blocker's hands and forearms are tilted backward.
9. At the moment of contact the blocker's hands and forearms are straightened, and the ball rebounds from spread and tensed fingers.
10. The moment of contacting the ball in the block should coincide with the spike.
11. At the moment of contacting the ball the blocker or blockers must give a verbal signal, such as "Touch," to indicate to the players with the pick-up assignments that the ball has been at least partially contacted.
12. The momentum of the ball rebounding off the solid hands of the blocker should be enough to carry the ball back into the spiker's own court.
13. The blocker must land with both feet touching the floor at the same time and with the weight controlled on the balls of the feet to avoid net and center line fouls and to enable her to jump back into the air to replay the ball whenever the subsequent play demands it.

Picking Up. The pick-up or "save" is an essential skill in defending against the spike when the block has failed, has been only partially successful, or there has been merely a deflection of the ball. The main objective of the pick-up is to get the ball back up into the air from its downward spiked course so that a teammate can assist and, if at all possible, begin an attack. An obvious way to pick up the ball is through use of an overhead volley or pass. However, only weak spikes can be handled in this manner. An underhand volley, when used at all, more often than not results in a holding or lifting foul. Therefore, against a strong spike the two-handed and the one-handed digs are recommended ball-handling techniques. These two digs, and practice methods for each, have been presented in Chapter 2.

The main coaching hints for using the dig to pick up the spike are:

1. The players with the picking-up assignments should be in a state of individual readiness: the body should be crouched low; the feet in a forward-stride position; and complete attention should be given to the ball.
2. The players with the picking-up assignments should study the spiker to learn what they can about how hard the ball is going to be hit; where the ball is going; and the angle of penetration of the ball.
3. The players with the picking-up assignments must listen for the signal of the blocker or blockers and for the sound of the block and judge whether the block has been completely or only partially successful.
4. The players with the picking-up assignments must move instantly to the place where the ball is directed.
5. The players with the picking-up assignments must execute a two-handed or one-handed dig that propels the ball back up into the air.
6. Whenever possible, the momentum of the dig should carry the ball to a front-line player so that it can next be set.
7. Immediately after executing the dig the defensive player must recover her balance and be ready to meet the demands of the next play.

DEFENSE AGAINST THE KEY-SPIKER AS LEFT FORWARD

Regardless of the basic offensive pattern (pair-partner, two-for-one, two-for-one interchange, five-to-one interchange, or all-set-spike) used by a team, it is likely that its most powerful spiker will be selected to begin the game in the left forward position. Therefore, each team must be organized and practiced in a defensive pattern adequate to meet this anticipated attack. The defense may try to stop the spike with a one-man, two-man, or three-man block combined with a pick-up or "save." The one-man block is usually effective against weak spikers only and multiple blocks are to be preferred. If the one-man block is to be attempted, the assignment should go to the defending right forward, who is playing directly opposite to the Key-Spiker. The center back, in this situation, should be alerted for the possibility of a dink, and the right and left backs stand by to pick up when the block is missed or is only partially successful or for a faked spike which develops into a high lob.

Two-Man Block. Whenever a two-man block is to be attempted as the defense against a spike coming from the player occupying the position of left forward, the right forward and the center forward of the defending team are responsible. The center back maintains her position and watches for a dink. Again, the right back and left back are both alerted for duties involving the pick-up (see Fig. 6–4).

Three-Man Block. After meeting with success in the use of two pairs of hands and forearms above the net in a two-man block, more and more girls'

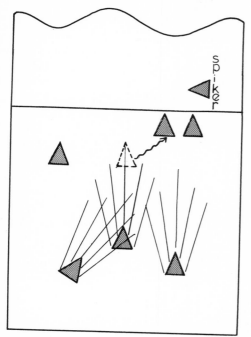

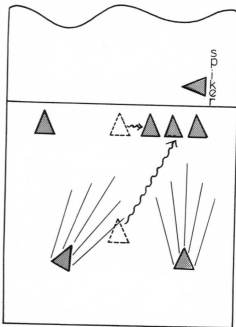

Fig. 6–4. Two-man block against a spiking left forward.

Fig. 6–5. Three-man block against a spiking left forward.

and women's teams are experimenting with and proving the worth of a three-man block, in which another set of hands and forearms is elevated in establishing a more solid barrier against the spiking offensive weapon. A three-man block against the Key-Spiker playing left forward involves the right forward, the center forward, and the center back. The center back rushes to the net and occupies a blocking position in between the two forwards. The picking-up assignments fall into the hands of the left forward and the right and left backs of the defending team. The left forward moves away from the net to assist in the pick-up and to help guard against a dink. In addition to picking up, the right and left backs are alert to a possible lobbing volley (see Fig. 6–5).

DEFENSE AGAINST THE KEY-SPIKER AS THE CENTER FORWARD AND RIGHT FORWARD

Center Forward. Whenever the Key-Spiker is the center forward, a one-man blocking assignment goes to the center forward on the defending team. The two-man block would be made by the center forward and right forward of the defending team, with the left forward and the three backs all in on the pick-up, dinked ball, or recovery of a long, high volley. The three-man block would be attempted by the center forward, the center back, and

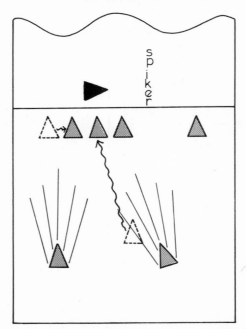

Fig. 6–6.   Three-man block against a spiking right forward.

the right forward. The center back rushes to the net and assumes her blocking position in between the two forwards. The left forward falls back from the net to help with a dink or the save, and the right and left backs brace for the pick-up or the lobbing volley.

Right Forward. When the set is made to the player in the right forward position to be spiked, a one-man block, if attempted, is the duty of the left forward on the defending team. A two-man block against the right forward involves the defending left forward and center forward. The three-man block calls for the center back to move forward to the net and to take a position in between the left and center forwards to assist. The right forward fades back from the net to help with a dink or to save the ball and the right and left backs pick up and guard against a lob (see Fig. 6–6).

INSTRUCTIONAL AND INTRAMURAL PROGRAMS:

Organization and Management

7

Teaching Preparations
and Techniques

Volleyball, as well as other worthwhile physical-recreational activities, has many potential values for the individual and the group as a part of the instructional physical education and voluntary intramural programs offered by secondary schools and colleges. However, skillful organization and management must obviously join knowledge and enthusiastic teaching if these values are to accrue.

Rather than being concerned with the general principles involved in organization and management of physical education classes and intramural competition, the objective of this chapter is to offer suggestions that will lead to the enrichment of the experiences provided by the game of volleyball in both programs.

TECHNICAL PREPARATION

Before the volleyball teacher or the volleyball intramural advisor faces her charges for the first time, two major aspects of technical preparation must be met. The first of these is to see that students are properly costumed for the activity and the second is to see that facilities and equipment are available, clean, safe, and in a good state of repair.

COSTUMES FOR VOLLEYBALL

While it is inconceivable that a physical education instructor would move to have a separate gymnasium costume adopted for volleyball units, certainly participation in this kind of activity should be considered when selecting a uniform for general physical education use.

The same type of physical education uniform can be worn for most individual and dual sports classes, providing that the one selected meets the primary requirements of freedom of movement, comfort, attractiveness, and is economical. The student in a volleyball class and the player in the intramural program are potentially very active persons. Therefore, the gymnasium clothing worn by them should in no way restrict their movements nor cause them discomfort in the running, jumping, twisting, turning, and swinging activity basic to the game.

The high school girl and the college woman are as conscious of the way they look as they are of the way they feel. The attractiveness of the uniform will affect what they think about themselves and will influence their attitudes toward volleyball. Attention to style and color in the choice of gymnasium costume assumes importance, and it is good planning to have students participate with faculty members whenever the selection of a uniform is to take place. Two-piece uniforms, consisting of a blouse and shorts of regular, jamaica, or bermuda length, are by far more popular than one-piece suits. The volleyball player will need a short-sleeve blouse with a loose fit and a long shirttail. Her shorts, regardless of length, should be loose enough to allow complete movement.

In selecting the costume, attention should be given to long-wearing, practical materials which give best possible service and quality for the money to be spent. To be economical the volleyball uniform must be one that launders nicely and easily.

Shoes and Socks. The shoes of a volleyball player should be of the canvas tennis shoe type. A heavy shoe with a good tread is preferred over the lighter kind, for it makes it easier to stop, turn, and land after jumping. Certainly, the shoes of the volleyball player should fit properly, and the wearing of the shoe for general use should be discouraged. White shoes are preferred, as well as white socks, in order to avoid sometimes harmful or irritating dye products. In addition, socks should be clean and free of holes. Any darned or mended spots should be flat and smooth to avoid blisters. The socks should fit the feet without wrinkling. If a student-player has feet that perspire freely, she should be encouraged to wear two pairs of socks to absorb moisture.

Knee Pads. While it is not expected that the student of the general volleyball class or the participant in the intramural program will have much occasion to wear them, the highly competitive volleyball player will find that knee pads are helpful when called upon to make plays that demand falling to the floor.

Glasses Guards. Although volleyball is strictly a noncontact sport, added protection for the student who must wear glasses during play is gained through the use of glasses guards. She may be encouraged to secure her own guards to hold glasses in place, but the physical education department should provide check-out privileges on some glasses guards for the volley-ball students who need them.

FACILITIES AND EQUIPMENT

Generally speaking, the volleyball teacher or intramural advisor must organize and manage her classes or program within the framework of the facilities and equipment which are available to her. Nevertheless, there are certain basic principles to be followed in the use of facilities and equipment so that the best possible results of each program can be obtained.

Facilities. The volleyball teacher or advisor should acquaint herself with the facilities that are available. She must know the location, size, and condition of these facilities. The location of the volleyball courts in relation to the locker room will affect planning of time to be spent in actual activity. Adjustments have to be made in equipment if the courts are located outdoors rather than indoors. Too, many suggested practice methods cannot be used on outdoor courts unless there is an adjacent wall-space available. The number of courts must be considered in arriving at numbers of students who can be handled in classes or in concurrent intramural play. The size of the courts, regulation or not, determines the playing of regulation games or necessary modification of rules. The condition of the courts must be thoroughly investigated from the standpoint of safety precautions. Outdoor courts should be washed down frequently to remove accumulations of sand, dust, and grit. The floor of indoor courts should be cleaned regularly, and wall obstructions offering safety hazards should be removed or covered. If the volleyball experience is to fulfill its possible values to the individuals and groups involved, every effort should be made to see that students have an opportunity to play on courts that are regulation, properly lined, clean, and attractive.

Equipment. The current rules of the game is the best possible source of information on the type of equipment desirable for volleyball play. Necessary new equipment should be ordered far in advance so that it will be available when time comes for its use in the volleyball class or intramural program. As most buying of equipment in public institutions is through an outside purchasing agency, the teacher or advisor must be prepared to specify down to the most minute detail the type of equipment desired.

Balls. Manufacturers have three kinds of balls on the market today which meet the general qualifications demanded by the rules. These are the stitched leather ball, the molded leather ball, and the rubber ball. While most skilled players prefer to handle leather balls, they are more expensive. Too, the rubber ball holds up better against the wear and tear of outdoor use; is more resistant to natural outdoor dampness; and is easier to clean. In purchasing new balls, the volleyball teacher should check to see that dimension and weight requirements are met. The ball should not be less than 26 inches nor more than 27 inches in circumference. The leather ball should not weigh less than 7 ounces nor more than 9 ounces. It should require not less than 7 pounds or more than 8 pounds of air pressure. The rubber ball should carry not less than 5 pounds nor more than 7 pounds of air pressure. Upon arrival of new leather balls, the teacher should check each one to make sure that each panel is good; that a high quality leather has been used; that there are no needle holes, valve leakage, sponginess, broken stitches, or wrinkles; that the valve is flush with the surface of the ball; and that there are no holes, cuts, deep scratches, flaking, or peeling of the leather. Any ball that does not meet these standards should be immediately returned to the manufacturer for correction or replacement.

Inflation of Balls. In inflating balls, careful attention should be given to the manufacturer's instructions. Air pressure directions are usually stamped on the ball. A hand pump should be used, and many school and recreation programs are finding that electric hand pumps save man-hours and are economical in the long run. Moistening the needle with glycerin is recommended. When saliva is used, care should be taken to remove excess moisture around the valve.

Cleaning of Balls. Saddle soap should be used in the cleaning of leather balls. A light vegetable oil or mineral oil may be used to treat dryness or harshness. It is best to allow the ball to dry at normal temperatures with almost normal playing pressure to prevent shrinkage and hardening of the leather. Wiping with a damp cloth or the use of warm water and soap when necessary is recommended procedure for cleaning rubber balls.

Storage of Balls. Expert care should be taken of the volleyball during the off-season. Leather balls should be stored in mesh-wire cages or bins, within a cool, dry room. Plenty of air circulation should be provided and crushing of balls should be avoided. It is best to leave the ball partially inflated to help maintain normal shape. Rubber balls should be stored in a cool, dry place in a chest, bin, or closet, away from any window where the sun shines through or from a hot roof. The air pressure should be reduced to avoid strain.

Nets. Volleyball nets should be constructed of dark brown or black No. 30 thread woven into 4-inch squares. A 2-inch double top binding of white canvas or duck is essential. If the net is to be used on an outdoor court, a good preservative should be added to guard against moisture and mildew.

A wire cable or cord is suggested to hold the outdoor net in position. Manila cord is adequate for indoor usage. Center strings, or ties, and bottom strings, or ties, are necessary if the net is to be held in the taut position highly desirable for play.

Care of Nets. Nets will last longer if they are taken down and stored properly. A yardage-fold is recommended, followed by a roll from the bottom of the net to the top. Finally, the cord should encircle the net to hold it together until it is to be used again. The nets should be stored on shelves in cool, dry rooms. In addition to preservatives for outdoor use, every effort should be made to see that these nets are kept tight and fully erected to prevent sagging and stretching.

Standards. Much progress has been made in recent years by manufacturers in designing standards which are serviceable and easier to manage in classes for girls and women. Three types have been developed: the wooden, the iron, and the aluminum. Due to its light weight and easy maneuverability, the aluminum standard is gaining in popularity for use in girls' and women's programs. If the standards, wood, iron, or aluminum, are of the screw-in type, the gymnasium floor must be reinforced to handle this additional pressure. The bottom of standards should be covered with felt, rubber, or sponge rubber cushioning and tape wrapped around any sharp edges. When several courts lie adjacent to each other, it is a good procedure that end standards be placed at all end positions and that center standards be used between courts. When new standards are being ordered, consider purchase of a type that has a winding ratchet attached. These permit tighter nets and easier erection by use of a handle to wind the net to preferred height. It is also possible to have ratchets bolted to standards already in use. These operate in much the same manner as ratchets used on tennis standards.

In addition to selection and care of equipment, the volleyball teacher should be careful to keep a running inventory of all equipment under her supervision. Broken equipment should be repaired, and in the case of balls, time and effort will be saved by returning them to the manufacturer. The proper identification of equipment with a departmental or school marking is a safeguard against loss and theft. Finally, the teacher will save much time for instructional purposes by having an efficient method of handing out equipment. Suggestions are use of a student monitoring system, in which a student leader, or leaders, educated for the task is responsible for handing out and taking in the equipment; a check-out system, in which students are responsible for securing and returning equipment to be used; and pass-out systems, in which the teacher is involved in issuing and collecting the equipment.

BUILDING SAFETY CONSCIOUSNESS AND COURT COURTESY

In any discussion of potential values of the game of volleyball, references to knowledge, understandings, attitudes, and appreciations and their relationships to socialization skills will be abundantly made. If these values are to be truly effected, the volleyball teacher must be prepared to do direct teaching toward their attainment rather than leaving it to an incidental or chance approach.

SAFETY CONSCIOUSNESS

Knowledge of safety factors and procedures and an understanding of responsibility for self and others are parts of the socialization process that can take definite shape within a volleyball class or intramural program. The volleyball teacher cannot instill safety awareness in her students, but she can teach volleyball in such a way that she instigates an attitude conducive to the practice of safety, and together she and her students can fulfill this objective.

Teacher's Responsibilities. First, the teacher must fulfill her obligations in respect to the technical preparations: costuming and facilities and equipment. She should insist that each student be properly clothed in the gymnasium outfit previously described. If a student is financially unable to provide the costume for herself, the volleyball teacher should investigate the possibility of a special fund to meet this kind of situation. Unclaimed articles in the lost and found are a possible additional source. However, great care and tact should be practiced in handling such aid to avoid placing the student in a position of embarrassment. On cold days when the volleyball class or intramural game is to be held outdoors, students should be encouraged to wear sweaters or sweatshirts which permit freedom of movement. Long coats or jackets should be prohibited as they restrict activity and become a safety hazard.

Facilities and Equipment. As previously stated, the teacher is responsible for the technical preparation of facilities and equipment before use. At the time of use, she should supervise the setting up of nets and standards to see that they are securely fastened; she must be ready with masking tape or other suitable materials to put down markings which limited facilities or special activities necessitate; and she must be ready with appropriate rule modifications when limited or obstructed facilities and good safety practice dictate them. She must be prepared to follow all building rules for clearance of students in event of fire or other disaster.

Glasses Guards and Knee Pads. Glasses guards and knee pads should be considered as safety protective equipment, and students needing them for protection should be educated and required to use them.

Jewelry. The volleyball teacher will enforce a ruling against the wearing of jewelry in class or in intramural competition. However, the rulings must be reinforced with student understanding. The wearing of rings, bracelets, watches, earrings, and necklaces are a safety hazard for the wearer and her teammates. It is also questionable practice from the standpoint of care for the item involved. Rings, bracelets, and watches may cut into the fingers and arms while the ball is being played off the hands or forearm. An ear may be torn as an earring catches in the net or on the clothing of another player. Jumping and sudden falls to the floor may send a necklace up forcefully against the mouth causing damage to the lips and teeth. The jewelry, in turn, may be bent, broken, twisted, or crushed.

Fingernails. For full participation in volleyball, fingernails should be relatively short and smoothly filed. In teaching ball-handling skills, the teacher will emphasize playing the ball with finger "pads" rather than "tips," but even among the highly skilled, long, narrow nails will interfere with play. Students should understand that a long nail can be broken in a manner dangerous to themselves and that broken nails are a hazard for teammates as well.

Health Status. Only those students who have been deemed physically fit through medical or health examinations should be allowed full participation in the volleyball program. The teacher's responsibility in this respect is to check appropriate health record forms and to counsel out of the class or intramurals those students who do not meet the specific health requirements. On the daily class basis, the student should be encouraged to report health conditions which might affect full participation in class. The volleyball teacher should follow through on standard school policy in referral of students to the health office or the school nurse. She should be prepared to make alternate assignments of a worthwhile nature to students who are to remain within the class but who need to curtail activity for the day.

Conditioning and Warming Up. The volleyball teacher should follow sound scientific principles in building up the activity load of her classes, beginning with initial lessons and continuing through the unit. In each class or practice session, the student should warm up the fingers in ball-handling technique before attempting serving or spiking practices which use the hand as a forceful weapon. There should also be a general warming-up period in which the student reduces chances of injury and physiologically prepares the body for use in game practices and play.

Instruction and Safety. As the volleyball teacher initiates instruction in skill, she should emphasize that there can be no separation in correct technique performance and safety. The safe way to execute a skill is the correct way. The correct way to perform a skill is the safe way. This basic concept should be correlated throughout volleyball instruction and competition. In addition, instruction should lead the students to an understanding and appreciation of the rules of the game with the outcome of enforcement to ensure not only a better game but also a safer one.

Finally, the teacher's management and organization of the class should reflect complete recognition of what is acceptable from the safety point of view.

COURT COURTESY

The development of sports etiquette, or court courtesy, should be a part of the learning process of students involved in volleyball classes or intramural programs. Learning and practicing what is socially acceptable in behavior as a participant and as a spectator are essential if values involving socialization skills are to be gained. Again, the teacher is responsible for the setting of the stage for such development. She instills an awareness for the social situation and guides the student in making the appropriate response.

Relationships with Own Team. First, each player must gain a respect for individual differences. Volleyball demands that six individuals with differing abilities, personalities, interests, and ambitions work together as a unit or whole. Therefore, each student must develop a sense of responsibility in carrying her fair share of the team load. Loss of faith and resultant loss of team morale quickly occur whenever a team member fails to perform within what is known to be her top-level capacity. Respect for individual differences should be followed by recognition and appreciation of efforts by all teammates. Each player will develop genuine trust and confidence in the teammate who continually works to develop her own skills, knowledge of the game, and understanding of the rules. Each player owes her attention to the game being played.

Relationships with Opponents. Not only does the volleyball player have social obligations to her own teammates, but she is also expected to fulfill courtesies in her relationships with her opponents. She should be able to recognize and acknowledge outstanding play by her opponents. Aggressive play in the game of volleyball should be directed toward the ball itself and not to the opponents. Emotions should be controlled, and there should be a complete absence of distractions which might affect the play of the opposing team. These distractions, such as yelling to throw off the timing of the spiker or blocker, are not to be confused with strategic maneuvers, such as screening the server, which are legal and in no way violate standards of sportsmanship.

Every team owes its opponents the honor of playing at its highest level of performance. Regardless of the fact that the competition may become one-sided, a team never plays down to its opponents. In the sports world, this is the prime insult. At the end of the match, appreciation and thanks for the game and congratulations are in order. These should be delivered as warmly and sincerely as possible.

Relationships with Officials. Officials of the volleyball match should be treated as honored persons whose purpose it is to ensure an optimum pleasurable experience. Therefore, students are taught to accept and respect the officials' decisions. Whenever questions concerning a decision arise, these should be channeled properly through the team captain or coach. Players should be encouraged to call their own fouls, which is particularly helpful in regards to the net, the center line, and body fouls. Finally, acknowledgment and appreciation of the work of the officials should be expressed to them at the end of the match.

Relationships with Teacher or Advisor. Certainly, the volleyball teacher or intramural advisor deserves the attention of the players when she is giving instruction or directions. The class or intramural group, in turn, should be ready to make appropriate contributions and comments in discussion. Students should be ready to assist with equipment without having to be asked by the leader. Inflating balls and erecting nets and standards are time-consuming and often impossible for one person to handle and are the responsibility of the students as well as the leader.

Game Conduct. Certain other courtesies to be observed by participants will help matches to run more smoothly and satisfactorily. In informal matches, played without benefit of officials, it is considered appropriate for the serving team to indicate its intentions to serve with the verbal signal of "Ready?" In addition, the serving team is responsible for announcement of the score before the ball is put into play. Whenever adjacent facilities are in use, every effort should be made to keep balls and players from interfering with the game on a nearby court. If a ball does roll into another court, it is correct courtesy to wait until "point" or "side-out" has been called on that court to retrieve it. In returning the ball to the team which has the service, it should be rolled under the net in the general direction of the right back. Whenever time-out is called, for any reason, the player nearest the ball should secure it and put it in the hands of the referee.

USE OF PRACTICE FORMATIONS

As each new individual skill in the game of volleyball was presented in Chapters 2, 3, and 4, careful attention was given to possible and profitable practice formations. The general principles the teacher should use in selecting a particular drill formation are presented here. While the teacher of a beginning unit and the teacher of an intermediate or advanced unit in volleyball may have quite different intermediate objectives in the use of a drill or practice formation, the ultimate objective remains the same. Each teacher desires that the skill being practiced be used skillfully and meaningfully in the game. Game skills are isolated and practiced separately so that when returned to the whole game they can be used with more success and satisfaction.

Beginning Units. One of the popular reasons for including volleyball in the physical education instructional program is the ability to take care of large numbers of students in an activity which has a relatively small number of individual skills to be learned before participation in the whole game can be meaningful. However, this does not mean that the teacher has any less responsibility in enthusiastic and dedicated instruction. On the contrary, here is an opportunity to teach in a way that the students do gain skills, can put these skills into game play successfully, and do leave a physical education class with a real desire to pursue the activity at a more advanced level. There is absolutely no excuse for the teacher of a beginning volleyball unit, in spite of the fact of a relatively large number of students, to allow her class to degenerate into a "messy-mass" experience which no student could possibly like or be willing to pursue.

The selection and use of meaningful practice formations provide an answer to many of the problems presented in the large group. With the division of the class into teamlike groups, practice formations allow much profitable practice for each member. Too, the use of drills will help the teacher in the presentation of motor skills which require more difficult coordinations. The use of practice formations as a warming-up activity before actual game participation is both psychologically and physiologically sound. However, the most significant use of practice formations for the teacher of a beginning unit is the unlimited opportunity provided to observe student performance, to analyze errors, and to make helpful corrections. Although these opportunities do occur during game play, they are never as abundantly provided as they are during concentrated practice on the particular skill.

Advanced Units. Although many of the same uses of drill formations in advanced units are identical with those in beginning units, there is, of course, one major difference. The beginner is trying to learn the skill—that is, to add it to her repertoire. The advanced player, on the other hand, is attempting to master the skill, to perfect it to such an extent that it can be added to her game with complete ease and accomplishment. Therefore, with this kind of motivation the student in the advanced unit, as well as the competitive volleyball player, will work at long lengths on minute detail. The same kind of practice for the beginner would be less meaningful and might serve to turn her away from the game in boredom and frustration.

Planning Practice Formations. There are certain principles to be followed in the planning of practice formations regardless of the skill level of the class. These points include the amount of knowledge the teacher can bring to bear upon the subject, the space available for practice, the amount and condition of the equipment to be used, the number of students within the class, and the length of the class period. The good volleyball teacher will select practice formations based on the skill level and previous experience of the students within her class. To appeal to the intermediate and advanced students, she must follow the principle that the drill formation becomes more complex and challenging as skills increase. In order to attract the students' attention and secure more effective practice, it is wise procedure for them to understand the "why," or purpose, of the particular formation and how it will help their game. The teacher must be prepared to provide a great deal of variety in practice formations to capture the interest and imagination of the students. Finally, the adding of a competitive element, even in the most elementary of practice formations, will serve to promote interest and enthusiasm and to instill team spirit and the will to win.

LEAD-UP GAMES AND ACTIVITIES

Lead-up games can be used profitably in volleyball instruction when they involve or concentrate on one or more of the basic skills and when they help the student to become more familiar and proficient in the skill or skills. The purpose of the lead-up game is to permit use of the basic volleyball skills in a somewhat modified, and usually simplified, version of the game.

VALUES OF LEAD-UP GAMES

A lead-up game is valuable in volleyball instruction as long as it keeps up with the latest changes in skills, strategy, and rules. It must grow out of the needs of individuals and class needs and must lead to the fulfillment of the ambitions of the players. Volleyball lead-up games are more valuable when they present situations closely comparable to the actual game and require students to combine skills and points of strategy in a similar manner. One of the values of the lead-up game is that it presents competition in such a way that pressures involved do not discourage and frustrate the learner.

PLANNING LEAD-UP GAMES

Contrary to some thought, lead-up games have value for the intermediate and advanced player as well as the beginning volleyball student. However, it is in the area of low-organized games, such as those in which students on the elementary and junior high school levels engage, which offer the first introduction to the skills of the actual game of volleyball. For a particular lead-up game to be selected at these levels, it should present knowledge and parts of the game which are easy to learn and which arouse the interest of the students. Within beginning units the lead-up game should be geared to the capacity and skill level, concentrate on a particular skill to be learned; and provide competition in a gamelike situation. On intermediate and advanced levels the lead-up game may be used to perfect a particular skill or to provide variety or novelty-relief when players seem to have reached a plateau in learning and need a respite from concentrated practice and play. Many volleyball lead-up games offer additional use in rainy-day and coeducational programs because they can be easily adapted to facilities and equipment at hand and to large numbers of students.

SELECTED LEAD-UP GAMES

No attempt will be made to cover the many lead-up games which are available for use by the enterprising volleyball teacher. Instead, a selected few of the most popular have been chosen and will be presented along with suggestions for their use within the instructional volleyball physical education program.

1. *Curtain Ball.* Divide the width of a regulation volleyball court in half and use some easily removable tape to mark a depth of 15 feet into the court from the center line. Arrange the players on the court so that they are in reaching contact of each other. Any number may be allowed to play; however, "sides" should be kept evenly divided and players should not be overcrowded. The net is lowered to the height of a tennis net and should be draped with blankets, sheets, or drapes so that the two opposing teams are unable to see each other (see Fig. 7–1). Players are seated, and regulation balls, scoring, and rules are used. The contestants must seek modification of technique on their own.

Curtain Ball, with its modification of playing area permitting two

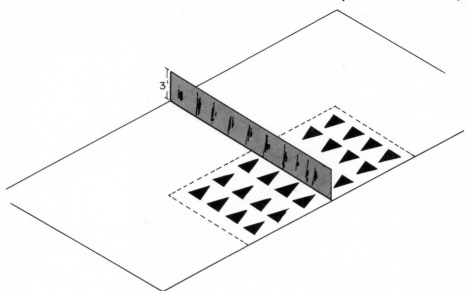

Fig. 7–1. Curtain Ball.

games to be conducted on a court at one time and its provision for a large number of players, is a fun-type game for rainy day and coeducational play. It can be used by the advanced unit teacher to help develop team alertness in watching for the ball. In addition, the seated position of the players demands more finger, arm, and shoulder power to make successful play, in spite of the fact that the net is lowered.

2. *Tailor Ball.* In Tailor Ball the players are arranged on a court of smaller size. The 15-foot by 15-foot area suggested for the game of Curtain Ball is appropriate, or a badminton court may be used. Sitting tailor-fashion with legs crossed in front of the body (see Fig. 7–2), the contestants must play the ball without leaving the floor. Again, any equal number per side may play, but players should be close enough to touch teammates' elbows on either side of them and to touch finger tips to players seated in the rows in front and behind them.

The net is lowered to a height of 5 feet. Generally, regulation volleyball rules, scoring, and balls are used. The ball is put into play by the player on the extreme right in the back row. She must use an underhand serving technique or toss. After the service has been lost and regained, the player on the original server's left becomes the server. The service continues down the back row of players until each has had her turn. Then, there is rotation by rows—that is, the back row becomes the forward row; the forward row, the second row; and continuing, until the second to last row becomes the last row.

The teacher in the beginning volleyball unit may allow players to in-

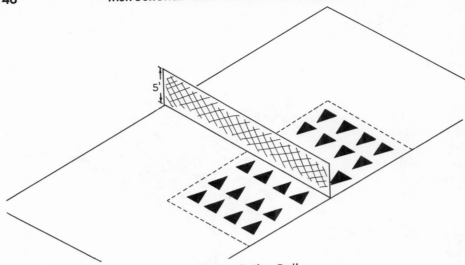

Fig. 7–2. Tailor Ball.

crease the number of volleys which can be made on each side of the net.
The advanced unit teacher will want to hold to three contacts and to use
this game as an additional means to develop fingers, arms, and shoulders.
Because of the limited space required and the larger number of contestants
which can be involved, this game lends itself to rainy-day, recreational,
and coeducational play. As an extra novelty measure, a large balloon may
be substituted for the regulation ball.

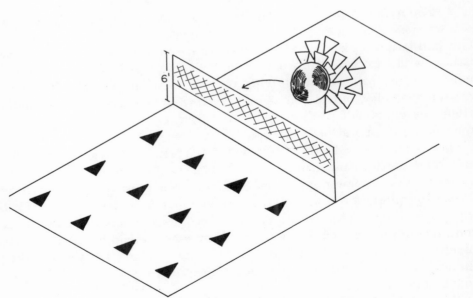

Fig. 7–3. Giant Volleyball.

3. *Giant Volleyball* (see Fig. 7–3). If the rainy-day, recreational, or co-educational program needs an amusing lift, dig into elementary school equipment and come up with a cageball. Or, if your school does not have a cageball, purchase a balloon which measures at least 36 inches in diameter when inflated. Then teach the students Giant Volleyball. Even the most sophisticated youngster will not be able to suppress the fun which a first exposure to the volleyball-oriented game will provide. The teacher in a beginning unit may use the game to add novelty and interest.

The number of contestants should be evenly divided, and on a regulation size volleyball court ten to twenty players per team will be satisfactory. The net should be lowered to 6 feet, and an agreement should be made on the termination of the game. A designated time may be set or a particular number of points. Regulation rules should apply with two major exceptions: First, the service can be assisted; and second, any number of volleys is permitted as necessary to get the ball over the net.

4. *Bounce Volleyball.* Bounce Volleyball is a lead-up game with many adaptable versions to meet requirements of the program in which it is to be used. Teams may number from six to fifteen; the court size may be adjusted at will; and the net height varies with the age and skill level of the contestants. If the players are of elementary school age, reduce the height of the net to 6 feet 6 inches and allow more players to cover less playing space. For junior high girls, reduce the net to 7 feet and reduce the number of players for a similar playing space. At the high school and other instructional levels, bring the net to standard height; use regulation court size; and adjust the number of players according to the purpose or use of the game. Bounce Volleyball is a good game to try among players who show some original fear of the ball.

In the basic game, the ball is served as in volleyball; the receiving team must allow the ball to bounce, but not more than once, before making its initial play; only three contacts with the ball can be made on each side of the net; and each time the ball crosses the net, it must be allowed to bounce before an initial contact is made. Regulation equipment is used and scoring is the same as in regular play.

Other modifications permit beginners to throw, not serve, the ball and to allow the ball to bounce between contacts by teammates. When the game is used by intermediates and advanced players as a novelty or recreational game, rule modifications allow freedom of choice in receiving the service after a bounce or on the fly and in relaying the ball on the fly or permitting it to bounce between teammates.

5. *Newcomb.* While the game of Newcomb is usually considered a game to introduce throwing and catching skills basic to the game of basketball, the teacher of both beginning and advanced volleyball units may profitably use some of its basic concepts and principals in her instruction.

Any playing space may be adjusted to a size suitable for playing the game, but usually a badminton size court is satisfactory. The net, or a rope, is elevated to a desired height of between 6 and 7 feet from the floor. The two teams are evenly divided and may number between six and sixteen. Although a utility or soccer ball may be used, the volleyball teacher using this game within her unit will want to provide regulation volleyballs for play.

The object of the game is to throw the ball over the net into the opponents' court; the opponents in turn must catch the ball on the fly and in one throw send it back into the original court. Play is started by the player in the right back corner of the court throwing the ball. Any player of the opposing team may catch it, but she must immediately throw it back into the other court. The ball is played only by throwing and catching and may not be kicked, volleyed, or bounced. No relaying is allowed, and no player may hold the ball. Long throws, or passes, near the baseline of the opponents' courts are desirable. Point or side-out is called upon the following fouls: a ball hitting out of bounds; a ball relayed or touched by two players on one side before going over the net; a ball touching the net on service; and a player holding or walking with the ball.

The teacher of volleyball in the beginning unit can use the game of Newcomb to teach position play, scoring, and rotation. The advanced unit instructor in volleyball can use the game of Newcomb to teach them offensive and defensive strategy. By modifying the game to allow each team three contacts with the ball on its side of the net, the teacher can promote good passing to teammates; advancing the ball from the back court to the net; covering and backing-up assignments; directing the attack at unprotected areas on the opponents' court; and the development of a 1-2-3 attack. Newcomb, as a novelty game requiring only limited space and allowing large numbers to participate, may also be used for recreational, rainy-day, and coeducational programs.

6. *Four Square.* The game of Four Square may be used as a volleyball lead-up game to encourage team cooperation and to develop underhand volleys which are legal and skillful. The Four Square playing area is a square 16 feet by 16 feet, and this area is divided equally into four smaller squares. Each of the four squares is designated as a letter: A, B, C, and D (see Fig. 7–4). One player is in each square and the object of the game is to advance to the A-square and remain there as long as possible. The player in the A-, or serving, square starts the game by bouncing the ball once and then hitting it with two hands so that it bounces in any of the other areas. The player within that square must keep the ball in play by striking the ball before it bounces a second time and by directing it to any one of the other areas. Play continues until one player fails to return the ball or fouls. A player who misses the ball or commits a foul must move

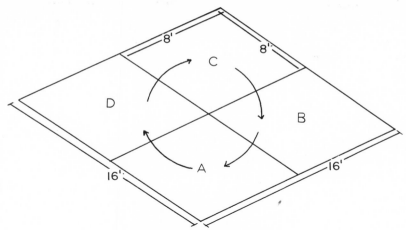

Fig. 7–4. Four Square.

out of the game if others are waiting to play. Otherwise, she moves to playing area D. For example, if player B fouls, player C moves to B; D to C; and B is demoted to the D square or out of the game if others are waiting to play. The first player in the waiting line would rotate into the game in the D-position.

A player misses the ball or commits a foul who fails to return a ball that comes into her square; fails to allow the ball to bounce before returning it; allows the ball to bounce more than once before returning it; fails to use both hands when returning or serving the ball; hits the ball so that it lands on a line; steps out of the serving area before the ball has been put into play; allows the ball to touch her body before it touches the ground; fails to play the ball with an underhand volley; or hits the ball more than twice in succession to any one player.

The game of Four Square can become a team game by using two teams of four players. Distinguish players by having one team wear red pinnies and the other wear blue pinnies. To start the game and after every point, each team lines up in alternate squares. The Reds start in A and C and the Blues in B and D. A red player stands first in the waiting, or challenge, line. Designate a number of points to constitute a game or set a particular length of playing time. In order to score, a team must fill all four squares with its own players. After a point has been scored, alternate the squares again with the team not scoring beginning in the serving square.

In addition to use of the game of Four Square to develop team cooperation and good underhand volleys, the teacher in the advanced unit may modify the game to permit use of the "digs" or playing the ball with a palm-down one-handed spiking motion. The playing area of Four Square may be drawn easily with chalk on outdoor playing surfaces and, because of its rapid pace, the game may be adapted for a large number of contestants.

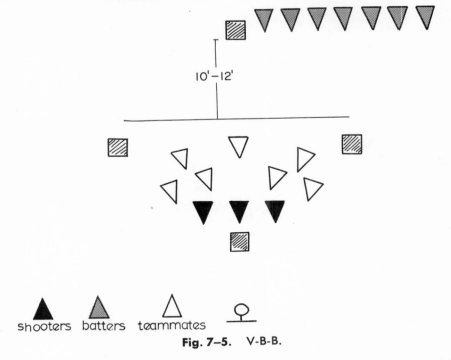

10'−12'

shooters   batters   teammates
Fig. 7–5.   V-B-B.

7. *V-B-B*.   The game of V-B-B is designed to permit the introduction of skills and playing principles involved in the games of volleyball, baseball, and basketball. Consequently, its usage will be primarily on the elementary school level. The offensive team lines up at home base, which is directly opposite to a basketball goal. The defensive team spreads itself out beyond the restraining line, 10 to 12 feet from the home plate. The three players who have been designated as shooters for the defensive team station themselves close to the basketball goal (see Fig. 7–5).

The batter puts the ball into play by a legal volleyball service and begins running the bases. The ball must land beyond the restraining line and must stay within the court boundaries. The defensive team must field the ball, complete three passes in getting the ball to its shooter, and score a basketball goal. If the goal is made before the runner reaches home, an out is made. If the runner reaches home before a goal is made, a run is scored for the offensive team. Three outs put the offensive team into the field. Each time the team assumes the defensive, different shooters should be designated.

V-B-B may be played either indoors or outdoors, and large groups of students may be involved in play at one time.

8. *Volley-Tennis*.   The playing area for the game of Volley-Tennis is that of either a regulation volleyball or tennis court: 60 feet by 30 feet for the former, 78 feet by 36 feet for the latter. In either case, there should

be a center line, 2 inches in width drawn from side to side underneath the net. Necessary equipment is a regulation volleyball and either a volleyball net or a tennis net adjusted to the width of the court.

The net is placed as in tennis, with the top of the net being 3 feet from the ground or floor at the center and not more than 3½ feet at ends. Six players are on a team. They take positions in two parallel lines, three in the front and three in the back. The players rotate counterclockwise. As in the regulation game, rotation occurs when a team wins the privilege of service.

The back center player is the server in Volley-Tennis and she stands with both feet behind the baseline of the court (see Fig. 7–6). She may use any legal means of service. The server may not step into the playing court until the ball has bounced. The ball must bounce one time inside the serving team's court and be assisted over the net by only the center front player. The center front player may use one or both hands in playing the

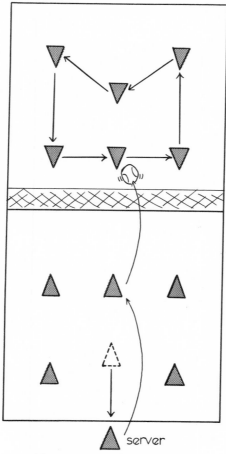

Fig. 7–6. Volley Tennis.

ball. The ball must not touch the net on the service and may not go over the net without the bounce. An assist, if necessary, can be given only by the center front player.

A ball in play after the service may bounce once inside of the court or may be returned directly from the fly. No more than three contacts are allowed on one side of the net. If two players contact the ball simultaneously, it is counted as two contacts. No player is allowed to contact the ball twice in succession. A ball that strikes a player and bounces off, making a direct as opposed to a rolling contact, may be continued in play as though that player had made a hand contact. A ball, except a service, striking the net and going over is still in play. The ball may be played when any part of it has crossed the top of the net. A ball, other than the service, may be recovered from the net, provided there is no net foul committed during the play.

The ball is dead when: It is played upon for the fourth time on one side of the net; it touches the net on the service; it bounces over the net without assistance (on service only); it touches any foreign object outside of court (ground, standards, wall, or ceiling); it is touched twice in succession by one player; it hits a player below the knee; it is caught, held, juggled, or pushed; it bounces more than once within a court without being played upon; a foul (net or center line) occurs on either side; it is kicked or bunted with the knee; it rolls on the body; a player reaches over or under the net; or any part of a player extends over or under the net during play. If the ball becomes dead as a part of the serving team's responsibility, side-out is called against the team. If the ball becomes dead as a result of the receiving team's play, the serving team scores a point. The scoring of the game is identical with that of regulation volleyball play.

Time-out may be taken by either team when the ball is dead. Each team is permitted two time-outs in a game. A team must take time-out in order to substitute. Any number of players may be substituted during a time-out.

Allowing the ball to bounce before volleying it tends to reduce fear of the ball as often exhibited by beginners. The teacher of advanced players may use Volley-Tennis to emphasize passing the ball to the center front player, which is comparable to passing the ball to the Key-Set in the regulation game. The game may also be used for novelty and recreation purposes on the senior high, college, and adult levels.

9. *All-Set.* All-Set is a lead-up game that follows all rules of the volleyball game in detail except for the number of contacts which are legal on each side of the court. Instead of the three hits in regulation play, All-Set requires that each player on the team contact the ball before it is returned across the net. No player may hit the ball twice in succession. Neither may any player contact the ball more than once before it crosses the net.

The teacher of a beginning unit in volleyball may find All-Set profitable when she is trying to encourage players to use all legal contacts on the ball open to them. The teacher in the advanced unit may use All-Set to encourage intelligent play reactions on the floor. To have all players make a contact and still execute an attack from the front line requires good planning and skillful play on the part of even the most advanced players.

10. *Volleyball Doubles* (see Fig. 7–7). The game of Volleyball Doubles is gaining popularity to the extent that it often provides competition apart from regulation volleyball play for girls' and women's doubles, boys' and men's doubles, and mixed doubles teams. It is an excellent game for the development of the 1-2-3 attack. It provides opportunity to develop the 1-2-3 attack in such a way that is beneficial to the Pair-Partner, Two-for-One, and Two-for-One Interchange patterns of offensive play. In addition, it provides opportunity to develop the defensive skills of the one-man block and picking up.

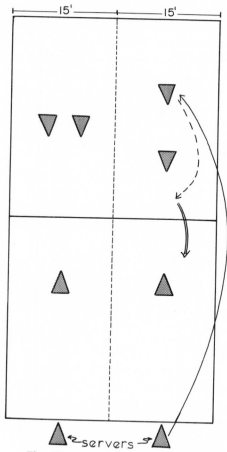

Fig. 7–7. Volleyball doubles.

The playing area consists of exactly one-half of a regulation volleyball court. Therefore, two games may go on at one time on each court. A regulation net and ball are used, and the net is elevated to regulation height. Two players oppose another pair of players. The rules and scoring are the same as in a regulation volleyball game. The service is put into play from behind the baseline. The player receiving the ball passes the ball to her teammate who has taken a position close to the net. The teammate then sets to the original player, who attempts to "kill" the ball. The opposing players attempt a block and a pick-up and, whenever possible, convert their own play into an attack. Volleyball Doubles is an excellent way to promote use of the running approach to spiking.

11. *Volleyball Skill Game.*[1] Volleyball Skill Game may be used profitably by teachers of intermediate and advanced units in volleyball. It is an excellent way to check on both individual and team effort in performance of advanced skills. A score sheet, which can be easily reproduced through the ditto or mimeograph process, should be available for use when the game is played (see Fig. 7–8). A successful spike scores 3 points; a successful block, 6 points; a successful pass, 1 point; a service which cannot be returned, 2 points; a service which falls on a boundary line without being touched, 2 points; a successful two-man net recovery, 2 points; a successful one-man net recovery, 3 points; and a "dig" which can be successfully passed, 2 points.

Regular volleyball rules apply. Set a particular number of points which

[1] Donna Mae Miller and Katherine L. Ley, *Individual and Team Sports for Women* (copyright 1955, by permission of Prentice-Hall, Inc., Englewood Cliffs, N.J.), p. 44.

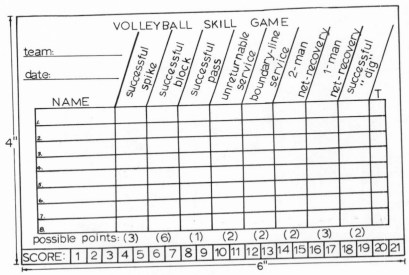

Fig. 7–8. Volleyball Skill Game.

a team must gain in order to win the game or play for the greatest number of points made within a particular time limit. At the end of the game the teacher may point out individual scoring to encourage perfection and use of these advanced skills. A score sheet, or method of scoring similar to this, can be used to "scout" opponents. It can also be used by the teacher when she is attempting subjective evaluation of individual effort during match or tournament play.

8

Teams and Tournaments

Today many high school girls finish their educational experience on that level and go to college without ever being a part of a real team sports effort. Furthermore, many college and university programs of physical education fail to provide this kind of experience. Largely, the lack of team sport fulfillment in schools and colleges has been caused by the great emphasis in recent years on the individual and dual sports with their acknowledged carry-over values. Certainly, the contributions of individual and dual sports in the building of skills for leisure-time use cannot be overemphasized. However, physical education teachers and administrators, given the charge of assisting with the total education of the young girl and woman, cannot afford to overlook possible carry-over in socialization skills as well.

In the cooperative-competitive atmosphere of a team sport class boundless opportunities will arise in which the alert and effective teacher can turn the incident or situation into a laboratory experience in group living. Volleyball, as such a team sport, will provide an adequate setting for the development of individual and group codes of behavior consistent with democratic ideals, for in this game exist many possible situations comparable to social activity—and governed by rules, regulations, customs, traditions, rewards, and punishments.

In volleyball the individual becomes a part of a team and assumes privileges and responsibilities. In being a team member a real sense of belonging grows. There is need to think and act independently but always in relation to the welfare of the group and to the goals of the game. The individual will give, take, cooperate, and conform. She must learn to give of herself and give to the fullest. She will gain much in the understanding of herself as she gains in the understanding of others.

TEMPORARY TEAMS

In the beginning of the unit, the volleyball teacher should make every effort to see that all of the students within the class have an opportunity to mix and mingle with all others. Therefore, the designation of permanent teams will be delayed. Instead, the instructor will employ a variety of methods for division into teams on a temporary basis until the arrangement of permanent teams becomes meaningful. In the mixing and mingling process, students will be encouraged to become acquainted with all the students in the class; to make some new and lasting friendships; to look for leadership qualities among classmates which will enable them to act intelligently in the selection of captains or leaders for the teams; and to begin an evaluation of the skill level of classmates and an assessment of their own playing abilities.

SQUADS

In many volleyball classes involving a large number of students, the teacher will rely upon the squad method for roll call and as an initial plan of class organization. These squads may be named by the teacher on the basis of cumulative records, brief observations of the students, the results of sociometric studies, or alphabetical alignment. These same squads may be used by the instructor in the introductory sessions of the class as temporary teams for both practice and play.

COUNTING-OFF SYSTEMS

One of the most popular methods of temporary team division is counting or numbering off. In this system, the members of the class count off as they sit or stand according to the teacher's directions. All of the "Ones" form a team; the "Twos" compose another team; and so forth until the number of teams needed or desired is completed. Counting-off systems are time-saving, efficient, and facilitate directions in the organization of the teams on the floor.

In the use of a counting-off system the volleyball teacher will want to vary the method so that the students cannot control assignments to teams by standing or sitting in a particular pattern or order. To provide variation the teacher may begin counting at the right of the group on one day, at the left of the group another day, and occasionally inject an activity which serves as a group mixer previous to the numbering-off procedure. Another variation is to move from one side of a line to the other, taking the specified number of players standing side-by-side as a team. Because of duplication of results, this variation will be more effective in classes where the squad system of roll call and organization is not used.

DRAWING SYSTEMS

Drawing for assignments on temporary teams rarely fails to arouse curiosity and interest in class response. Too, drawing systems are economical in time spent within the class. However, some preparation is required of the teacher. In drawing for teams the teacher should provide as much variation as possible. Numbers printed or typed on small strips of paper, folded, and dropped into a container is good for an initial trial. For a container a plain paper sack, an old, comical hat, or a large envelope will do. Again, the "Ones" or "A's" make up a team; the "Twos" or "B's" a second team; and so forth until the desired number is completed. The team should be given a minute or so to gather together; to organize for play or practice; and whenever desirable, to select a name for itself. The teacher should be ready to come up with some clever suggestions. For example, one day she may ask that each team be named for a popular sports car; another day, a television-advertised soap product; and another day, a favorite animal. The choice of a team name is a beginning for the unity and spirit that can be gained with the creative development of an appropriate yell or slogan for the team.

A variation of the drawing system is to print or type the names of colors on strips of paper, which are folded, dropped into an appropriate container, and drawn by the members of the class. The teams are then instructed to choose a team name that fits the color they received. Again, team effort in choice of name, yells, and slogans will do much to develop unity and spirit. Another form of the color system is through use of colored index cards in the 3 x 5 size. These are available for purchase with stationery supplies. This size of card fits the blouse pocket of many regulation gymnasium costumes, and each member of a team is identified through the color tag she is wearing. If colored index cards are not available, the same effect can be gained by cutting colored construction paper into the proper size.

Another variation of drawing systems is to make actual name tags, drop them into an appropriate container, and have the students draw for a temporary team assignment and name at the same time. This system requires more preparation on the part of the teacher. The wearing of name tags involving pins for attachment is definitely questionable from the safety point of view. Therefore, the name tag should be one that fits into the blouse pocket and shows. Although some time within the class may be saved through use of this system, the ones in which the teacher merely provides the framework and the class members function as a creative group in arriving at their own team names, are more highly recommended. In the drawing of colored name tags or regular name tags, students should not be able to see into the container from which they are drawing.

In the use of drawing systems the volleyball teacher should prevent the swapping of numbers, letters, colors, or names. Any color or name tags should be sturdy enough to be collected at the end of a class meeting and used in other sections of the activity or in successive meetings of the class.

In all of the proposed systems of temporary team division, the element of chance predominates. It is possible for the better players to end up on a team, the less skilled on a team, or the teams may be evenly divided in skill level. The latter outcome is the one most desirable from the standpoint of educationally sound competition.

PERMANENT TEAMS

Although the division of the class into temporary teams is important, it is through permanent team division that most of the socialization skills will begin to grow and develop. There is no set guide as to when permanent team division should occur. However, the length of the unit, the number and ages of the students, and the skill levels will be determining factors. Roughly speaking, the volleyball teacher should aim for permanent team division near the half-way mark in the length of the unit. The system used in permanent division should be one that allows maximum participation in social interaction and results in an equalization of skill level for sound competition.

DIVISION BY THE TEACHER

By the half-way mark in the unit, the volleyball teacher will be in a position to make relatively sound judgment as to the skill level of the individual members of the class and, consequently, ready to assume the responsibility of division into permanent teams. Her judgment may be augmented by the administration and results of skill tests. Division by the teacher has potential advantages in evenly balanced teams and in being economical in the saving of class time. However, these advantages are outweighed by the fact that the teacher may be somewhat prejudiced in her ideas as to the real identity of class leaders. In other words, the volleyball teacher's choices of group leaders may be far removed from the choices of the members of the class. Another disadvantage is that team division by the teacher prevents opportunity for social interaction in the choice of leaders and assignment to permanent groups.

DIVISION BY CLASS DIRECTION

Permanent volleyball teams may be arranged by a procedure in which the class members elect their captains, and these girls, in turn, are given the responsibility for the division. The potential advantage in this procedure is the opportunity for broad social interactions. On the other hand, drawbacks to such a plan include the question as to how well the elected captains would be able to fulfill their responsibilities. While prowess and ability in sports is a prime reason for sociometric choice of friends and teams among boys of the junior and senior high school level, girls and women tend to give more attention to already established friendships and cliques. Consequently, teams established under this procedure might well result in the entrenchment of cliques and teams of unbalanced skill level.

DIVISION BY TEACHER-CLASS METHOD

When the volleyball teacher and the captains, as truly elected representatives of the class, function together in the division into permanent teams, the results usually reflect satisfactory social interaction and equalization of skill level. In this method the teacher guides the class in looking for likely and logical prospects for leaders by outlining the desirable qualifications well in advance of the actual election date. When the election is held, the teacher sees that it is conducted under the best democratic principles. All nominations are accepted; each student has as many votes as the number of captains to be elected; and the voting takes place as a form of the secret ballot. After the election the captains may be given a class meeting or two to evaluate the skill level of the members of the class in order to function intelligently in making choices for the division.

The teacher works closely with the captains at the time of division. Preferably, the meeting is held out of class so that instruction time does not suffer. Choices will alternate in an order established by lot. As the captains choose, the order should flow from first choice to the last captain in order and then that captain should have the succeeding choice, with all captains making a choice in reverse order until the captain with the first choice is reached again. The procedure is then repeated until all the girls have been chosen. If the captains have been wisely selected and if the volleyball teacher has given adequate guidance, the skill levels of the teams will be fairly comparable. For example, when six teams are to be chosen, the first captain should come out with the players who rank first, twelfth, thirteenth, twenty-fourth, and etc., in skill; the second captain, second, eleventh, fourteenth, twenty-third, and etc.; and on, until the sixth captain gets the sixth, seventh, eighteenth, nineteenth, and etc. The captains make trial lists of the players as they choose them for their teams, and the teacher keeps a running account in her roll book of every girl selected.

When every member of the class has been assigned to a team and there has been a cross-check verification by the teacher and the captains, the captains make a new list of their team members in alphabetical order by last names and turn trial lists over to the teacher. The trial lists can be used by the teacher to mark permanent assignments in her roll book or on other record forms. The alphabetical listings of the captains are the ones posted for the class members to see or are read off in a class meeting.

Some volleyball teachers have successfully used a modification of this same procedure in which the team lists, once composed, are numbered, placed in a container, and each captain draws to see which team alignment will be hers. This modification provides an added incentive to the captains to work for equal division of playing talents. If this plan is to be used, each instructor should counsel with her leaders before actual division so that they understand fully what is to take place. It must be decided in each situation whether the merits of this plan outweigh possible merits when each captain works diligently to form a team of her own choosing.

Once the permanent team division has been completed, the volleyball teacher will allot a certain amount of time for the captains to meet with their new teams; to choose a team name, slogans, and yells; and to become acquainted. Consequently, the permanent teams will be used as the group unit for the practice of skills, the playing of lead-up games, the building of offensive and defensive strategy, the playing of games and matches, and tournament competition.

INTRAMURAL TEAMS

One means of measurement of the success of the instructional program in volleyball is the number of individuals and groups who want to pursue participation in the intramural, or voluntary phase. The purpose of a volleyball intramural program is to provide students of moderate, or above, ability and interest with additional opportunities for the satisfaction and enjoyment to be derived from participation in a competitive program. To ensure fulfillment in such a competitive program, a realistic and meaningful basis for participation must be adjoined to expert leadership, supervised practice periods, competent officiating, adequate and pleasant facilities, and high quality equipment.

In order to be realistic, volleyball participating units must be organized in such a way that as many girls or women who desire to be a part of the program can be. Therefore, in the large school, college, or university it is no longer feasible to have intramural teams which represent a grade level or class level. In order to have meaningful competition, participating units must be organized in such a way that the girls or women involved feel that they are actually representing a group to which they in some sense belong. Therefore, loose pick-up teams are apt to become demoralized in the face of opposition from groups which are unified through some common cause.

Intramural team organization can be based on homerooms, clubs, or class sections at the junior and senior high school levels, and at the college and university levels, clubs, sororities, dormitory floors, apartment houses, or other plans of residence-type organization may be utilized.

VALUE OF TOURNAMENTS

Tournaments will be used in beginning units of volleyball, as well as by the teachers of intermediate and advanced units and leaders of intramural programs, as worthwhile culminating experiences for the girls and women involved. Tournaments provide an easy framework within which games and matches can be conducted. After any competitive orientation, as is necessarily involved in the game of volleyball, the students' interest and imagination are captivated by the idea of pitting themselves against other teams in tournament play. They are encouraged to work harder to master the skills and strategies of the game, to capitalize on their own strengths, and to diagnose and correct their own weaknesses. In addition, through tournament play the volleyball teacher is in a better position to evaluate the learnings of her students and their abilities to perform under at least minimum pressure.

While tournaments for volleyball are of easily recognizable value, they should never be used by the teacher merely to relieve herself from instructional responsibilities. Neither should they be used as a "filler" by the teacher who lacks the knowledge or skill to lead her students beyond a certain point in the development of skills and strategy. Tournaments should be scheduled by the volleyball teacher only after the students have gained sound basic skills and feel some security in performance under game conditions. Tournaments, except the bridge or progressive type used primarily for organization of daily competition among teams, should not be introduced until classes have been divided into permanent teams and have had a chance to work together in developing at least a minimum of offensive and defensive strategy.

NON-ELIMINATION TOURNAMENTS

Although usually used in connection with individual and dual sports, the ladder and pyramid types of non-elimination tournaments have certain merits when used in volleyball instructional and intramural programs. The bridge and the round-robin types of non-elimination tournaments are quite valuable in volleyball—the former in the instructional program and the latter in both instructional and intramural play. In non-elimination types, play is scheduled around a timetable involving a beginning and an end, and all entrants remain in the competition until the tournament is officially declared finished.

LADDER TOURNAMENTS

Ladder tournaments will be useful in volleyball classes and intramural programs when the number of students involved is large enough to form six to eight teams. One of the main advantages of using a ladder-type tournament in a volleyball class is the flexibility that is permitted in scheduling matches. The teacher can set the beginning of the tournament and continue the competition as long as time permits or as long as it is meaningful to the individuals and teams involved. Too, there is less problem and worry about weather conditions interfering with the tournament schedule when the volleyball classes are conducted on outdoor courts. In intramural play the teams can arrange a time for challenge matches within a predetermined time limit and can carry on much of the initiative in the planning and organization of the match.

The ladder type of tournament is also of merit in the class or intramural program because it serves as a continuing incentive to the team. Striving to work its way to the number one position on the ladder (see Fig. 8–1), a team will compete against others with approximately the same or slightly higher skill level. Furthermore, as the ladder tournament allows the team to compete throughout the tournament, teams do not become frustrated and eliminated by an early season loss or two.

In the administration of a ladder tournament, the volleyball teacher or intramural advisor, along with the student leadership, must determine how the team entrants will be placed on the rungs and the particular rules and regulations for the tournament. Suggested methods for the placement of teams on the rungs are: first, by chance selections, where the name of the team is drawn from an appropriate container; second, by skill level, in which an evaluation of team prowess causes the group with the highest skill level to be placed either at the top or the bottom of the ladder; or third, by subjective judgment, in which the teacher, or the teacher and the student leadership, decides on the basis of observation.

Rules and regulations governing the tournament should include the number of rungs ahead that can be challenged. In a volleyball class or intramural program of six teams, a rung at a time will serve as a realistic challenge. However, with eight or more teams, challenges of two rungs

Fig. 8–1. Ladder tournament (using soap products for team names).

ahead may be permitted. A time limit must be set within which intramural teams must play challenges. In the class, the volleyball teacher will have clearer control over the timing of the matches. Certainly, the tournament rulings must indicate what shall be considered an official win—that is, will the unit of competition be an official match or less? Because of the limited number of teams involved, rather stringent rulings on the number of successive challenges are recommended for volleyball play, and no team should be allowed to accept more than one challenge at a time.

PYRAMID TOURNAMENTS

The pyramid type of non-elimination tournament is quite similar in nature to the ladder tournament and has some of its same merits. The pyramid will be useful in those volleyball experiences, instructional or intramural, where a large number of students and teams are involved. A special merit of the pyramid tournament is that there is additional opportunity for competition among the teams in the lower rankings. The names

Fig. 8–2. Pyramid tournament (using animals for team names).

of the teams are placed in an appropriate container and the first one drawn becomes the top team, and the successive ones occupy positions on the pyramid as illustrated in Fig. 8–3. The object of the tournament is to gain the top team position and hold it. Challenges must first be issued to another team on the same horizontal row. If the challenging team wins the match, it is then eligible to challenge a team on the row directly above. A victory over a team on the higher plane gives the lower team that position on the pyramid and causes the losing team to move down to the position previously occupied by the winning team. When the challenging team loses to a team on a higher plane, it cannot issue another challenge to that team until both have played matches against other entrants in the tournament.

BRIDGE TOURNAMENTS

The bridge, or progressive, type of non-elimination tournament is especially valuable in volleyball classes. It can serve as an informal method of arranging competition among teams within the daily lesson as well as serving as a culminating activity for the unit or class. The teacher will find it particularly helpful in the early stages of game and match participation

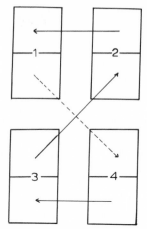

Fig. 8–3. Bridge tournaments.

when she is trying to see that individuals within the class have an opportunity to play with and against as many others in the class as possible. Through this type of competition, which is lacking in any real pressures, the students experience their first taste of competition; begin to evaluate individual and team strengths and weaknesses; and have an opportunity to look for leadership potential on the part of classmates which will help them to function intelligently when the time comes to elect team captains and to divide the class into permanent teams.

In a bridge tournament the courts must be numbered and should fall into a pattern that makes rotation from court to court easy and sensible (see Fig. 8–2). The number one court is designated as the top court, and the object of the tournament is to progress from one court to another until the top court has been reached and then to remain there to defend against all teams making their way up to issue a challenge. On each court except the top one, the winning team progresses to the next court. The losing team remains at home with the exception of the top court, where the losers must drop down to the bottom court and begin the climb to the top court again.

The teams are placed in their original positions on the court by chance with the student leaders drawing for places. If the bridge is used as an informal method of arranging competition, it is suggested that play be designated on a time basis with regulation 8-minute games. When the bridge is being used as culminating play, full matches should be permitted. Whenever matches on a court are finished ahead of other matches, the players should finish up the time allotment with predesignated practice or play. The teams should have pretournament knowledge of the time to be spent in the tournament so that they understand the opportunities they will have in advancing to the top court.

ROUND-ROBIN TOURNAMENTS

Of the non-elimination types of tournaments, the round-robin decidedly has the most advantages for use as a culminating experience in a unit of volleyball instruction or as basis of competition in the intramural program. In the round-robin tournament every team has the opportunity to pit its prowess against the ability of every other team entered in the competition. After every team has met every other team, the winner is decided as the team that has the greatest number of wins and the least number of losses. It is possible for a round-robin tournament to end in a tie, and there should be previous agreement as to whether ties should be permitted to stand or on a method of play-off.

One of the advantages of the round-robin tournament is that there is no particular significance given to the placement of teams in original positions. Therefore, there does not need to be any pretournament evaluation for placement, and chance drawings are fair in every respect. Since a team remains in the tournament from beginning to end with a chance to improve its record of wins along the way, the incentive and motivating features of the competitive experience gain rather than lose in strength.

The volleyball teacher who wants to use team accomplishment as an evaluation technique will find the round-robin tournament the best in making a fair assessment. The volleyball intramural advisor will end tournament play with a team ahead that has truly proven itself in competition against all others.

On the disadvantage side, the round-robin tournament can be quite time-consuming when a large number of teams are entered in the class or intramural competition. Therefore, the teacher or advisor must carefully evaluate the use of time in terms of accomplishment of objectives.

There are two ways of setting up the tournament. One is the number system, and the other is the square system. Under both systems the same formula is used to determine the number of matches to be played. With N equaling the number of teams participating, use the following formula: $\frac{N(N-1)}{2}$. When the number system is to be used, the team captains draw for a number and the numbers are arranged in vertical system. After the first match, the teams are rotated according to number with the number one team remaining constant (see Fig. 8–4).

I	II	III	IV	V	VI	VII
1 vs. 2	1 vs. 4	1 vs. 6	1 vs. 8	1 vs. 7	1 vs. 5	1 vs. 3
3 vs. 4	2 vs. 6	4 vs. 8	6 vs. 7	8 vs. 5	7 vs. 3	5 vs. 2
5 vs. 6	3 vs. 8	2 vs. 7	4 vs. 5	6 vs. 3	8 vs. 2	7 vs. 4
7 vs. 8	5 vs. 7	3 vs. 5	2 vs. 3	4 vs. 2	6 vs. 4	8 vs. 6

Fig. 8–4.   Round-robin tournament: number system.

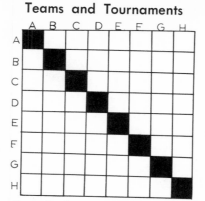

Fig. 8–5. Round-robin tournament: square system.

In the square system arrange the teams so that alphabet letters indicate the team and that numbers are used to point out the round. Each succeeding horizontal row is filled by numbering the squares consecutively. In the square system it is easy to record the scores of games and matches right on the tournament schedule (see Fig. 8–5). In either system it is important to keep an up-to-date account of standings, and this information should be posted for student observation.

ELIMINATION TOURNAMENTS

Elimination-type tournaments are based on the elimination of losing teams until a winner is named. For volleyball purposes, each match results in the complete elimination of the losing team; the transference of the losing team into another bracket with still another chance left for the championship; or the opportunity to win in a less important championship.

SINGLE ELIMINATION TOURNAMENTS

The single elimination tournament is rarely used for competition in a team sport class. Its main advantage lies in the fact that it can be conducted in a limited period of time. Therefore, in a class situation without restrictions enforced by a large number of teams, the time factor will not make this type of tournament mandatory. On the other hand, the single elimination tournament may prove quite profitable in a large intramural program where the time factor, the ability of the tournament to lend itself to play of short duration, simplicity of administration, and demands upon space and facilities are involved.

As a volleyball team is defeated in a single elimination tournament, it is eliminated from further play. Consequently, weaker teams who need additional play experiences are eliminated first. Too often eliminated teams lose all interest in the outcome of the tournament. In the single elimination tournament only the champion team and the runners-up are determined, and the comparative abilities of the teams eliminated early in the competition remain unknown.

In setting up this type of volleyball tournament, the number of matches which will need to be played may be determined by the formula $N-1$. N represents the number of entering teams. In drawing the tournament brackets, the teacher or intramural advisor will be working with powers of two. Enough brackets must be included to take care of the number of entrants, and the number of brackets must be divisible by two in order to end up with two teams playing each other in the finals. For example, with eleven teams entered in the tournament, there must be a sixteen-bracket tournament, with eight brackets in the quarter-finals, four brackets in the semifinals, and two brackets in the finals (see Fig. 8–6). When the entries are not sufficient to fill all the brackets, as in the case of the eleven teams and sixteen brackets setup, it is necessary to fill the empty lines with byes. The number of byes is determined by subtracting the number of entrants from the number of brackets, and in this case the number is five. Whenever the byes are even in number they should be evenly divided between the top and bottom halves of the tournament chart. For uneven numbers, the extra bye is placed in the bottom half of the tournament chart. Teams appearing on the brackets opposite a bye do not play in the first round, and all byes must be taken care of during the first round of play.

Unless some evaluation procedure has proceeded the establishment of the tournament chart, the captains of the volleyball teams involved draw for bracket positions. If some evaluative procedure has taken place, such as use of a ladder, pyramid, bridge, or round-robin tournament, the teams may be placed according to demonstrated ability. The best teams are scattered equally on the tournament chart so that they will not meet and eliminate each other in the early rounds of play.

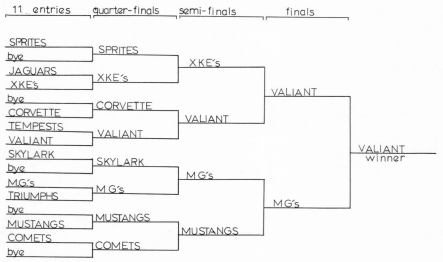

Fig. 8–6. Single elimination tournament (using sports cars for team names).

If the setting up of the tournament chart is to be a learning experience for the students, it should be drawn up and position placements made in their presence. Then, the chart should be posted in a prominent place where all students may study it.

CONSOLATION-ELIMINATION TOURNAMENTS

Consolation brackets held in connection with single elimination tournaments give the volleyball teams losing in the first round an opportunity to win in a less important championship. Consolation rounds provide additional competitive experiences for teams that need them the most and guarantee every team at least two matches before elimination. Therefore, the number of entrants after the first round remains stabilized for one additional round rather than being cut in half as occurs during a single elimination tournament.

In the consolation volleyball tournament all teams losing in the first round and losers of the second round who had byes in the first round are eligible for consolation competition. In this case it is necessary to wait until teams drawing byes have played their initial matches to complete the consolation draw.

Consolation types of elimination tournaments are recommended when the number of teams entered does not exceed sixteen. A sample tournament chart for seven teams is illustrated in Fig. 8–7.

Fig. 8–7. Consolation-elimination tournament (using colors-birds for team names).

DOUBLE ELIMINATION TOURNAMENTS

The volleyball teacher and intramural advisor can profitably use the double elimination type tournament when it is desirable to give every team a second chance in competition and when it can be assumed that the teams are fairly equal in skill level. This type of tournament is generally used when the number of team entries does not exceed eight and is rarely used if there are more than sixteen entrants.

In the double elimination tournament any team losing a match in the winner's bracket is transferred into the loser's bracket, but still holds on to the chance of working its way through losing bracket competition back to a culminating match with the winner of the winner's bracket. If the winner of the loser's bracket should take this match, each of the two teams has

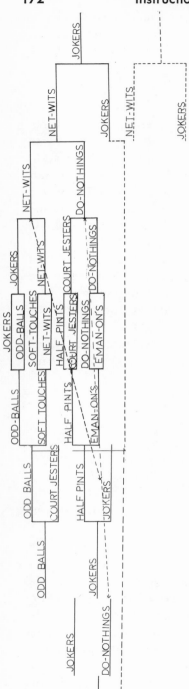

Fig. 8–8. Double Elimination: back to back (using free choice for team names).

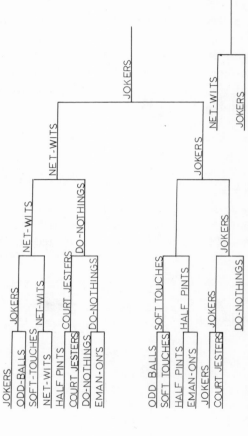

Fig. 8–9. Double Elimination: over-and-under (using free choice for team names).

then suffered a single loss and there is a rematch with the winner designated as the tournament champion.

There are two methods of drawing up the chart for a double elimination tournament: the back-to-back method and the over-under method. In the back-to-back method, the winners' brackets advance toward the right and the losers', following broken lines and arrows, to the left (see Fig. 8–8). In the over-under method, a loser's bracket is arranged under the winner's bracket. As teams lose, they are transferred to the loser's bracket, and the winner of that bracket moves up to challenge the winner of the winner's bracket (see Fig. 8–9).

When setting up a double elimination tournament the volleyball teacher or intramural advisor should be careful to arrange brackets to prevent teams from playing each other a second time until absolutely necessary. Crossing losers from the top and bottom half of the winner's bracket should take care of this situation.

Placement of teams on the brackets for the double elimination should follow the same principles as hold true for the single elimination tournament—that is, chance drawings or the seeding of teams on the basis of some evaluative procedure.

9

Audio-Visual Aids and Testing

Whether it is to direct a student or students toward correct performance in skills or to attract the attention of student groups toward offerings in the voluntary program, the competent volleyball teacher and advisor must know and follow principles of selection, construction, and use of audio-visual aids as a means of enriching educational experiences. The chief purposes of visual aids are to captivate interest and to make the learning involved more realistic for the intended group. Certainly, visual aids increase tremendously the scope of experience that can be brought into instructional volleyball units. Few students will ever have a chance to attend Olympic volleyball competition, for example, but the alert teacher will be able to announce dates and times when television cameras will relay pictures made on the scene to viewers at school or home. The number of students who will be able to follow in person the experts in volleyball competition will be limited, but through good visual aid devices, they may become acquainted with the expert and be able to study her form.

In addition to purposes of motivating and advertising, visual aids are part of the actual teaching procedure of the good volleyball teacher. Through them she will be able to show interrelationships among complex wholes. For example, a diagram of the entire defensive team as it moves to combat a spike will provide the players a clearer picture of individual responsibilities and relationships to the group effort. With this understanding, the learning will be reenforced and retained.

With a variety of visual and motivating aids at her command, the volleyball teacher is able to capture and maintain student attention; to create new interests; and to overcome some of the problems presented by individual differences in the rate and pattern of learning.

PREPREPARED AIDS

Preprepared aids are those that the volleyball teacher designs and constructs, causes to be constructed, rents, or purchases previous to use in the program. In the group of aids constructed as a result of the teacher's direct or indirect efforts are bulletin boards, posters, teaching devices, and worksheets. If the teacher has an artistic or creative flair, her own know-how in the technical aspects of the game may lead to the development of aids superior to those created by the commercial artist who possesses artistic ability but little knowledge of the game. However, in many educational institutions faculty and students within art and industrial arts departments can be counted on for valuable assistance in the creation and design of visual aids. Prepared aids rented or purchased by the teacher previous to class use include films, film strips, and technique charts.

BULLETIN BOARDS AND POSTERS

Generally speaking, the bulletin boards and posters used in volleyball programs will be of two types: the central type, which is located in some prominent place where students pass frequently during the day; and the class type, which is used within the class in connection with instruction in some phase of the game. The time, effort, and cost of the construction of bulletin boards should prohibit haphazard planning and shoddy work. The device should be built in such a way that it can be used on several occasions or until the material or information is no longer meaningful. Therefore, the teacher must select materials which will stand up under wear and tear, and the finished product should be one that can be stored easily and returned to active duty when desired.

In addition to the economy of the device, the other requirements of an effective bulletin board or poster are originality, attractiveness, and technical correctness. To accomplish originality and attractiveness, the device must attract the attention of the viewer to the extent that she wishes to absorb its full message. A central theme; simplicity; orderly presentation; a title that stands out in large print, is brief, and arouses curiosity; a minimum of writing; adherence to simple color rules; and the use of a variety of materials to give a feeling of texture, third dimension, or any desired effect are guiding principles which should be followed. To ensure technical correctness the information should be timely, accurate, and in accordance with the best current knowledge of the game.

Students should be encouraged to participate in the building of bulletin boards, as well as to take advantage of those constructed by, or at the direction of, the volleyball teacher. They should help in the search for appropriate materials, and many of them will have artistic and creative abilities which will be useful to the teacher or advisor in arranging the board. The teacher may use the setting up of such displays as an effective alternate assignment for the student who is well enough to be in school on a particular day but unable to engage fully in activity.

FILMS AND FILM STRIPS

Films and film strips can prove quite profitable to the teacher of a beginning unit of volleyball instruction if major emphasis is an introduction to the whole game. While an exhibition game by reasonably skilled players may attempt the same purpose, films and film strips may be stopped, restarted, and slowed in motion, allowing concentration on points of desired emphasis. The teacher in an intermediate or advanced unit may use films or film strips to illustrate in detail skills and strategy in which she is giving instruction.

Because of the expense involved in such an undertaking, the volleyball teacher should discourage outright purchase of a film until she is sure that it meets the particular needs of the program. In the renting of a film to be shown to classes, the teacher should order it in time to preview its contents. In addition, she should read any printed material available on the film and prepare a list of questions on contained information so that she can guide the students in the film experience.

After the showing of the film, she should lead the students in discussion of the materials covered. As soon as possible the students should be allowed to carry through on what they observed and learned from the film presentation in their own playing experience.

The *Volleyball Guide,* published biennially by the DGWS, the American Association for Health, Physical Education, and Recreation, carries in each issue an up-to-date listing of films and film strips available on the commercial market for purchase or rental. The listing also provides a description of the content of the film, the time required for showing, and instructions on how to order.

TECHNIQUE CHARTS

In addition to technique charts, constructed by, or at the direction of, the volleyball teacher, a set of black and white charts illustrating volleyball serves, volleys, and other techniques are available for purchase at a nominal fee through the DGWS. Additional information on these charts can be gained through the previously mentioned *Volleyball Guide.*

WORKSHEETS AND RULES DIGESTS

The combination worksheet-rules digest or separate worksheets and rules digests have become one of the most popular and meaningful teaching aids to be used in the volleyball instructional program. Many teachers distribute the aid during the introductory phase of the unit to give the students a more complete idea of the total learning experience in which they will be engaging during the activity. Others withhold the aid until later in the development of the unit so that it serves as a recall sheet of experiences already completed and as a preview of others to come. Still other teachers may reserve the worksheet-rules digest until nearer the unit's end and then distribute it for study and review purposes.

A combination worksheet-rules digest requires an outstanding job of condensation of information by the volleyball teacher. Materials or information spread over more than four typewritten pages will begin to look too burdensome to the average high school student, and there will be a tendency to belittle or ignore actual perusal of its contents. If the teaching aid is divided into two parts and distributed upon different occasions, more information and greater detail may be accomplished.

The worksheet, or the worksheet phase of the combination aid, should include: a brief description of the game; a compact history of volleyball and a concise statement of its current recreational status; an assessment of potential game values; a listing of all the individual skills to be introduced in the unit; an outline of the offensive and defensive team patterns which the students will have an opportunity to learn; a statement of the etiquette or sportsmanship standards of conduct which each will be expected to follow; and an overview of the student's responsibility toward safety for herself and others in the class.

In addition to brevity, the material should be presented in a positive manner, emphasizing "do's" rather than "don't's"; should utilize diagrams and eye-catching illustrations when space provides; and should motivate the student to seek out additional information from other sources.

The rules digest should be a condensation of the current rules of the game and should cover rule information that is essential in making play meaningful for the student. The rules digest should follow as closely as possible the presentation of the official rules. Therefore, the headings will include:

1. Object of the game.
2. Starting the game.
3. Playing area, net, and ball.
4. Team composition.
5. Substitutions and time-out.
6. Scoring.
7. The game and the match.
8. Service.
9. Rotation.
10. Point and side-out.
11. Dead ball.
12. Changing courts.
13. Double fouls.

In the use of this type of visual aid the volleyball teacher will be reinforcing one of her objectives and a valued student outcome by emphasizing, through the printed word, knowledge leading to a more complete understanding and appreciation of the game and its possible contributions to the total development of the participant. In actuality, she is offering to the student a substitute textbook for a course in which the purchase of one is not required.

The worksheet-rules digest can be mimeographed or duplicated through some other economical process at comparatively little expense to the school for the value received. It should contain a bibliography for the interested and enterprising student who wishes to pursue additional reading resources. The bibliography should contain a complete listing of the books, pamphlets, and major articles dealing with volleyball and associated activities which are available within the school library. When the teacher owns materials she would like to make available to students, she should include this information, along with the procedure to be followed in the use of her personal library.

AIDS DEVELOPED IN CLASS

In contrast to the visual aids which are preprepared, constructed, purchased, or rented, and brought into the volleyball class are those which may be developed during the actual instructional period. This does not mean that these aids are totally impromptu and improvised on the spot without any previous arrangement and planning by the teacher. On the contrary, class developed aids will involve much preparation so that the desired purposes may be accomplished.

CHALKBOARDS

The use of chalkboards to list items; to draw diagrams; to make illustrations; and to develop ideas, point by point, is as effective a teaching device for the volleyball teacher in the gymnasium or on the outdoor playing court as it is for the classroom teacher. Visualizing in this form leads to stronger retention of points; makes ideas more clearly understood; and tends to capture and hold the interest of the students. Consequently, the volleyball teacher who must conduct her class in a teaching station where there is no permanent board attached to a wall should secure use of a movable chalkboard on wheels or a portable chalkboard of a smaller size. The latter type is used in most outdoor teaching stations.

The major asset of a chalkboard can be its main liability unless the teacher engages in preplanning. Materials presented on the chalkboard can be erased and the board used over and over. However, it is most difficult to keep material over any length of time because of easy erasing and smearing, and it is next to impossible to retain any aid for another class period or section to see. Therefore, the volleyball teacher planning to illustrate an offensive or defensive pattern through a chalkboard diagram should first plan it on paper so that the master copy is available for repetition in the next showing. The volleyball teacher must also be concerned with technical correctness and the prevention of hasty and shoddy reproductions in her chalkboard work. Therefore, she should start with a clean board and have collected everything she will need to develop the aid during class. She will avoid overcrowding the board, make wording simple, print and draw on a large scale, and use colored chalk when she wants to lend emphasis. As she proceeds in the development of the illustration, she should stand to one side as much as possible so that the students can observe fully; use a pointer when she is referring to parts of the illustration; and underline when she wants to focus attention on a particular part.

MAGNETIC BOARDS

The use of a magnetic board as a teaching device offers unlimited possibilities within a volleyball class. Its unique contribution to team sport teaching is the fact that materials can be moved about readily and effectively. Usually of portable size, the magnetic board can be carried by the volleyball teacher to her teaching station, indoors or outdoors. There it can be used to introduce the elements of team play after a minimum of fundamental skills have been learned. For example, the team defense against the service is a primary defensive pattern to become a part of a team's strategy, and the magnets on the board can be utilized to illustrate team positioning in receiving the service and the backing-up assignments of each player. After the introduction of team play, the magnetic board can be used over and over again to point out new elements of offensive and defensive team patterns.

The volleyball teacher will also be able to make good use of the magnetic board in class discussion and testing situations. In oral review, for example, the volleyball teacher may show the offensive team with the Key-Spiker and Key-Set in particular forward line positions and ask the players to outline for her the blocking and picking-up responsibilities of the members of the defensive team. Or the teacher may show a team in various stages of positioning on the court and point out that a player has sent the ball into the net with two remaining contacts left on it. Should the team try for a two-man offensive or two-man defensive net recovery and what players will be directly involved?

While it is possible to have a magnetic board serve a variety of classes with no permanent lines drawn on it, the volleyball teacher will be able to make best usage out of the board which has the playing court permanently outlined in proportionate size. Shaded or broken lines should be drawn in on at least one half-court to represent the six equal playing areas to be covered by the team. If a board without permanent lines is to be used, the teacher must prepare the board with temporary lines before class to ensure technical accuracy in her presentation. Magnets of two different colors should be secured. These can be used to advantage in showing two opposing teams, to point out players occupying spiking as opposed to setting positions, to illustrate Key-Spikers and Key-Sets in the lineup under the various patterns of play, and the like. A white magnet, contrasting with the two other colors, can represent the ball.

In addition to the teacher's use of the magnetic board to develop visual aids within the class, the device should be made available to captains and teams for experimental use in developing their own strategies whenever feasible.

SKILL TESTING

A volleyball unit of instruction, planned for the beginning, intermediate, or advanced level, which has objectives in skills, abilities, knowledges, and understandings as pupil outcomes, must involve testing as a culminating activity. Consequently, the volleyball teacher must concern herself with finding or devising skill tests which will accurately and objectively measure the student's level of achievement and the acceptance of standardized tests, or construction of her own written tests, which will allow her to evaluate the knowledge and understanding gained through the unit of instruction.

In measuring the skills of the individual student participating within a volleyball team sport class, the teacher will need to depend heavily upon three types of testing devices: objective skill tests, rating scales, and incidence charts. The truly objective volleyball skill tests available today are those which evaluate volleying and serving skills. While many attempts have been made by experts in the field to come up with instruments which measure the spike, net recovery, blocking, and picking-up, the resulting tests have involved other players and therefore have been negated as objective devices. Thus, the volleyball teacher may select from several available volley and service tests the ones most appropriate for her particular situation, but to evaluate in the other skills, she must turn to rating scales or incidence charts she has adopted or constructed for use.

VOLLEY TESTS

Certainly, the volley as a pass and as a set is an important and crucial skill which the teacher on any level, grade or skill, will wish to measure. Some of the tests available today and an assessment of their respective uses and values are presented here. Others may be found, with a little research, by the enterprising teacher.

1. *French-Cooper Repeated Volleys Test.*[1] Devised for measuring the volleying ability of high school players, the French-Cooper Repeated Volleys Test meets many characteristics of a good skill test. It demands that the skill be performed in a way that approximates the game situation; it can be administered to large numbers at one time when wall space is available; it is easily understood and requires comparatively little time for instruction and administration; it allows enough trials so that chance errors do not effect the grade; it requires little equipment; its results may be easily recorded; and its simplicity allows the teacher to use student help in its administration with a feeling of confidence.

1. Equipment needed:
    a. Balls.
    b. Wall space.
    c. Stop watch.
2. Markings (see Fig. 9–1):
    a. A line 10 feet long drawn on a wall 7½ feet above the floor.
    b. A line 10 feet long drawn on the floor 3 feet from the wall.

[1] Esther French and Bernice Cooper, "Achievement Tests in Volleyball for High School Girls," *The Research Quarterly*, VIII, 2 (May, 1937), pp. 150–157.

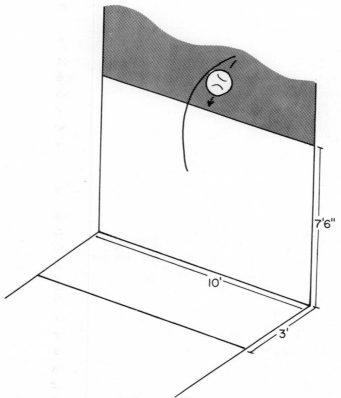

Fig. 9–1. French-Cooper Repeated Volleys Test.

PROCEDURE. The player stands behind the restraining line on the floor and puts the ball into play against the wall with an underhand toss. As the ball rebounds from the wall, she repeatedly volleys it for 15 seconds. If the ball goes out of control, the player recovers it and restarts with an underhand toss.

SCORE. The score is the number of times in each trial that the ball is volleyed on or above the wall line. The underhand toss starts should not be counted. A volley in which a ball-handling foul is committed should not be counted and neither should volleys in which the player steps on or over the restraining line. Ten trials are given. The test score is the sum of the five best trials.

2. *Russell-Lange Volley Test.*[2] The Russell-Lange Volley Test is an instrument devised to test volleying ability at the junior high school level. Its originators claim as merits the reliability, validity, and objectivity of the test. They also point out that it is easy to administer; it is helpful in the diagnosis of player weakness; it can be used to measure progress; and it can be used as a teaching aid as well as a testing device. Another advantage is that students can be easily taught to assist in administration and scoring.

1. Equipment needed:
   a. Balls.
   b. Stop watch.
   c. Wall space.
2. Markings: same as for the French-Cooper Repeated Volleys Test (see Fig. 9–1).

PROCEDURE. The player being tested stands behind the 3-foot restraining line and with an underhand toss puts the ball into play against the wall. On its rebound, she volleys the ball above the line on the wall for 30 seconds. The ball may be caught or set up to oneself as is desired or necessary. If the ball is caught or goes out of control, the restart is made with an underhand toss from behind the restraining line.

SCORE. The score is the number of legal volleys made from behind the restraining line to the wall on or above the scoring line. Each girl is given three trials. It is recommended that trials do not immediately follow each other because of the fatigue factor. The best score within the three trials becomes the test score.

3. *Trotter Self-Volley Test.* Almost all the volley skill tests available to the volleyball teacher require use of wall space. The Trotter Self-Volley Test was designed to help meet the particular needs of the teacher who conducts her unit of instruction at an outdoor teaching station with no

2 Naomi Russell and Elizabeth Lange, "Achievement Tests in Volleyball for Junior High School Girls," *The Research Quarterly,* XI, 4 (December, 1940), pp. 33–41.

available wall space. However, there is no reason why the test cannot be administered indoors if the teacher, upon evaluation of the testing procedure, feels that its merits are desirable in her particular situation.

In addition to the fact that no wall space is required, the test has merit in that it can be easily administered to a large class within a matter of minutes; student assistance in administration and scoring can be utilized with a minimum of instruction; the grade and skill levels of the students can be met through the test's provision for adjustment of net height; and the test requires that the player being tested gain and maintain control over the ball in a gamelike situation.

1. Equipment needed:
   a. Balls.
   b. Stop watch.
   c. Volleyball courts.
   d. Whistle.
   e. Score sheets or cards.
   f. Standards holding nets at recommended heights for grade and skill levels:
      (1) Junior high school—6 feet, 6 inches.
      (2) Average high school group—7 feet.
      (3) Advanced high school and college units—7 feet, 4¼ inches.
2. Markings (see Fig. 9–2):
   a. Divide one half of the regulation playing court into six equal portions by measuring 15 feet down the sidelines from the center line and then, parallel with the center line and baseline, at the 15-foot markings, finish the division by marking off cross marks at the 10- and 20-foot intervals.
   b. Use chalk on outdoor courts and chalk or masking tape indoors. The chalk or tape should be a contrasting color, and the crosses should be large enough (15- to 18-inch strips) so that they are easily discernible from behind the baseline at the opposite end of the court.

PROCEDURE. A player stands in each one of the three 10-foot by 15-foot areas adjacent to the net. At the sound of the whistle signal to "Go," blown by the test administrator, she volleys the ball into the air above her own head so that it clears a minimum of net height. As the ball descends, she continues to volley it to herself until the whistle sound indicates the end of the 30-second time limit. The ball is put into play at the beginning of the test, and after each loss of control, with an overhead volley.

Three players may be tested on each court at one time. Each must perform her volleys within the confines of her own particular area.

Each player has a partner who acts as her judge and counter. The partner stands with her feet completely behind the baseline at the opposite end of the court and counts aloud the legal volleys of the player taking the test. She should distinguish her voice so that the student taking the test will realize when her contacts do not meet requirements to be counted.

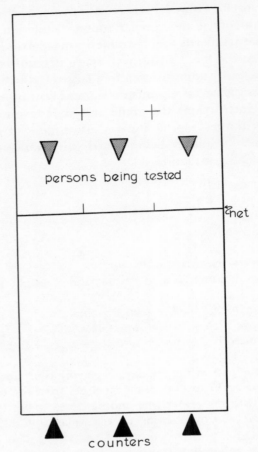

Fig. 9–2. Trotter Self-Volley Test.

The test administrator—the teacher—assumes a position central to all courts, times the 30-second time limit by means of a stop watch, and indicates through the means of a whistle the "Go" and "Stop" signals.

SCORE. The score is the number of times in each trial that the ball is legally volleyed above the height of the net. The partner-judge will count only those volleys in which there is definite space between the bottom of the ball and the height of the net; in which the student remains within her own respective area; and in which no ball-handling violations are committed. The regulation rules of the game will be strictly adhered to in assessing the ball-handling violations of holding, catching, lifting, scooping, and pushing.

The test will consist of three 30-second trials and the score will be the number of volleys in the best trial. It is recommended that no more than two trials be administered on the same day. The two trials on the same day should be separated by having the player taking the test and her partner-judge exchange places, or by having the students work in groups of three with the third player recording the score and having all three players rotate to exchange duties.

4. *Brady Volley Test.*[3]   Although it is initially designed for use with instructional units for college men, there is no reason why the volleyball teacher of an advanced high school girls' or college women's class cannot effectively use the Brady Volley Test as an instrument to measure volleying ability.   The Brady Volley Test demands that a volley be of a height greater than 11 feet and 6 inches in order to score on the test, but this is certainly not unrealistic in the intermediate or advanced units at the high school and college levels where desirable volleys to be used as sets for the spiker are elevated to a height of 12 feet or better.

[3] George F. Brady, "Preliminary Investigations of Volleyball Playing Ability," *The Research Quarterly*, XVI, 2 (March, 1945),   14–17.

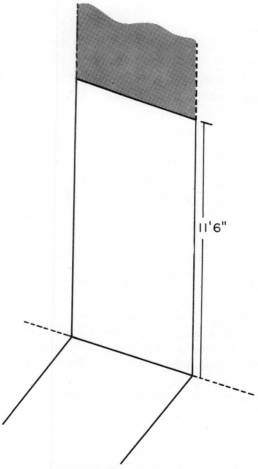

Fig. 9–3.   Brady Volley Test.

1. Equipment needed:
   a. Balls.
   b. Stop watch.
   c. Smooth wall space.
2. Markings (see Fig. 9–3):
   a. A horizontal chalk line 5 feet long and 11 feet, 6 inches from the floor.
   b. Vertical lines extending upward toward ceiling at the ends of the horizontal line.

PROCEDURE. The player stands where he or she wishes and puts the ball into play by throwing it against the wall. As the ball descends, it is returned to the wall with a volley and the volleys are continued for a 1-minute time limit.

At any time the ball goes out of control, it is put back into play by a throw.

SCORE. The score is the number of times the volley lands in the target above the 11-foot 6-inch level. The throws to put the ball into play do not count.

Each student is given two trials with sufficient rest in between so that the fatigue factor does not influence the score of the test. The best of the two trials stands as the score.

5. *Liba and Stauff Volleyball Pass Test.*[4] The Liba and Stauff Volleyball Pass Test was devised to test concurrently both height and distance, the two most desired qualities in the volleyball pass. The originators offer two versions of the test: one to be used at the college level, and the second to be used at the junior high school level. The tests require a rather elaborate administrative procedure, involving ropes elevated to certain heights, restraining lines, and a canvas strip target (see Figs. 9–4a and 9–4b).

1. Equipment needed:
   a. Balls.
   b. Standards holding ropes elevated to these heights:
      (1) College women—11 feet and 13 feet
      (2) Junior high school girls—10 feet and 12 feet
   c. Targets made out of canvas strips:
      (1) College women: 2 feet wide and 30 feet long; lined off in 2-foot squares; and each square numbered one to eight to one.
      (2) Junior high school girls: 2 feet wide and 28 feet long; lined off in 2-foot squares; and each square numbered one to seven to one.
2. Markings:
   a. College women: a restraining line 10 feet, 6 inches from standards holding ropes.
   b. Junior high school girls: a restraining line 6 feet, 6 inches from standards holding ropes.

4 Marie R. Liba and Marilyn R. Stauff, "A Test for the Volleyball Pass," *The Research Quarterly*, XXXIV, 1 (March, 1963), pp. 56–63.

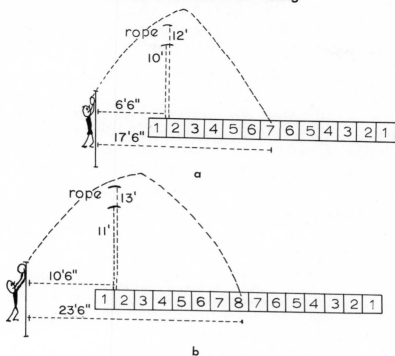

Fig. 9–4. Liba and Stauff Volleyball Pass Test. (a) Junior high school level. (b) College level.

PROCEDURE. The player stands behind the restraining line and puts the ball into play with a self-toss. She then volleys, or passes, the ball, attempting to clear the top rope and to have the ball land in the target with the highest value.

She must handle the ball legally. Although there is no foul for stepping over the restraining line, she should be encouraged to remain behind it.

SCORE. The player is given a height score on the following basis:

1. College women:
   3 points—over the 13-foot rope
   2 points—between the 11-foot and 13-foot ropes
   1 point—under the 11-foot rope
   0 point—fails to reach ropes
2. Junior high school girls:
   3 points—over the 12-foot rope
   2 points—between the 10-foot and 12-foot ropes
   1 point—under the 10-foot rope
   0 point—fails to reach ropes

The player is given a distance score according to the number on the target in which the ball lands. When a ball lands on a line, the higher score counts.

The combination score is gained by multiplying the height score by the distance score. For example, a college woman whose volley cleared the 13-foot rope and landed in the number eight target would receive a test score of twenty-four.

Two practice trials are given and then ten trials in each of two days or class meetings.

6. *Mohr and Haverstick Repeated Volleys Test.*[5] Mohr and Haverstick's Repeated Volleys Test is a modification of the Russell-Lange Volley Test with an expressed effort to make the test more realistic for college women and to reduce the advantage given to taller players because of height.

    1. Equipment needed:
      a. Balls.
      b. Wall space.
      c. Stop watch.
    2. Markings (see Fig. 9–5):
      a. A line 10 feet long drawn on a wall 7½ feet from the floor.
      b. A line 10 feet long drawn on the floor 3 feet from the wall.

[5] Dorothy R. Mohr and Martha J. Haverstick, "Repeated Volleys Tests for Women's Volleyball," *The Research Quarterly*, XXVI (May, 1955), 179–184.

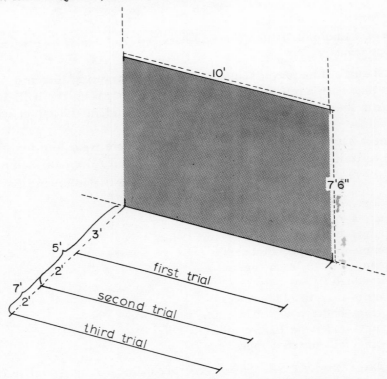

Fig. 9–5. Mohr and Haverstick Repeated Volleys Test.

c. A line 10 feet long drawn on the floor 5 feet from the wall.

d. A line 10 feet long drawn on the floor 7 feet from the wall.

PROCEDURE. The player stands behind the 3-foot restraining line and with an underhand toss puts the ball into play against the wall. On its rebound, she volleys the ball above the line on the wall for 30 seconds. If the ball is caught or goes out of control, the restart is made with an underhand toss from behind the restraining line.

During the second trial, the player moves behind the 5-foot restraining line and repeats the same procedure. The 7-foot restraining line is used for the third trial.

SCORE. Legal volleys made from behind the restraining line to the wall on or above the scoring line are counted. The player is given three trials at each line. The test score is the sum of the three trials.

7. *Trotter Wall Target Volley Test.* The Trotter Wall Target Volley Test was designed to test volleying ability in the intermediate and advanced player at the senior high school and college levels. Emphasis is given in

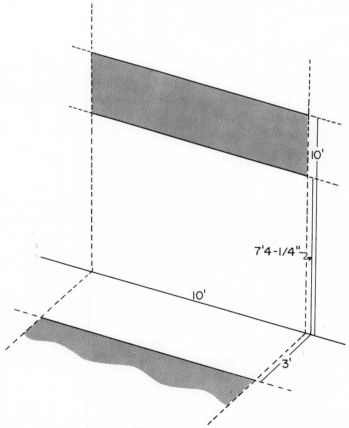

Fig. 9–6. Trotter Wall Target Volley Test.

the test to volleys that meet standards high enough to qualify as sets for the spiker as distinguished from those that meet minimum game requirements: namely, height of the net. Volleys that qualify as sets are given double value while the net-height volley earns single value. Therefore, the player who attempts the most desirable type of volley is not penalized as is often true on tests requiring only minimum height. Too, the test demands such control of the ball, through rewarding consecutive efforts, and a combination of skill and stamina, through the 1-minute time limit, that intermediate and advanced skill level players are challenged.

While the time limit for trials run to 1 minute in length and require more time for administration than the tests of 30- and 15-second duration, student assistance in administration and scoring help to make the Trotter Wall Target Volley Test economical on a timewise basis.

1. Equipment needed:
   a. Balls.
   b. Stop watch.
   c. Whistle.
   d. Score sheets or cards.
   e. Pencils.
   f. Wall space.
2. Markings (see Fig. 9–6):
   a. Line 10 feet long on the wall 7 feet, 4¼ inches from floor, representing net height line.
   b. Line 10 feet long on the wall 10 feet from floor, representing desirable set-volley height.
   c. Line 10 feet long on the floor, 3 feet from the wall, representing the restraining line.
   d. Use chalk, masking tape, or paint for wall lines and removable tape for the restraining line.

PROCEDURE. The player stands behind the restraining line and on the whistle signal to "Go," puts the ball into play by tossing it up against the wall. As the ball descends she volleys the ball so that it repeatedly makes contacts until the whistle sound indicates the end of the one-minute time limit. Should the player catch or lose control of the ball, she recovers it and starts the volley procedure again with an underhand toss.

Two helpers work with the player taking the test at the testing station. The duty of one helper is to count and record the "high" volleys, those hitting on or above the 10-foot line. The other helper counts and records the "low" volleys, those hitting on or above the 7 foot, 4¼-inch line but not reaching the 10-foot line.

The test administrator—the teacher—assumes a position central to all testing stations, times the 1-minute time limit by means of a stop watch, and indicates through the means of a whistle the "Go" and "Stop" signals.

As many students can be tested at one time as there are available testing stations. Working in groups of three, they rotate in duties until all have been tested.

SCORE. The "low" volleys receive single point value and the "high" volleys receive double point value. As the object of the test is to determine control of the ball, as well as height of the volley, scores are given on the basis of the "high" and "low" points earned in a consecutive interval within the time limit. For example, a student gets forty-five high volleys and twelve low volleys and then loses control of the ball. The helpers record those scores on the score sheet and start counting over at one. Consequently, the student gets eighteen high volleys and twenty-two low volleys, and then the whistle sounds to indicate the end of the time limit. Her consecutive score during the first interval is double forty-five plus twelve, equaling 102. The second interval produced double eighteen plus twenty-two, equaling forty-eight. Obviously, her first interval score of 102 is best and becomes the test score.

No credit is given a volley in which there is either a ball-handling violation or in which the student steps on or over the restraining line.

Three trials should be given with adequate rest in between trials so that the fatigue factor does not influence test scores.

SERVICE TESTS

Service tests available for teachers range from those in which the inexperienced player is given a score for each service she can get over the net and into the court and a zero for those she does not to courts rather elaborately marked with target areas in which varying points are awarded the player who can direct her services to these areas. The three service tests presented here are the French-Cooper, the Trotter, and the Odeneal.

1. *The French-Cooper Service Test.*[6] The French-Cooper Service Test divides the court into seven target areas and gives point value to the ball as it lands in the target areas. It permits the use of any legal service.

1. Equipment needed:
   a. Regulation court.
   b. Net at regulation height.
   c. Balls.
2. Markings (see Fig. 9–7):
   a. A chalk line across the court 5 feet inside and parallel to the baseline.
   b. A chalk line across the court parallel to the net, and 12 feet, 6 inches from the center line directly under the net.
   c. Chalk lines 5 feet inside and parallel to each side line, extending from the line under the net to the line described in "a".
   d. Chalk in numbers in the center of each area to indicate its value:
      (1) The space nearest the net in the center of the court—value: one.

6 Esther French and Bernice Cooper, "Achievement Tests in Volleyball for High School Girls," *The Research Quarterly*, XVIII, 2 (May, 1937), 150–157.

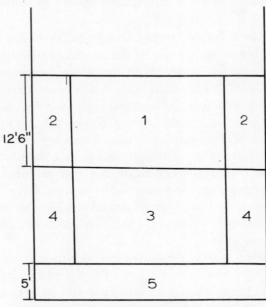

Fig. 9–7. French-Cooper Service Test.

(2) The spaces on either side of this area—value: two.

(3) The area directly behind space "one"—value: three.

(4) The area directly behind spaces "two" and on either side of space "three"—value: four.

(5) The entire end space farthest from the net—value: five.

PROCEDURE. The player being tested stands behind the baseline opposite the target and is given ten trials to serve the ball into the target in the court across the net. Any legal serve is permitted. Foot faults shall count as trials; "let" serves shall be reserved and do not count as trials. The scorer stands on a chair near one side line about 15 feet from the net.

SCORE. The scoring is indicated in the test markings. A ball landing on a line separating two spaces scores the higher value. A ball landing on an outside boundary line scores the value of the area the line bounds. Trials in which foot faults occur score zero.

2. *The Trotter Service Test.* The Trotter Service Test is the result of an effort to simplify court markings, to retain emphasis on placement of the service, to test specific serving techniques, and to provide for economical administration. The student will be tested in the serving skills in which she has had instruction and adequate experience during the volleyball unit. For example, in beginning units the underhand service will be emphasized and possibly the sidearm introduced. The teacher's judgment will determine whether both skills should be tested. In an intermediate unit, the students gain experience in all three serving techniques, and the teacher

may designate the underhand and a choice of the other two services to be tested. Or she might allow the student to choose her two best out of the three services on which to be tested. In advanced units it is expected that students would be tested in all three of the basic serving techniques.

1. Equipment needed:
   a. Balls.
   b. Regulation court.
   c. Nets elevated to regulation height for appropriate grade and skill level group.
   d. Score sheets or cards.
   e. Pencils.
2. Markings (see Fig. 9–8):
   a. A line across the court 5 feet (inclusive) inside and parallel to the baseline.
   b. Lines 5 feet (inclusive) inside and parallel to each side line and extending from the center line to the line lying parallel with the baseline.
   c. On outdoor courts use chalk or paint to mark off the target areas. On indoor courts, use chalk or masking tape. An alternate suggestion is to use oil cloth, cut into 2-inch strips and stitched together into the appropriate 30-foot and two 25-foot lengths, or carpet binding in a distinguishable color, cut into the proper lengths. Both the oil cloth and carpet binding have the advantages of being easy to put down; clinging to the floor or being held in place by attaching masking tape; and being easy to remove, reroll, and store for future use.

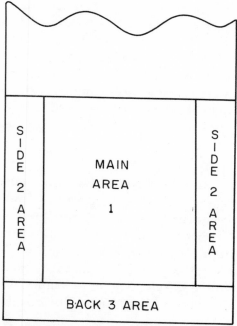

Fig. 9–8. Trotter Service Test.

PROCEDURE.   The student is tested in one of the three types of service skills at a time.

The player being tested stands at any point she desires behind the baseline opposite the target areas. Using the serving technique designated for the test, she takes one practice trial, and then serves ten trials in succession.

Any service faults in the game, such as foot fault, moving back more than the allowed 6 feet, or giving forward impetus with the holding hand, are also test faults, and cause the trial to result in a zero score.

SCORE.   A legal service landing in the main area, "good" as far as game requirements are concerned is valued as one point. A legal service landing in either of the side areas, "better" as far as game requirements are concerned, is valued as two points. A legal service landing in the back area, "best" as far as game requirements are concerned, is valued as three points. Balls landing on target area lines count as the higher value. Illegal services, out-of-bounds, into the net, and striking standards or overhead obstructions count as zero. The test score is the sum of the ten trials.

With only a minimum of instruction, students working in groups of four can administer the test to each other with the teacher serving in a supervisory capacity. One student takes the test; two helpers judge where the ball lands, call out the numerical value of the service, and return the balls to the server; and the fourth student records the score on the score sheets or cards. Then there is a rotation of duties.

4. *The Odeneal Service Test.*[7]   Designed primarily for use with boys' and men's groups the Odeneal Service Test sets aside target areas which represent identical space coverage as those outlined in the Trotter Service Test (see Fig. 9–8), which was originated as an evaluation instrument for girls and women. However, the Odeneal Service Test differs in that any legal serving method can be used in each of the ten trials allowed and in that five points are awarded for services landing in the baseline target area; four points, for the right side line target area; three points, for the left side line target area; and two points, for the main target area.

INCIDENCE CHARTS

Because of the lack of objective skill tests to measure student ability in spiking, blocking, picking up, and net recovery, as well as performance in offensive and defensive assignments, the volleyball teacher can use incidence charts to record achievement in these skills and use of strategy during actual game play. The enterprising volleyball teacher will devise her own incidence charts emphasizing the game points that she considers most important to good play. Her initial efforts may be as simple as scoring the lead-up game, Volleyball Skill Game (see page 156). The best incidence charts, how-

---

[7] William T. Odeneal and Harry E. Wilson, *Beginning Volleyball* (Belmont, California: Wadsworth Publishing Company, Incorporated, 1962), p. 49.

ever, should reveal attempts and failures as well as successes. The use of incidence charts as a means of subjective student evaluation is fairer when records are kept for some length of time. Thus, the student has a measure of her progress as well as a chance to prove herself on a given date. Incidence charts are also valuable when students are taught to evaluate the efforts of individual teammates and team strengths and weaknesses.

RATING SCALES

Rating scales may be devised by the volleyball teacher and used to supplement incidence charts in revealing the ability of students to perform in certain skills. Rating scales are of a subjective nature, and consequently will be used more often in the evaluation of spiking, blocking, picking up, and net recovery, in which no valid objective tests are available. Rating scales attempt to evaluate the performance of the player according to prescribed standards for each skill in which it is to be used. Miller and Ley have designed such a diagnostic checklist to be used in rating the volley, the underhand service, and the attack.[8] In order to be completely fair with the student, the individual teacher should draw up her own rating scales emphasizing the points she stressed during instruction in the unit. The rating scale should be in written form so the student can study what is expected of her, can study the results of her effort, and can use the results to correct errors in her performance and to capitalize on her own strengths. Used in this way, the rating scale becomes a motivating, as well as a measuring, device. When rating scales are to be utilized in arriving at a grade evaluation for the student, they should be applied on several occasions with each student. In addition, a truer picture of the player's ability and achievement will be gained when it is used in connection with game play as well as in practice formations.

KNOWLEDGE TESTS

Certainly a volleyball unit of instruction with an established objective of imparting rewarding knowledge and understandings centered around history, rules, regulations, skills, strategies, values, safety, and court courtesy should have as a culminating experience the testing of such knowledge and understanding. As volleyball classes tend toward comparatively large numbers, the teacher will find that economy from the standpoint of time in grading papers points to the construction and use of objective tests.

USE OF TEST

The use that one wishes to make of the test must be considered before the actual construction begins. The volleyball teacher may use a knowl-

[8] Donna M. Miller and Katherine I. Ley, *Individual and Team Sports for Women* (New York: Prentice-Hall, Inc., 1955), p. 44.

edge test at the beginning of a unit of instruction to determine the information level of her new students. She will find this of particular value when she is teaching a group of students which has moved to a different school level—for example, in a high school class when the students have recently moved up from the junior high school level. Another occasion might be the teaching of an intermediate or advanced level unit when students had a different instructor for the beginning level unit. In addition, the teacher may use the written test as a teaching device to help students summarize what they have learned. Finally, she may use the tests as a partial basis for assigning grades.

CONTENT

The unit outline and the combination worksheet-rules digest should help the volleyball teacher in deciding the distribution of content which is to be considered for purposes of the written test. Both the outline and worksheet have as a purpose the placing of emphasis on the kinds of knowledges and understandings which should result from the volleyball instructional experience. Nothing should appear on the test that has not been noted within the unit. Emphasis in content distribution on the test should correlate with the emphasis the teacher has made within the course.

TYPES OF ITEMS

Selecting the types of items to use on the test is very important to the well-written examination. Naturally, the types of items depend upon the content the test is to cover and the purpose for which it is given. The most frequently used types of items for an objective volleyball test are multiple choice, alternate response, recall, and matching. A test may consist of only one type of these items, or it may be a combination of no more than three types.

PREPARATION OF ITEMS

In order to avoid ambiguity and poorly worded items, test statements should be written with conciseness and logic. Long and involved statements should be avoided, for they have a tendency to mislead the student. Test statements should steer away from the trivial or from the absurd. Questions should be checked to ensure that they do not give away the answers to preceding or succeeding questions. The test should progress from the simpler questions to the more difficult and should contain some questions that all students can answer and some questions that no students can answer. In writing a volleyball test the teacher will want to steer clear of questions that sound "rule-bookish" in language and will strive to have questions which are in keeping with the grade level of difficulty. The number of items will depend upon the purposes of the test, the grade level undertaking it, and the time to be allotted for its administration.

TEST DIRECTIONS

Although the teacher plans to give oral instructions for taking the test, test directions should be included on the test itself so that they can be read and referred to at any time during its administration. These test directions should include such general instructions as to whether answers are to be recorded on the actual test; how to use the answer sheet if one is available; and how to identify the test or answer sheet with name, class section or period, and the date. Specific instructions should be given for each type of test item. For example, in alternate response, such as true and false, include information on: how the answer is to be recorded; whether a partially false statement is to be considered as completely false; a brief definition of what is to be considered as "true" and as "false"; how the items are to be scored in terms of points; and if there is to be any penalty for guessing. In multiple choice, the directions should include: how the answer is to be recorded; whether there is more than one answer possible; whether there is one best answer; and how the items are to be scored in terms of points. The same detail should be given in connection with each type of item included on the test.

PREPARATION OF COPY

Every effort should be made to see that the copy which goes to the typist is correct and edited as far as possible. Certainly, the copy should be readable and should be in the form wished for presentation to the students. More often than not, typists responsible for multiprocessing of examination papers are lay people to the sport involved and therefore cannot be expected to make professional corrections as they process the test.

ANSWER SHEETS

When administering tests to several sections or periods in which there are comparatively large numbers of students involved, as is usually the case in volleyball instruction, the teacher will find it worthwhile from the standpoint of economy to furnish an answer sheet on which the students record answers. Not only will it save the department financially by cutting down on costs in multiprocessing of the examination, but it will also cut down on the time and effort expended by the teacher in the correction of papers. A single page constructed properly can hold the answers to hundreds of questions.

KEYS

Time-saving test keys can be devised for scoring both actual tests and answer sheets. In the former, a strip-key or a cut-out key, which fits down over the correct answers, will work. In the latter, a punched key or an overprinted key is appropriate. In either case, the volleyball teacher will work for a key that contains the correct answers and will be durable under prolonged use.

COMPETITION

10

Principles and Planning

Every girl who participates in volleyball in an instructional program of physical education, or even every girl who engages in some phase of a voluntary program, is not expected to present herself for the interscholastic or intercollegiate program, however modified. Indeed, the percentage of students who have this need and interest and are competent for this experience will be relatively small. Nevertheless, the reduced numbers do not relieve the school, college, or university of the responsibility of providing a program of volleyball competition conducted on a high level of performance, sportsmanship, and fair play for the more gifted individuals who have the interest and need for this kind of experience.

Educational systems which have denied competitive experience to girl and women students have often been responsible for their seeking outlets for the expression of athletic skills in environments lacking in the wholesome supervision and controlled conditions that the school or college can and should provide. Therefore, it behooves educational institutions to make provisions for those students who are ready physically, socially, mentally, emotionally, and healthwise and are competent in the skills of volleyball by providing educationally sound extraschool and extracollegiate experiences. It also behooves recreation departments, church leagues, and industrial and civic organizations to provide for a continuation of these experiences in competitive programs in which full values may be realized. This does not necessarily mean the sponsorship of long, drawn-out seasons and schedules which command full and absolute attention and leave the participant with little time to pursue other needs and interests. It does mean enough breadth and depth so that the would-be competitor is stimulated, challenged, and satisfied.

PLAYER SOURCES

In educational institutions with sound instructional and intramural programs of volleyball, a natural and valuable source of skilled, interested, and stimulated players awaits tapping by the competitive program. However, the faculty member who is assigned the responsibility of conducting the interscholastic or intercollegiate phase cannot sit idly and wait for players to come to her. On the contrary, each new volleyball season will represent an interval in a succession in which the older and more experienced players are lost through graduation or dropouts and must be replaced by promising new arrivals.

INTRAMURAL PROGRAMS

The volleyball player who chooses to participate in the school's or college's intramural program has in essence selected herself as a possible choice to be weighed and evaluated for further competitive experience. Participation in a voluntary-type of program usually indicates enough skill to make additional play satisfying and rewarding. Further significance lies in the fact that the player seeks out volleyball to fill potential leisure time. Often the faculty member who is to be responsible for the interscholastic or intercollegiate volleyball program will be more willing than reluctant to conduct the volleyball phase of the intramural program so that she has firsthand knowledge of potential competitive players. In any case, she will assuredly establish the best possible relationships and contacts with the faculty member who is in charge of intramurals.

INSTRUCTIONAL PROGRAM

Although participation in the instructional program is not as potentially selective as the intramural program, the volleyball coach should not underrate its possibilities in the development of skilled and enthusiastic players. In fact, if she is concerned that players come to her with sound skills and thorough knowledge in the game, she will often insist on instructing classes as well as directing the competitive program. From this vantage position she is able to discover early and develop students who show unusual promise in the game. When other demands upon her time and effort prohibit class instruction, she will make every effort to establish and maintain cordial professional relationships with the teaching personnel. In addition, the volleyball expert will find that her assistance, when needed and requested, in the in-service education of the teaching personnel will pay handsome dividends through improved relationships and information of potential players.

LOWER GRADE LEVELS

At every grade level the volleyball coach will search out possible player sources at lower grade levels. Thus, at the junior high school level, the volleyball teacher who directs the limited extramural experiences of her students with students from other schools will look to the upper elementary grades as a potential player source. At the upper elementary level students will receive initial experiences in the basic skills of the game, and the players who have accomplished these skills to a more polished degree are likely prospects for the junior high school extramural experience. At the senior high school level, the members of the junior high school extramural team are a possible source of interscholastic competitors. In the colleges and universities offering intercollegiate volleyball experiences, the faculty member in charge will keep abreast of the interscholastic programs in her area; seek out players who have accumulated impressive or creditable records in the game; use personal data records of students to supplement her knowledge of player potential; and will make herself available as a visiting expert in the conduct of volleyball clinics, workshops, and master lessons.

The role of the coach in player "recruitment" in volleyball programs sponsored by recreation departments, church leagues, and industrial and civic organizations is somewhat different. Generally speaking, only those girls and women who are completely "sold" on the game will be willing to undergo the rigorous and detailed training, conditioning, practice, and play characteristic of competition at this level. Therefore, the players who present themselves for this kind of competition are self-recruited through their own playing needs, interests, ambitions, and skills. However, this does not mean that the coach in this situation is free of effort in establishment of potential player channels. On the contrary, she will be in continuous contact with school and college programs in the area and will seek out players who have accumulated creditable and impressive records in the game. As school and college competitors are likely prospects to continue participation in posteducational experiences, it will prove worthwhile to capitalize on their interest before it has a chance to subside. A skilled and enthusiastic competitive team is its own best motivating factor. Therefore, potential players should be invited and encouraged to visit the team in action. In addition, the coach should make herself available as a visiting expert to conduct in-service education, clinics, and workshops in order to cement sound and cordial relationships with other personnel with vested interests in the game of volleyball.

NATURAL FINDS

The program sources of players may be supplemented by natural finds made by the coach. A natural find is a player who has a combination of several of the following qualifications: ability in the ball-handling skills; good basic neuromuscular coordinations; height and jumping ability; a sense of where and how to move; competitive spirit; the will to win; aggressiveness that is easy to channel into proper directions; and a social awareness that makes working with others toward a common goal easy and satisfying.

PRACTICES AND SCHEDULES

The setting of times for practice, the arrangement and conduct of the individual practice session, and the schedule of matches and tournaments for the team deserve and demand careful attention and planning on the part of the volleyball coach and the administration of the sponsoring organization.

SETTING THE TIME FOR PRACTICES

At first glance the setting of a time for the volleyball practice session seems perfunctory. However, in the coaching of girls and women several principles should be considered before a choice of time is made. When the competitive program is sponsored by a school or college, the coach will avoid setting an early morning session. At this time of the day the average girl or woman has arrived at the institution at the top level of her physical appearance. She is freshly groomed and neatly dressed and will not be attracted by the idea of immediately changing into gymnasium costume and undergoing rigorous practice which will at once tear down the effect she has often worked hard to achieve.

Midday Practices. Neither will the volleyball coach find practice sessions scheduled for the middle of the day too satisfactory. Often when the session is scheduled previous to the lunch hour, the energy level of the participant is at its lowest ebb. The smell of food coming from cafeterias and snack bars is distracting and, instead of concentrating on the game, the players may be looking ahead to their own lunch time. Certainly, a period coming too soon after partaking the midday meal is to be avoided. Having just finished with eating, there is a definite tendency for the reactions of the players to be sleepy and sluggish.

End of School Day. The end of the school day is also a questionable time for the volleyball practice. Besides a drop in the energy level resultting from the activities of a normal school or college day, there is natural concern about buses and other forms of transportation. The players may feel pressures from parents, girl friends not on the team, and boy friends to cut short practice. Often when the session is held during afterschool hours many fine potential players are lost to the team because they do not have transportation of their own and cannot afford to miss that provided by the school system.

The solution to this rather negative approach in arranging practice time indicates a choice of a midmorning or midafternoon session.

When the competitive program is one sponsored by non-educational institutions and organizations, practice sessions are held at late afternoon or evening hours or on Saturday mornings so that women holding working positions can attend. Because of tradition and precedence in established programs the self-recruited player with loyalty and interest in the game will fit her time to coincide with the scheduled practice.

PRACTICE SESSIONS

One of the basic principles in building team spirit and morale is the organization and conduct of a practice session which is stimulating and appealing to the players. The establishment of the length of time and how it is to be used at the beginning of the season, prior to competition, during competition, and during culminating tournament experience should be thoughtfully planned and smoothly executed by the volleyball coach.

Length of Session. A 1-hour period when working with girls and women is an absolute minimum. However, this length of time is less than satisfactory if pre- and postpractice dressing time must be included. On the other hand, the long, drawn-out session in which there must be a slower pace to ensure completion results in a loss of time and stimulating procedure. A 2-hour session, providing for pre- and postpractice dressing and leaving approximately 1½ hours for actual activity, may prove quite satisfactory. Generally speaking, the older and more mature the girls and women are the longer the practice session can be without loss of attention and interest. When the practices can be arranged with greater frequency, as is possible within educational-type programs, the length need not be quite as long as for groups when practices are held on a weekly or twice-weekly plan.

Type of Practice. The type of practice to be conducted by the coach differs as the volleyball season progresses. At the beginning of the season major emphasis will be placed on conditioning and building of the individual skills basic to the game. As the season progresses toward the beginning of competition, there is an increased pace, if not time, in the conditioning activities; a reduced continuation of work on individual skills; and emphasis on the building of team offensive patterns of play, followed by concentration on team defensive patterns of play. During the actual competitive season there is a continuation of all of the previous activities, often at a highly quickened pace, and more and more emphasis is placed on scrimmages. During the culminating experiences, such as sports days and tournaments, practices should stress the keeping of reactions primed and interest and morale high, and often rest and relaxation are indicated as much as drill on skills and strategies.

Practice Activities. The percentage of time allotted to the type of activities within the individual practice session is determined by the emphasis of that stage within the season. For example, in the early practice sessions conditioning activities (see pages 210–13) and the development of individual skills (see Chapters 2, 3, and 4) will occupy the entire session. Later in the season, both conditioning and individual skills will be relegated to secondary importance and together will occupy no more than twenty-five per cent of the practice time. The building of team strategies and scrimmages will consume the other seventy-five per cent. The basic pattern of the practice session calls for beginning the practice session with conditioning and warming-up types of activities; moving on to the stressing of individual skills; effecting the development of the team offensive and defensive systems of play; scrimmaging in short-term, game, and finally match periods of time; and ending with additional conditioning activities with endurance as the primary objective. Whenever possible, preseason scrimmages with outside groups should be scheduled in order to give the team an opportunity to function as a unit and with the coach to evaluate progress and to discover any weaknesses that need to be eliminated before league play begins.

SCHEDULES

Almost all institutions and organizations have available to them an established system of scheduling matches and arranging for tournaments. Educational institutions are organized, however loosely, into districts or boundaries which include all like institutions in grade level and size in the area. These districts provide a natural basis for competition from within and frequently provide a chance for the outstanding teams of each to compete with the outstanding teams of other districts. Non-educational institutions and organizations usually provide self-contained programs of competition. Recreation departments, church leagues, and YWCA volleyball programs, for example, sponsor programs involving a number of teams. Thus, the first unit of competition is established, and similar setups in nearby areas provide a second, or regional, level when the champion teams from each meet.

The round-robin type of arrangement (see pages 168–69) is by far the most popular provision of play at the first unit of competition level. Depending upon the number of teams involved, the regular season of matches may be scheduled by having each team compete against every other team a specific number of times. The round-robin arrangement is often supplemented at the end of the season by an elimination-type of tournament in which all, or only a predetermined number of the top regular season, teams play. The number of matches per day and per week and the length of the season are firmly set for educational institutions sponsoring volleyball programs under the jurisdiction of the DGWS. These standards, along with others governing conduct of the program, are featured in the *Volleyball Guide,* published in alternate years.

TRAINING AND CONDITIONING

To gain and maintain the strength, endurance, agility, flexibility, co-ordination, and balance required for competitive volleyball play, the girl or woman athlete must undergo rigorous programs of training and conditioning. She must have in reserve vast resources of energy and stamina which she can call into play when the occasion demands without undue fatigue or strain.

TRAINING

The volleyball competitor should not be interested in seasonal training only. The athlete who prizes personal success in the sport, has competitive spirit, has pride in the team, and has the will to win will be interested in keeping regular and temperate living habits throughout the year, not just during the volleyball season. However, such habits must be established and enforced during the regular season of play. Training rules will be accepted, and thereby enforced more easily, when they are the combined effort of the coach and players rather than a written list of rules handed down to the team members by the coach. In setting up training rules the volleyball coach must be prepared to guide the players' thinking so that they understand and appreciate the reasons behind each rule as well as its detail. Because the training rules must cover all aspects of daily living, more often centered away from the sponsoring institution or organization than not, they are more practically enforced by teammate pressures and opinions than they could possibly be by firsthand supervision of the coach. Infractions of training rules should result in immediate and appropriate disciplinary action, predetermined with the rules.

Diet. The objective of training rules concerning diet is to keep the participant at her highest energy level and to provide for current needs in her pattern of growth and development. Junior and senior high school players must understand that competition for them is occurring at the time in their lives when growth and development demand greater food intake than that at any other time. Diet training rules should be kept simple. Effort should be made to have food in the following kinds and amounts: from breads and cereals, four or more servings per day; from milk products, four or more servings, which may include ice cream or cheese as alternates; adequate but not excessive protein, with meat as the basic source; and from vegetable and fruits, four or more servings per day, including citrus fruit, or others high in Vitamin C, potatoes, and at least on alternate days, deep-green or deep-yellow vegetables. Some additional general diet rules are: Food should be cooked simply; no supplementary vitamins should be used unless the need is medically determined; extra salt may be required in hot, muggy weather; and carbohydrates may be stepped up to combat fatigue.

Division of Food Intake. Generally speaking, the kind and amount of food intake on a daily basis should be divided into the following type meals. Breakfast should be a solid meal, consisting of bacon, eggs, toast, cereal, fruit juice, and beverage. While it would be foolish to insist upon the adult player changing from long established coffee or tea habits, the young high school girl should be encouraged to stick with milk. Lunch should consist of soup, sandwich, fruit for dessert, and beverage. The evening meal should be composed of the bulk of caloric needs, and should consist of meat, potatoes, vegetables, salad, choice of dessert, and beverage. The young, growing volleyball player can be encouraged to have a bed-time snack of a milkshake, glass of milk, malted milk, a small sandwich, or a piece of fruit.

The noon meal must be relatively small and easily digested when the practice session is to take place in the afternoon. Otherwise, the players will become sleepy and sluggish and will not be able to devote full attention to participation. When the practice session is scheduled for the end of the school day or after school hours, the player must have a period of rest and relaxation before she partakes of the evening meal so that the digestive processes may adjust from the practice to the handling of a substantial food intake. Among adult groups practicing at night some adjustment must be made in the plan of having the bulk of caloric needs in the evening meal.[1]

Before the Game. Careful attention should be given in the training rules as to what the player should consume on the day of the game and particularly in the pregame meal. As much as possible, the changing of an established food pattern should be avoided. Unless the match is to be in midmorning, as may often be the case in large tournaments, breakfast should be emphasized. The pregame meal should occur 3 to 4 hours before the match and should consist of easily digested foods. Rich pastries, fried foods, and highly seasoned foods should be avoided. Carbohydrates, the energy-giving foods, should be emphasized, but not excessively. As the emotional outlook of the players at this time will greatly affect not only what the player may eat but also how her body will handle it, the coach should allow players to control the amount of intake. The atmosphere of the pregame meal should be happy, pleasant, and free from tension. Conversation about the match should be avoided.

Sleep. Sleep, nature's restorer, is needed more by the high school age girl volleyball competitor than it is by the average adolescent. It is in this area that the coach should be suspect when there is a noticeable slump in

[1] Edward O. O'Donnell and William A. Krehl, "Ideal Meals for the Athlete," *Scholastic Coach*, XXIV, 3 (November, 1954), 48–49.

the performance of the player. Medical research indicates that the young athlete has more sleep motion in tossing and turning than does the non-athlete. Therefore, additional sleeping hours are required to compensate for the increased motility. The volleyball player should be encouraged to spend 9 hours in bed each night, resting if not asleep.

Rest and Relaxation. Rest and relaxation are as vital to the total training program of the volleyball player as are diet and sleep. Positive relaxation rules should guide players in the period before eating the dinner meal, before matches, and between matches in tournament play. The coach should control the rest and relaxation before matches by calling the team together at least 2 hours before play and by having planned activity to occupy the time prior to dressing for pregame warm-ups. In tournament play the team should be withdrawn from the competitive scene between matches. Swimming, going to a movie, or some other recreationally oriented activity will provide much needed release from the tensions and excitement involved in such highly competitive experience.

Smoking. Girl and women volleyball players at the school and college levels should be discouraged in smoking by very stringent training rules against it. While athletic coaches have frowned upon smoking for years without concrete evidence to support their views, they can now make absolute claims against the habit. Smoking does influence athletic performance. Some are more resistant to its hazards than others, but all are affected to some degree. Smoking irritates the mucous membranes; absorbs carbon monoxide, leaving less oxygen in the blood; constricts small blood vessels; produces digestive disturbances; increases the heart rate; and irritates the nervous system. More recently, the relationships between cancer and heart and blood vessel victims and smoking have been clearly established.

The best way to stop smoking is not to start. The young girl athlete, and even the mature woman, should be guided in the knowledge that her playing is affected by the habit. If she is a good volleyball player as a person who smokes, she could be better as a nonsmoker. As the standard of training and conditioning is often a determining factor in the win or loss of a highly competitive match, the individual player or team cannot afford to overlook smoking as a hindrance to complete effort.

Alcohol. In setting up training rules concerning use of alcohol, appeal to the commonsense of the girl and woman should be made. The coach should guide the players in understanding how alcohol works in the body. It passes immediately into the blood stream and into all organs of the body. The brain is dulled and neuromuscular coordination is impaired. As loss of coordination results, the volleyball player will not only lose her finesse in game play but is also more prone accident-wise. Alcohol intake often results in nutritional shortages which subsequently bring on both mental and physical deterioration.

CONDITIONING

Since maximum performance in volleyball depends upon a broad and solid structure of all-round strength, endurance, agility, flexibility, balance, and coordination, the activity involved in practices, scrimmages, and play is not sufficient to produce the high level of physical performance demanded in skillful competition. These activities must be supplemented and complemented by an expertly planned and executed program of conditioning.

Effects of Conditioning. Research proves that conditioning of the body leads to increased economy of exertion by perfecting coordinations, by eliminating unnecessary motion, and by accomplishment of results with a minimum of energy. Medical experimentation in the area of conditioning has shown that voluntary muscles become stronger and more efficient in ridding themselves of fatigue products. Consequently, they are able to withstand without damage intensive demands put upon them. The heart, the major muscle to be considered in a program of conditioning aimed toward the building of endurance, shows increased efficiency in its pumping action. Pulmonary ventilation is increased and other body systems also improve. As a result, the conditioned player is able to carry on more rigorous activity over a longer period of time and to perform moderate activity with less effort and fatigue. Additional benefits are greater chance of preventing injury, improved performance in game skills, and increased enjoyment of the game.

Overload. The overload principle is the universally accepted method of building strength and endurance. Thus, in a conditioning program for competition, the volleyball player will be asked to push herself beyond physical levels easily reached. Although the coach should understand and practice in method the difference in fatigue and exhaustion, the conditioning program should help the individual player to overcome fear of fatigue. All-out effort producing fatigue in the healthy and normal player is absolutely necessary in the establishment of new physiological limits. However, the physiological limit is different for each player.[2]

Long-Range Effort. The building of the conditioned volleyball player able to compete at all-out performance level in the full match, and probably more than one match per day during tournament play, is best effected

2 C. Etta Walters, "Scientific Foundations of the Overload Principle," *Scholastic Coach,* XXVII, 8 (April, 1958), 20, 22.

gradually and over a long period of time. Consequently, the conditioning program will receive impetus in the initial session of practice and will increase in intensity of pace, if not time devoted, throughout the season. As a major emphasis in early practices, conditioning activities must be based upon the results of the medical examination and the starting condition of the players. Primary and intermediate targets can be levels necessary for all-out performance in a single game, then two games, and the three-game match. The demands of concentrated tournament play is the ultimate objective.

General Programs. Although competition in volleyball calls upon concentrated use of specific muscles—namely, fingers, hands, arms, shoulders, back, feet, and legs—it is accepted that maximum performance will demand an all-round high standard of physical fitness. Thus, the conditioning program will be composed of general activities designed to meet the needs of the entire body structure and of specific activities with particular muscular emphasis. During recent years professional efforts in the development of total fitness programs have produced some excellent results. Among these is the XBX program developed by the Royal Canadian Air Force.[3] Devised to cover girls and women beginning at the age of seven and continuing through to the age of fifty-five, the ten calisthenic-type activities involved stress general warm-up, agility, flexibility, abdominals, arms, shoulders, backs, chest, buttocks, upper legs, lower legs, feet, and endurance. In addition to the completeness of its fitness approach, the XBX plan is especially adaptable to competitive programs because it demands such a small part of the practice session time. Complete execution of the activities of the XBX plan takes a total of 12 minutes, and the overload principle is fulfilled not only by increasing the number of repetitions within the time limit designated for each of the activities but also by progressing in the difficulty and demand of the calisthenics after a certain accomplishment level has been reached. The XBX plan makes some allowance for individual physiological and physical differences by the setting of standards according to age. Other total fitness programs worthy of attention include the fitness tests designed by the American Association for Health, Physical Education and Recreation, the California Performance Tests, the Steinhaus series, and others too numerous to mention but available through professional journals and literature of physical educators, physiologists, and medical doctors.

Such conditioning activities usually include running, with warming-up and concluding purposes; calisthenics, with limbering-up, warming-up, strength, agility, and coordination objectives; and additional activities, which include drills, with repetition of the more vigorous volleyball game

[3] Royal Canadian Air Force, *Exercise Plans for Physical Fitness* (Canada: Crown Copyright, 1962).

elements; stunts, especially those emphasizing use of the hands, fingers, arm, and shoulder muscles; and contests, including relays, races, and running.

Specific Activities.   Since volleyball is a game built primarily on handling a ball under specialized conditions, it is absolutely essential that competitors develop hands, fingers, arms, shoulders, and backs above and beyond the degree emphasized in any program of general total fitness. The coach must have a variety of activities, emphasizing development in these muscles, at command to supplement the general conditioning program conducted in each practice session. A selected few are presented here:

1. Rub the hands vigorously together for a 30-second time limit.
2. Clap the hands vigorously together for a 30-second time limit.
3. Perform finger flexions and extensions with the hands and arms held in front of the body, overhead, at sides, and down for 1 minute.
4. With the body in a front leaning rest position, use hands and arms only to move around on the floor. Allow the feet and legs to drag behind.[4]
5. Perform animal stunts emphasizing use of arm and shoulder muscles, including the Frog Hop, Rabbit Hop, Bear Walk, Elephant Walk, Lamed Dog Walk, Measuring Worm, and Crab Walk.
6. Modify traditional calisthenics so that additional emphasis is placed on hands, fingers, arms, and shoulders. For example, while using straddle hopping as an endurance exercise, add vigorous clapping of the hands at the side of the thighs and overhead. While running in place, swing the arms and shake the hands vigorously.
7. Use isometric-type exercises: [5]
   a. Stand with back to the wall with the elbows held at shoulder height and the hands held at chest level, with the palms down. Press the elbows hard against the wall.
   b. Stand with the elbows at shoulder height and the hands held at chest level with the palms gripping each other. Press the palms hard against each other and then relax.
   c. Use the basic position as listed in "a." Instead of pressing against a wall surface, have a partner grasp the elbows and pull them back. Relax the elbows and repeat.
8. Stauff conditioners: [6]
   a. Use elliptical hand-dynamometer to test and increase strength. Begin by taking one grip for each hand and then increase the load by adding one more grip per day.
   b. Finger pushups against a wall. Players establish an arms-length distance from the wall by standing erect with their palms flat on the wall

[4] William T. Odeneal, "Conditioning for Volleyball," *Athletic Journal*, XXX, 6 (February, 1950), 46, 48–49.

[5] Ken Doherty, "Basic Training for All Sports," *Scholastic Journal*, XXVII, 6 (February, 1958), 16, 18.

[6] Marilyn Stauff, "Developing Skill in the Volleyball Pass Through Conditioning," *Volleyball Guide, 1963–1965* (Washington: The Division for Girls and Women's Sports), pp. 30–31.

surface and with elbows extended. By slightly spreading the fingers and using only the fingertips to support the weight of the body, lower toward the wall, hold, and push away using a slow count of ten. The intensity of the exercise can be increased by keeping the number constant but by increasing the distance away from the wall. Three inches at a time is the recommended distance increase.

c. Rubber ball exercise. Use rubber balls about 2 inches in diameter and have the players squeeze the ball tightly and then completely relax and extend the fingers. Increase the number of trials per session by five.

d. Passes over rope. Using a rope elevated to a height of twelve feet have the players volley a ball over the rope ten trials each day. On the first day use a volleyball; on the second, a volleyball for five trials and a soccer ball for five; on the third, use a soccer ball exclusively; on the fourth, use a soccer ball for five trials and a basketball for five; and on subsequent days, use a basketball exclusively.

Conditioning and Morale. Since it is highly desirable that the competitors link conditioning and success in the game, the atmosphere in which the conditioning program is held is of utmost importance. While some of the exercises and activities, because of limitations in equipment, necessitate participation on an individual basis, team morale will be much improved when conditioning activities can be conducted for the group as a whole. Upon occasion the coach herself may want to lead and participate in the activities. At other times the team captain or manager may be called upon for the leadership, and sometimes individual players may be selected to direct a particular exercise or activity. Occasionally, the coach might use a procedure in which she merely posts the conditioning activities for the practice session and allows each player to fulfill her own obligations within a set time limit. High levels in achievement in conditioning activities should be recognized. Performance score cards can be kept on the individual player, and whenever some noteworthy level has been reached, the score card of the particular player should be posted as a means of recognition and to motivate the other teammates to high accomplishment.

BUILDING TEAM MORALE

There is little chance of producing a winning or successful team, regardless of the talent of its individual players, unless there is an accompanying esprit de corps. Certainly, there are no hard-and-fast rules for building team spirit. It cannot be instilled or enforced by the coach or captain. It must grow and evolve naturally to be long and lasting. However, there are some guides in the promotion of team morale that the coach should be aware of and try to effect with the cooperation of the members of the playing squad.

LOYALTY

First, there is pride and loyalty to the sponsoring group. Although school and college spirit are fairly infectious and easy to promote, there must be conscious effort in the promotion of the same feelings on the part of participants in noneducational types of competition. The chance to represent one's school, college, industrial, or civic group is one of the most attractive aspects of competition and should be used by the coach to promote team unity and morale.

POSITIVE ATTITUDES

There should be conscious effort to build positive attitudes in each player toward her responsibility as an individual player and a contributing member of the team. Each player must be ready to perform to the best of her ability. This means strict attention to the development of individual skills and to her duties within the framework of the team's offensive and defensive strategies. She must also be a student of the game, continually increasing her knowledge and her potential as a player. Thus, she earns the confidence of her teammates, and team morale is enhanced. In this type of team atmosphere there is no place for the individual "star" or "goat," and victory or defeat is shared and shared alike.

COMPETITION FOR POSITIONS

The players should never be allowed to feel that their positions in the starting lineup are unchallenged. Competition for positions should open at the beginning of the season and should remain open until its close. As new players come on to the squad and as other players develop in individual skills and in working into the offensive and defensive play of the team, they serve as additional challenges to the more experienced players to improve their own game. The coach would be foolish to shake up an effective team lineup without cause. However, in thinking of future seasons, the knowing coach will give inexperienced players opportunities to get in game experience at opportune moments.

PLAYING MORALE

Game morale should be kept at a high level. Teammates should be encouraged to "talk the game up" on the floor. Team chatter is helpful in overcoming natural tensions and pressures. A silent team is usually one that is deflated in morale and defeated in play. An expression of encouragement and confidence passed from one teammate to another is invaluable in keeping spirit high and is essential when the team is momentarily behind its opponents. Players should never be allowed to criticize the play of each other. There is nothing more damaging to the team than to have players begin to find fault with each other. On the other hand, the coach does criticize play whenever necessary. However, she will usually find a constructive suggestion more effective. The champion athlete usually recognizes her own errors and is ready and willing to try to correct them as soon as possible. A gentle reminder by the coach, or a vote of confidence, may be all that is needed to return the player to her usual high caliber of play.

PRACTICES

The practice sessions of the team should be as stimulating and challenging as possible. Drill and repetition of practice must be meaningful to the competitive player. She must understand the "why" as well as the "what" and the "how." She should leave each practice session fatigued, but not exhausted, and with a feeling of accomplishment and eagerness to return.

TRADITIONS

Finally, there should be an effort to build meaningful and educationally sound traditions and customs for the volleyball team. The traditions may include such simple acts as the coach passing through the dressing room before or after practice to give words of encouragement and to cement closer personal relationships with the players; the establishment of a customary meeting place where the team gathers for the beginning of each practice session; a traditional yell for themselves and opponents before and after a match; and the practice of the coach and squad members standing to talk to the team during time-outs or as a player leaves the game when a substitute is entered. More involved traditions may include the practice of special social events for the team and coach; the establishment of a sound system of publicity for the team; a system of record-keeping which emphasizes team and individual accomplishments, such as winning streaks, consecutive services without faults, and high scores on fitness and skill tests; and team recognition through awards, banquets, and other special events.

THE COACH

No program of volleyball competition can be any stronger than the coach, hired or volunteer, who is in charge. Without doubt the volleyball coach should be an enthusiastic expert in the game. No teacher, recreation leader, or volunteer should accept a coaching function until she knows that she is qualified. Although the coach's relationships with players and the coaching procedures should be as democratic as possible, coaching is highly specialized teaching and once given the charge, the coach must prove to the players that she is in command and control and that she is worthy of the assignment.

PROFESSIONAL QUALIFICATIONS

Coaches at the secondary level are required to be certified teachers by most state athletic associations.[7] The Educational Policies Commission goes a step beyond by asking that athletic leadership be properly certified and competent teachers of physical education, who possess understanding of growth and development, the purposes and principles of teaching and learning, and other knowledges, understandings, attitudes, and appreciations that characterize competent teachers, in addition to technical knowledge of the game involved.[8] In addition, the DGWS standards rate as an essential prerequisite that the volleyball coach be a woman. Although the coach has been consistently referred to within this text as a woman, it would be extreme folly at this time to propose that only women should coach volleyball for girls and women, in or out of education programs. Such leadership is simply not available, and until it is, competency and sound principles and procedures are more desirable characteristics than sex.

OBLIGATIONS

In addition to professional qualications, the volleyball coach should exercise obligations in respect to membership in local, state, and national organizations associated with the coaching function; should attend and help conduct clinics, workshops, or demonstrations which promote and upgrade the volleyball experience; and should keep abreast of current literature, directly and indirectly, associated with the sport. Such literature includes *Standards in Sports for Girls and Women* and the *Volleyball Guide* published by DGWS, the *Official Rules and Reference Guide* published by the USVBA, the *International Volleyball Review*, and volleyball articles appearing in the major sports journals.

RELATIONSHIPS WITH PLAYERS

The first step undertaken by the coach in establishing sound relationships with players is to gain their respect. Essential in gaining the respect of the players is knowhow in the game. The knowhow should be reflected in the conduct, organization, and management of each experience within the competitive volleyball program. It will take little time for players to discover a coach with limited knowledge and understanding of the game. The living habits and the moral and ethical behavior of the coach are also

[7] George E. Shepherd and Richard E. Jamerson, *Interscholastic Athletics* (New York: McGraw-Hill Book Co., Inc., 1953), p. 48.

[8] *School Athletics: Problems and Policies* (Washington: Educational Policies Commission, National Education Association, 1954), p. 61.

instrumental in gaining or losing player respect. The coach, especially on the secondary school level, serves consciously or unconsciously as a model for various social roles. Therefore, she should exemplify femininity, clean living, and socially acceptable behavior. Respect once lost is seldom re-gained. In addition to gaining and keeping student respect, the coach should know each player individually and should establish personal and friendly relationships with her. As a competitor finishes her playing career, she should leave with the feeling that in the coach she has a firm and lasting friend.

HEALTH, SAFETY, AND WELFARE OF PLAYERS

The volleyball coach and the administration of the sponsoring organization must jointly assume responsibility in the establishment and enforcement of sound policies and procedures protecting the health, safety, and welfare of the players.

HEALTH

One of the most important requirements of the potential volleyball athlete is the medical examination. A complete medical examination is comparatively easy to arrange and conduct in schools, colleges, universities, and industries, where there is a school or industrial doctor or a physician engaged for this specific purpose. If private family physicians or public health doctors must be depended upon, there may be increased difficulty. Three essentials of the examination are: administration at the beginning of each season previous to practices; it must be complete and inclusive, with all physical conditions stringently evaluated; and use of an official medical form used to record the results of the examination and made available for study as a part of the permanent record of each player involved in the program. The sponsoring group should be ready to assume at least partial financial responsibility for the examination when private family physicians must be used.

First Aid Attention and Supplies. During every volleyball practice and match the health of the volleyball player should be further protected by the availability of first aid attention in attendants and supplies. Attendants may be doctors, nurses, private physicians "on call," or qualified first-aid attendants. Minimum supplies on hand should include the recommended kit list of the American Red Cross. The legal ramifications of failure to provide such attention and supplies are of increasing severity today.

Illness and Injury. A girl or woman player who has been absent from volleyball practices or play because of illness or injury should be required to have a statement of written permission by a qualified physician before returning to the activity of the team. The medical examination, properly conducted and with good resultant records, and understanding of the effect of competitive pressures upon the emotional and physical well-being of players will do much to eliminate many problems previously associated with the menstrual period. The coach will need to know which players suffer difficulties and the nature of the care needed. Some, on the recommendation of a physician, should be withheld from activity. A man in charge of a girls' or women's team must become thoroughly familiar with each player's medical record and should arrange for a woman faculty member in educational institutions, or a woman manager in non-educational programs, to assist him in keeping informed of current menstrual period difficulties. At no time should the volleyball coach put herself or himself in the position of administration of a sedative, however mild or for whatever seemingly harmless purpose, because of the legal implications involved.

SAFETY AND WELFARE

Many facets of the volleyball competitive program have both direct and indirect bearing upon the safety and welfare of the participants. Some guidelines to sound policies and planning are outlined here. In regard to facilities and equipment, the coach and the administration should make every effort to see that the facility in which practices and play are to be conducted is clean, safe, free from obstruction, and in a good state of repair. There should be a regular schedule for the cleaning of the gymnasium or outdoor surface. The cleaning should be in the hands of well-trained and properly supervised personnel. In addition to the regular schedule, cleaning should occur immediately after all home matches in which there has been a large audience in attendance. Obstructions should be removed or covered in such a way that they do not present safety hazards. The gymnasium floor should be refinished on a regular schedule to be free of splintering and to provide a surface with good traction. The outdoor surface should be smooth, washed down, and completely dry before use.

Equipment. The game and personal equipment for the competitive program should follow the same standards outlined for the instructional program (see pages 135–39). However, the competitive program indicates enforced addition of two types of protective equipment. Glasses guards, personally or program provided, should be worn by the player who needs glasses to compete effectively, and knee pads are essential for the competitive player who may drop or fall to the floor frequently.

Permissions. Whenever the competitive program involves players who are under age, as is the case in school and often college, university, and civic or industrial sponsorship, it should be the policy of the coach and administration to secure written permission from parents for the girl to participate. A special form should be devised for this purpose and should be circulated previous to the beginning of formal practice sessions. Written parental permission should also be required to cover the method and conditions of travel when playing out-of-town games. If the same type of transportation is to be used throughout the season, the permission form can be written to cover the entire season and distributed before the first road-trip. If the mode of transportation changes, individual trip permissions must be obtained.

Insurance. The crying need to have insurance coverage is the major determining factor in the type of transportation to be used. A bonded carrier, such as school buses or athletic station wagons on the college and university level, is indicated. Whenever private vehicles are to be used, as is often the case in civic or industrial programs, "bodily injury liability" to cover all players is an absolute minimum. In addition to transportation insurance, there should be some provision made to pay for expenses incurred through injury to volleyball players in practices or matches. Where school and college insurance plans cover all student activities, each volleyball player should be required, as a part of her eligibility, to participate in the program. Where such programs do not exist, the coach and administration should investigate and instigate one at the earliest possible moment. Industrial organization employees are usually covered by insurance plans. Care should be exercised to see that benefits are in effect when the player is representing her organization in volleyball competition as well as on the actual job. Civic organizations should encourage adoption of separate insurance plans to which the involved players must subscribe.

Retention. It is important to the welfare of participants, as it is to the ongoing of teams, that as many players who have the interest, desire, and meet the eligibility requirements be allowed to try out for the volleyball team. Often open tryouts reveal player potential missed in the previously outlined selective recruitment procedures. In addition to open tryouts, the player should be retained on the volleyball squad as long as she deems it personally desirable. At all times she should be kept well informed of her chances for varsity competition. Thus, the coach will practice squad cutting to a minimum degree, and then only when disciplinary action and leadership, time, and facility limitations demand it. To provide additional competitive experiences for those desirous of them, it is an excellent practice to maintain a "B-team" and conduct matches when such experiences can be arranged without demanding too much time, distance, and expense involvement.

Recognition. The social and personality welfare of the player is enhanced when she has an opportunity to engage in pleasant social relationships with her opponents and members of her own team. Informal "get-togethers" planned for visiting opponents by the home team provide a setting for the former. Informal gatherings and parties in the coach's home; team parties planned and executed by the group; and banquets, parties, and picnics planned in honor of teams by the sponsoring agency offer opportunity to improve relationships within the team as well as recognition of team members. Additional recognition may come through the practice of bestowing awards on players at the end of a season. These awards should be important not because of their monetary value but because they are symbolic of personal and team achievement. Recognition should also come to players through proper promotion of the volleyball program and wise publicity.

SOUND COMMUNITY RELATIONS

It should be immediately recognized that athletic events within themselves attract a great deal of public attention. Therefore, the general policies, aims, and objectives of the competitive program of volleyball should be determined in advance and made known to the general public. A continuous effort should be made to interpret to newspaper reporters, parents, and community leaders, as well as to the players and their associates, the aims and desirable outcomes of the program.

PUBLICITY

To ensure the proper kind of publicity for competitive volleyball, it is best to have the initiative come from within the program itself. Colleges, universities, industries, and some civic organizations support full-time public relations directors. Schools often have one faculty member with released time to fulfill this function. A close professional tie between the volleyball coach and the director of public relations should be maintained. Together they can plan and release publicity stressing the educational benefits of volleyball; supporting clean athletics and good sportsmanship; emphasizing team effort rather than the accomplishments or failures of individual players; varying in appeal in order to reenforce points without monotony; reaching all possible agencies, such as newspapers, bulletins, radio, and television; and approaching presentation through interesting news stories rather than mere statements of fact or principle.

RECOGNITION

Whenever community agencies want to play a part in the recognition of teams at the end of season by the giving of awards or events conducted in honor of the team, the volleyball coach and the administration of the sponsoring organization should keep firm control. For the morale of individual players and the team as a whole, no one or two individuals should be isolated and honored to the exclusion of others. It is also essential that such occasions occur at the end of losing, as well as winning, seasons.

Glossary

The volleyball terms in this glossary are defined according to their use in this text.

ALL-SET-SPIKE PATTERN: An offensive system of play in which all six players set and spike the ball according to the given game situation.

BACKING-UP: A planned system of assisting the player who assumes the responsibility of making the initial contact with the ball after the service or a spike.

BLOCK: A defensive play at the net in which one or more players jump to elevate hands and forearms above the top of the net and to meet the spiked ball by: (1) returning it immediately to the spiker's court, or (2) deflecting it so that it can be played by a teammate.

CROSS SET: A set directed to a Key-Spiker which travels parallel with the net and in front of the player to her natural-hand side.

DIG: A contact of the ball below the waistline with a solid surface formed by the forearms or the heel of the hand. Primarily, the dig is used to meet forcefully propelled balls (services and spikes) with the momentum of the rebound enough to carry the ball forward and upward with little, if any, backswing or follow-through involved. Other uses of the dig are in net recovery situations.

DINK: A faked spike in which the attacking player merely taps the ball down on the opposite side of the net or over the out-stretched hands of the waiting blockers.

DOUBLE-V POSITIONS: A team formation used in defending against the service; so named because the six players form an inverted "double-V" in relation to the net.

FADEAWAY POSITIONS: A team formation used in defending the service; the forwards are stationed in a parallel line some 8 to 10 feet away from the net.

NET RECOVERY: The legal play of a ball that has fallen into the net. An underhand volley is used under limited conditions. The digging skills are preferable. Strategic orientation occurs as a result of the number of previous contacts and the positioning of the team at the time the ball goes into the net.

ONE-TWO-THREE ATTACK: The use of the pass, set, and spike in sequence as the basic form of attack.

OVER SET: A set in which either the right forward directs the ball over the head of the center forward to be spiked by the left forward or the left forward directs the ball over the head of the center forward to be spiked by the right forward.

OVERHEAD VOLLEY: A volley in which the ball is contacted above shoulder height and preferably in front of the player's upturned face. The direction of the ball flight is forward and upward.

PAIR-PARTNER (THREE-THREE) PATTERN: An offensive system of play in which three players are designated as setters and three as spikers. Alternate positions are assumed in the rotating order.

PATTERNS OF PLAY: A basic framework within which the team organizes its system of offensive and defensive strategy.

PASS: The initial contact of the ball by a team within its own court. The objective of the pass is to send the ball to a player on the forward line to be set. An overhead volley is the preferable skill. However, the underhand volley and the digs may be substituted under certain conditions.

PICK-UP: A save; the meeting of a forcefully spiked ball. One of the digging skills is preferably used.

REVERSE SET: Use of the reverse volley in directing the set to a Key-Spiker.

REVERSE VOLLEY: A volley in which the player directs the ball over her own head in the direction opposite to the one she has been facing.

SCREEN: The use of three or more players in providing a cover for the server so that her actions are not easily discernible by the receiving team.

SERVICE: The act of putting the ball into play. Generally speaking, four techniques are used:

1. Underhand—the ball is contacted below the server's waistline.
2. Sidearm—the ball is contacted at a height approximate to the shoulder level of the server.
3. Overhead—the ball is contacted from above the server's head.
4. Roundhouse—the ball is contacted from above the server's head in a movement pattern similar to the hook pass or shot in basketball.

SET: Usually the second contact of the ball by a team within its own court. The objective of the set is to direct the ball to the attacking player to be spiked. The overhead and reverse volley skills are used.

SPIKE: Usually the third contact of the ball by a team within its own court. The ball is met with a one-hand, whiplike contact taken at the top of a jump, and often with a preliminary running approach. The objective is to direct the ball with such power and/or placement that the opponents' return, if any, is irreparably damaged.

TWO-FOR-ONE (FOUR-TWO) PATTERN: An offensive system of play in which two players fulfill setting assignments for four spikers.

TWO-FOR-ONE INTERCHANGE PATTERN: An offensive system of play in which the interchange privilege is used to put the Key-Set, a Key-Spiker, or a combination of the two in a more advantageous position on the forward line.

UNDERHAND VOLLEY: A volley in which the ball is contacted from below the waistline. While the underhand volley is still legal and acceptable in purely recreational play and at a beginning skill level, it is almost obsolete among skilled players.

VOLLEY: The basic skill of the game in which the ball is contacted by the finger pads of both hands simultaneously and is propelled forward and upward into the air.

Index